A Coast Guardsman's
HISTORY *of the*
U.S. COAST GUARD

A Coast Guardsman's
HISTORY *of the*
U.S. COAST GUARD

C. Douglas Kroll

NAVAL INSTITUTE PRESS
Annapolis, Maryland

Naval Institute Press
291 Wood Road
Annapolis, MD 21402

ISBN: 978-1-61251-876-3 (eBook)

Library of Congress Cataloging-in-Publication Data
Kroll, C. Douglas.
  A Coast Guardsman's history of the U.S. Coast Guard /
C. Douglas Kroll.
      p. cm.
  Includes index.
  ISBN 978-1-59114-433-5 (alk. paper)
  1. United States. Coast Guard—History. I. Title.
  VG53.K76 2010
  363.28'90973—dc22

                              2010018338

Printed in the United States of America on acid-free paper

20 19 18 17   9 8 7 6 5

All photos are official U.S. Coast Guard photos except where
otherwise indicated.

Book layout and composition: Alcorn Publication Design

To all who serve—
Yesterday, today, tomorrow,
especially my two sons:
LTJG Timothy N. Kroll, USCGR, and
LTJG Matthew M. Kroll, USCG

CONTENTS

A COAST GUARDSMAN'S PREFACE

In the 1960s, as a young cadet at the Coast Guard Academy, I learned to recite from memory the mission of the academy. I can still remember the closing words of that mission, "to be strong in the resolve to be worthy of the traditions of commissioned officers in the United States Coast Guard in the service of their country and humanity." Sadly, however, the inspiring stories of those men and women who preceded me were not part of the curriculum. My classmates and I knew there had to be stories about the individuals whose names were on the buildings: Yeaton, Satterlee, Billard, Munro, and others. I remember on an exchange weekend visit to the Naval Academy in Annapolis, I was struck by the number of monuments to U.S. Navy officer heroes on that campus. My alma mater, the Coast Guard Academy, had no similar monuments, at least at that time.

I always wished I had known some specific Coast Guard heroes. After serving for a number of years as a commissioned officer in the service and even now, as a Coast Guard Auxiliarist and a member of Team Coast Guard, I realize that many of my service's men and women think they are short on heroes. Those who do know some history about our branch of the military know mostly about famous cutters and rescues—the focus of most Coast Guard histories. Only a few individuals are well known. Every member of this service knows about Signalman First Class Douglas Munro. As former Coast Guard commandant Adm. James Loy said to the Corps of Cadets at the Coast Guard Academy in 2006: "We are intensely proud of Signalman First Class Douglas Munro and his heroic exploits at Guadalcanal during World War II that earned him the Congressional Medal of Honor. But in a service more than 200 years old, many are too aware or even ashamed that we have only one Medal of Honor recipient."

The reality is that there are thousands of Coast Guard heroes. The problem is that the service seldom talks about or learns about them. They served in various roles: Some were active duty, some Reservists, some Auxiliarists, and some civilian employees. These heroes represent a great diversity in age, sex, race, and ethnicity. They are both commissioned officers and enlisted personnel. But all are heroes and role models for today's Coast Guard men and women.

In this book, *A Coast Guardman's History*, I attempt to tell the story of the service and its predecessor services through the stories of some of these Coast Guard men and women, rather than focus on the history of an agency, famous cutters, or rescues. In learning their stories, the reader can gain much insight into the history of the Coast Guard. This is a book about heritage more than history. My hope is that will make my fellow service members stand a little taller and feel a little prouder every time they put on their uniforms.

Most histories of the Coast Guard start at the beginning, with Alexander Hamilton and the founding of the Revenue Cutter Service, and move forward through time. In this book I have chosen to explore our heritage by way of themes rather than chronology. My goal is not to make readers experts in history, but to share a heritage that makes our agency proud and special. However, a chronological account of combat history is included, as the final chapter titled "Battle Streamers." Chapter 1 of the *Coast Guardsman's Manual* also provides a brief overview of the service's history.

Finally, I would like to emphasize that the views expressed are my own and do not reflect those of the Department of Homeland Security or the United States Coast Guard.

ACKNOWLEDGMENTS

This book could not have been written without the help of many important and impressive people who took time out of their busy lives to provide suggestions, help me locate information, and encourage me. Each played a vital role, and I am indebted to all.

Adm. Thad W. Allen, USCG: commandant of the U. S. Coast Guard and U.S. Coast Guard Academy classmate (Class of 1971)

Capt. Rob Ayer, USCG, Ph.D.: senior military professor, U.S. Coast Guard Academy, New London, Connecticut

Master Chief Petty Officer Bruce R. Bradley Jr., USCG: Command Master Chief, Coast Guard Training Center, Cape May, New Jersey

Capt. David Brimblecom, USCG (Ret.): director, Coast Guard Leadership Development Center, New London, Connecticut (2005–8)

Robert M. Browning, Ph.D.: chief historian, U.S. Coast Guard

Capt. Andrea L. Contratto, USCGR: chief, Office of Reserve Affairs, U.S. Coast Guard

Jonathan Dembo, Ph.D.: special collections curator, Eastern Carolina University

Capt. John Fitzgerald, USCG: commandant of cadets, U.S. Coast Guard Academy, New London, Connecticut

Christopher B. Havern: assistant historian, U.S. Coast Guard

Capt. Fred F. Herzberg, USCG (Ret.): founder and executive director emeritus, Foundation for Coast Guard History

Tara King: editor, Coast Guard Academy Alumni Association *Bulletin*

Lana G. Kroll: editor, critic, creative consultant, and loving wife

Chief Warrant Officer Edward J. Kruska, USCGR: editor, *Coast Guard Reservist*

C. Kay Larson: Coast Guard Auxiliary historian

Master Chief Petty Officer John F. Niece, USCG: command master chief, U.S. Coast Guard Academy, New London, Connecticut

Senior Chief Marine Science Technician Dennis L. Noble, USCG (Ret.),
    Ph.D.: author, historian and independent scholar
Cdr. John O'Conner, USCG: chief, Officer Candidate School, New London,
    Connecticut
Lt. Corina Ott, USCG: instructor, Officer Candidate School, New London,
    Connecticut
Jerry Patton: president, College of the Desert, Palm Desert, California
Vice Adm. David P. Pekoske, USCG: commander, Coast Guard Pacific Area
Scott Price: deputy historian, U.S. Coast Guard
Food Service Specialist 1st Class Mark H. Reis, USCG: USCGC *Bertholf*
    (WMSL-750)
Capt. Mark D. Rizzo, USCG: chief, Office of Auxiliary and Boating Safety
Dave Rosen, Ph.D.: historian, Coast Guard Pacific Area
Master Chief Petty Officer Jeffrey D. Smith, USCGR: master chief petty offi-
    cer of the Coast Guard Reserve Force
William H. Thiesen, Ph.D.: historian, Coast Guard Atlantic Area
Vice Adm. Howard B. Thorsen, USCG (Ret.): chairman of the board,
    Foundation for Coast Guard History
John A. Tilley, Ph.D.: professor of history, Eastern Carolina University
Rear Adm. Paul F. Zukunft, USCG: commander, Eleventh Coast Guard District

PART 1. CORE VALUES

During March 1993 at a meeting of those involved in Coast Guard leadership development activities, it was recognized that an absence of commonly stated core values was problematic to developing service leaders. Work was immediately begun to identify appropriate core values. In 1994 the Coast Guard formally articulated those that the service holds dear: honor, respect, and devotion to duty. These were approved by the commandant of the Coast Guard, Adm. Robert Kramek, and officially promulgated in April of that year. The values may have been stated formally relatively recently, but they are deeply rooted in the heritage of commitment and service that distinguishes the U.S. Coast Guard. They define the organization's very character. From the days of the first revenue cutters, lifesaving stations, and lighthouses, Coast Guard people have embraced and lived these values.

Individual members bring their personal values to the workplace. As with all organizations, the Coast Guard has a tendency to attract and retain people who hold values aligned with those of the organization. As the service continues to embrace different ethnicities and backgrounds, it is reassuring to know that members share the same values. These have been and will continue to serve as the Coast Guard's foundation.

The service may look different in the years ahead, but the core values will endure. They will provide the strength and character to build on the service's reputation as the world's premier maritime service.

The values are more than just rules of behavior. They are deeply rooted in the heritage that has made the organization great. They demonstrate who Coast Guardsmen are and guide their performance, conduct, and decisions every minute of every day. Members of the service seek to embrace them in their professional undertakings as well as in their personal lives. The official service statements of the core values follow:

Honor

Integrity is our standard. We demonstrate uncompromising ethical conduct and moral behavior in all of our personal actions. We are loyal and accountable to the public trust.

Respect

We value our diverse work force. We treat each other with fairness, dignity, and compassion. We encourage individual opportunity and growth. We encourage creativity through empowerment. We work as a team.

Devotion to Duty

We are professionals, military and civilian, who seek responsibility, accept accountability, and are committed to the successful achievement of our organizational goals. We exist to serve. We serve with pride.

The current commandant, Adm. Thad Allen, has often described these core values as being like concentric circles. At the center is honor, a compact you have with yourself. These are your values; it is how you conduct your life. Beyond that is respect, a compact with others—those with whom you interact. The outer circle is devotion to duty, a compact with the public and nation. They are all interrelated and key to the identity and character of every member of the Coast Guard.

1. HONOR

Integrity is our standard. We demonstrate uncompromising ethical conduct and moral behavior in all of our personal actions. We are loyal and accountable to the public trust.

OFFICIAL COAST GUARD STATEMENT OF THIS CORE VALUE

Coast Guard members demonstrate honor in all things, never lying, cheating, or stealing. We do the right thing because it is the right thing—all the time. The temptation is frequently to do what is easy or would benefit us. Doing the right thing is not always easy, because in addition to not benefiting us, it may even cost us.

Countless Coast Guardsmen have done the right thing, and sadly many have been forgotten. But at the time of their actions, they inspired others. One of these, even though it cost him a great deal later in his life and even his legacy, was Ellsworth "Todd" Bertholf.

Ellsworth P. Bertholf

Born in New York City on 7 April 1866, Bertholf grew up in Hackensack, New Jersey. In September 1882 he received a congressional appointment to attend the U.S. Naval Academy in Annapolis, Maryland. A little less than a year later he was court-martialed and dismissed for his involvement in a hazing incident. Two years after that, he competed and won appointment as a cadet in the U.S. Revenue Cutter Service at their School of Instruction in New Bedford, Massachusetts. Graduating with the Class of 1887, Bertholf was not immediately commissioned due to his many conduct infractions. But finally, in June 1889 he went on to have a distinguished career. In 1895 he became the first Revenue Cutter Service officer to attend the Naval War College in Newport, Rhode Island.

Todd Bertholf gained nationwide fame for his participation in the Alaska Overland Relief Expedition of 1898–99. He was awarded a Congressional Gold Medal for his role in this heroic rescue of stranded whalers near Point

Barrow, Alaska. During 1901–2 he made a round-the-world trip, including across the breadth of Russia, to secure a new species of reindeer for importation to Alaska and supervised their transport across the Bering Sea. He later commanded both the USRC *Bear* and *Morrill*.

In June 1911, as a junior captain Bertholf was selected to be the captain commandant of the Revenue Cutter Service, over twenty-two officers who were senior to him. He was the equivalent of a lieutenant commander at the time and was promoted immediately to the equivalent of captain, skipping the rank of senior captain (equivalent to a modern commander). As captain commandant of the Revenue Cutter Service, he helped create its merger with the Life-saving Service to become the United States Coast Guard in 1915. He then was appointed as the first commandant of the Coast Guard, a position he retained throughout the service's participation in the First World War.

Following its end, the new Coast Guard faced a major crisis. The wartime mixing of Coast Guard and Navy officers had created serious agitation among the officer corps. When the war had begun, the laws in place fixing the relative ranks of officers resulted in a Coast Guard captain ranking below a lieutenant commander in the Navy. By September 1917, Bertholf had corrected the relative rank problem.

A further irritant to the Coast Guard was that only naval officers were eligible for temporary promotion during the war. They also received sea pay, while Coast Guard officers did not. When Bertholf learned that the Secretary of the Navy refused to support a change to the legislation to provide temporary promotions for Coast Guard officers, he dropped the matter there, on the grounds it was not essential to the war effort and would not apply to enlisted men. He was convinced that in time the law would be changed, but his officers criticized him for failing to promote the interests of the service.

In July 1918, temporary promotions in the Coast Guard were authorized. Bertholf, as a captain commandant, was temporarily promoted to the rank of commodore, becoming the Coast Guard's first flag officer.

In many respects Bertholf's biggest battle came after the war. The Coast Guard had become part of the Department of the Navy during the war, and following it many congressmen and members of the Wilson administration—including a young assistant secretary of the Navy named Franklin Delano Roosevelt—thought the service should remain there. Many senior Coast Guard officers also supported the permanent transfer of the Coast Guard to the Navy Department. According to one estimate, 70 percent of Coast Guard officers were in favor of permanent transfer. They had enjoyed the increased resources, larger commands, faster promotions, and other benefits.

Commodore Bertholf disagreed. He feared that because his officers had not been trained for naval service, they would not be selected for promotion in the Navy. He also was concerned that the proposal would demote and reduce the pay of a large number of enlisted men. Furthermore, Bertholf believed that his service's absorption into the Navy would destroy the esprit de corps and identity of the Coast Guard. But he was a lone voice before Congress. Even his most senior officers testified in favor of transfer to the Navy Department. They publicly criticized Bertholf, alleging that he opposed the transfer to retain his power over the service.

In reality, it would have been in Bertholf's self-interest to support the permanent transfer. The provisions of the bill were distinctly advantageous to him from a monetary and rank standpoint. The fact that he opposed the transfer should have absolved him from suspicion that he acted from self-interest, but it did not. Bertholf retired in June 1919, confident that the Coast Guard would return to the Treasury Department, which it did two months later.

"Todd" Bertholf paid a high price for acting in the best interest of the Coast Guard, rather than to gain popularity and support among his officer corps. Although he cared about how his subordinates and colleagues thought of him, he never allowed a desire for personal popularity to compromise his principles. As commandant, first of the Revenue Cutter Service and later the Coast Guard, Bertholf's primary concern was always what was best for the service, especially the enlisted personnel. He frequently displayed a courage that was often misunderstood and maligned by those who disagreed with him. As a result, following his death, he was ignored and virtually forgotten by the service he had fought to save. Until a few decades ago, no one in the Coast Guard even knew of him.

Completed in 1992, Bertholf Plaza at the Coast Guard Academy is named after the first commandant of the modern-day Coast Guard. The plaza, located near Waesche Library, is unmarked, the site of several plaques commemorating Coast Guard personnel who served in World War II. Visitors would never realize this was Bertholf Plaza without consulting the walking guide.

On Coast Guard Day, 4 August 2008, the USCGC *Bertholf* (WMSL-750) was commissioned in honor of this service member who epitomized the core value of honor.

Dorothy C. Stratton

Dorothy C. Stratton was born on 24 March 1899 in Brookfield, Missouri, daughter of Anna Troxler Stratton and the Rev. Richard Stratton, a Baptist preacher. She attended high school at Lamar, Missouri, and Blue Rapids, Kansas.

Graduating from Ottawa University, Kansas, in 1920, she went on to earn an MA in psychology from the University of Chicago and then, in 1932, a Ph.D. in student personnel administration from Columbia University. While earning her graduate degrees, she taught at public high schools in Brookfield,

Capt. Dorothy Stratton, head of SPARS during World War II

Missouri; Renton, Washington; and San Bernardino, California (where she was the dean of girls). In 1933, Stratton joined the faculty at Purdue University as the institution's first full-time dean of women and assistant professor of psychology. She became a full professor in 1940.

At Purdue, Dr. Stratton had already begun to hone the leadership skills for which she would later become famous as director of the Coast Guard SPARs (named after the Coast Guard motto Semper Paratus—Always Ready). She recalled that part of her role as dean of women was to act as disciplinarian. "I tried from the beginning to establish a more positive atmosphere," she says. She began by moving her fourth-floor office to the ground floor, in an effort to make it easier for students to visit. At a university where the ratio of men to women was seven to one, Stratton understood that having an open-door policy provided a learning experience that would benefit both her and her students.

The university was renowned for its agricultural and engineering studies, but did not offer a bachelor of arts. Its curriculum largely attracted students interested in science, so Stratton adopted a vision to make this field more appealing to women. She devised an experimental curriculum tailored specifically to women. This proved successful, as female undergraduate enrollment increased from 600 to more than 1,400. Stratton also managed the construction of three new residence halls and an employment-placement center for women. With Helen B. Schleman, a Purdue colleague who would later become a commander and assistant director of the SPARs, Stratton coauthored an undergraduate social-usages book titled *Your Best Foot Forward.*

With these successes at Purdue already behind her, the black cloud of World War II loomed, and, like many veterans, she felt an urgent need to serve her country. So in June 1942, Stratton took a leave of absence and joined the Women Appointed Volunteer Emergency Service (WAVES), otherwise known as the Naval Women's Reserve.

Stratton was commissioned into the Navy as a lieutenant after completing the first WAVE indoctrination class at U.S. Naval Training Station, Smith College, Northampton, Massachusetts.

While serving as assistant to the commanding officer of the radio school for WAVES in Madison, Wisconsin, Lieutenant Stratton received a telegram to come to Washington, D.C. On 23 November 1942, President Roosevelt signed an amendment to Public Law 773, thereby establishing the Coast Guard Women's Reserve. She became its director with the rank of lieutenant commander on 24 November. Simultaneously, Stratton became the first female officer to be accepted for service in the history of the Coast Guard.

She immediately took to the task of creating another first. In a November 1942 memo to wartime Coast Guard commandant Adm. Russell R. Waesche, Stratton wrote: "The motto of the Coast Guard is 'Semper Paratus—Always Ready.' The initials of this motto are, of course, SPAR. Why not call the members of the Women's Reserve SPARs? . . . As I understand it, a spar is often a supporting beam and that is what we hope each member of the Women's Reserve will be. . . . I like SPARs because it really has meaning."

Stratton's choice of a name for women in the Coast Guard was in every way appropriate. The service was well aware that no ship can function without its support, and indeed the Coast Guard might not have succeeded in its war effort had it not been for the dedication of all its SPARs.

Because of her good humor and reputation as a "talented raconteur," Stratton easily earned the affection and admiration of all who knew her. Promotions came quickly for Lieutenant Commander Stratton. She was promoted to commander in December 1943 and to captain two months later. During the war her only brother, Capt. Richard C. Stratton, served in the Medical Corps Reserve of the U.S. Army.

During her four years as director of the SPARs, Dorothy Stratton recruited and led 10,000 enlisted women and 1,000 commissioned officers. She guided the service through World War II and until the SPARs' demobilization was completed on 30 June 1946. As director of the Women's Reserve of the United States Coast Guard, Captain Stratton was primarily responsible for originating policies for the procurement, training, utilization, and maintenance of morale of the Women's Reserve.

At the peak of Coast Guard strength, one in every fifteen or sixteen enlisted persons was a woman, and one in every twelve or thirteen officers was a SPAR. This was the highest ratio of women to men in any of the wartime armed services. Enlisted SPARs served in thirty different Coast Guard ratings, and many of them achieved the distinction of becoming first class and chief petty officers in their particular specialty.

While most enlisted women served as yeoman and at storekeeper ratings, others were trained as sound-motion-picture technicians, link-trainer operators, parachute riggers, chaplains' assistants, air-control tower operators, as well as cooks and bakers, radiomen, pharmacist's mates, radio technicians, and drivers of motor vehicles who knew how to maintain their own cars. The greatest number of SPAR officers—37 percent—held general duty billets. About 23 percent served as communications officers, and 17 percent as pay and supply officers. Seven percent were involved in recruiting (including the recruiting of men). As soon as Congress permitted women of the naval services to volunteer outside the continental United States, relatively large numbers did so and were assigned to Hawaii and Alaska.

When Captain Stratton completed her service to the Coast Guard in January 1946, commandant Adm. Joseph F. Farley awarded her the Legion of Merit. The accompanying citation, signed by Secretary of the Navy James Forrestal, includes the following comments: "Through her qualities of leadership, Captain Stratton inspired the finest type of woman to volunteer her services to her country. Through her keen understanding of the abilities of women, her vision of the jobs which they could perform, and her consummate tact in fitting women in a military organization, she was able to direct the efforts of the women of the Reserve into channels of the greatest usefulness to the Coast Guard and to the country."

Upon receiving her award, Captain Stratton's response epitomized a core value by honoring others, rather than herself. She stated:

I am glad this medal is called the Legion of Merit, for it is to the Legion that it is awarded, the Legion of 11,000 who volunteered to do a wartime job. As representative of the Legion of SPARs, I am happy to accept this award and to say how much we have appreciated the opportunity to serve in the Coast Guard. The Coast Guard utilized the highest percentage of women of any of the services. This is adequate testimony to the adaptability of the Coast Guard, and to the ability of the women who entered its service. We have liked serving in the Coast Guard and we shall always be interested in its future.

Stratton went on to serve as the director of personnel for the International Monetary Fund (1946–50), and then as national executive director of the Girl Scouts of America (1950–60). She died in 2006 at the age of 107, in West Lafayette, Indiana, where she had lived since 1985. She had survived the entire tumultuous twentieth century.

In 2001 the Women Officers Professional Association (now the Sea Services Leadership Association) created its Captain Dorothy Stratton Leadership Award in her honor. It is presented to a female officer (W-2 to O-4) of the Coast Guard who shows leadership and mentorship and shares the service's core values.

In 2005, the Ottawa University Alumni Association presented its Outstanding Achievement Award to Stratton. In 2008, the Coast Guard announced it would name its third national security cutter *Stratton* (WMSL-752) in her honor.

Thomas James Eugene Crotty

"Jimmy" Crotty (born 1912) grew up in Buffalo, New York, heavily involved in team sports. Following his 1930 graduation from the city's South Park High School, he was appointed a cadet at the U.S. Coast Guard Academy in New London, Connecticut. At the academy, Crotty excelled in athletics, becoming captain of the football team in his last year, and of the basketball team for three years. Graduating in 1934, he spent the next six years serving on board cutters based out of New York, Seattle, Juneau, and Sault Ste. Marie.

In the late 1930s, diplomatic tensions between the United States and Japan increased. This caused the military to send additional personnel and units to overseas Pacific outposts. In April 1941, Crotty received orders to undertake studies at the Navy's Mine Warfare School in Yorktown, Virginia. After additional training at the Navy's Mine Recovery Unit in Washington, D.C., Crotty became the Coast Guard's leading expert in mine operations, demolition, and the use of explosives. In early fall he departed for his new assignment in the Philippines, as a member of a Navy mine-recovery unit near Manila.

Arriving on 28 October 1941, Lieutenant Crotty's unit served under the commandant, 16th Naval District. He was attached to In-Shore Patrol Headquarters at the U.S. Navy Yard, Cavite.

Not even two months later, the Imperial Japanese Navy launched surprise attacks on American military installations in the Pacific, including those in the Philippines. On 10 December, Japanese aircraft bombed and damaged most of the facilities at the Cavite Navy Yard, where Crotty was assigned.

With enemy ground forces advancing, American and Filipino forces moved behind fortified lines on the Bataan Peninsula and onto the island fortress of Corregidor. During this evacuation, Lieutenant Crotty, because of his special qualifications in handling explosives, supervised the demolition of the USS *Sea Lion* (SS-195), the Navy yard's ammunition magazine, and other naval, military, and important civilian establishments, to prevent them from falling into the enemy's hands. Then Crotty and the other Cavite personnel were evacuated to Fort Mills, on Corregidor.

There Crotty served in the local guard unit but also participated in night raids on the mainland, to demolish more American equipment and facilities before the Japanese arrived. During February and March 1942, he served as executive officer of the Navy minesweeper USS *Quail* (AM-15), which swept minefields so that U.S. submarines could surface at night to deliver goods and remove critical personnel. The vessel also provided antiaircraft cover and fire support for the land-based units defending Bataan and Corregidor. By the end of March, Bataan's defenders were exhausted from five months of Japanese attacks; on 9 April the American and Filipino defenders of Bataan finally surrendered.

Corregidor held out for another month. Crotty served with honor up to the bitter end, fighting alongside the island's Army, Navy, and Marine defenders. But with Corregidor's surrender on 6 May, Crotty became the first Coast Guard prisoner of war since the War of 1812 , when the British captured members of the U.S. Revenue Cutter Service. The Japanese loaded Crotty and his fellow prisoners into a landing craft that took them to Manila. There the POWs were herded into boxcars for shipment to the infamous prison camp at Cabanatuan, Mieva Ecija, Luzon.

Throughout his defense of the Philippines, Lieutenant Crotty had served with honor and displayed a sense of humor and unwavering optimism. This continued through the rigors and trials as a POW. But then, late in the summer of 1942, a diphtheria epidemic swept through the camp, killing forty prisoners per day. Crotty was among those who contracted the disease. With the prison's lack of necessary medication and proper health care, he passed away only days after getting sick. To this day, no one knows exactly when he died or the precise location of his grave. His body lies buried beside those of thousands of other American and Filipino heroes who perished in the terrible conditions at Cabanatuan.

Lieutenant James Crotty serves as a great example of what it means to serve with honor under the most trying conditions. By doing so, he also brought honor to all those who wear the Coast Guard uniform.

Quentin R. Walsh

Groton, Connecticut, native Quentin Walsh's long and illustrious Coast Guard career began with his appointment as a cadet at the academy on 25 July 1929. Graduating with the Class of 1933, he took part in Rum War patrols to prevent the smuggling of alcoholic beverages into the United States during prohibition. During the early days of World War II, he navigated the transport *Joseph Dickman* (APA-13), carrying British troops from Halifax, Nova Scotia, to Bombay, India. Because the U.S. forces in England were concerned about having access to ports to augment their over-the-beach delivery of men and materiel, they needed Coast Guardsmen as part of the solution. In 1943 Commander Walsh was assigned to the U.S. Naval Forces staff in Great Britain, to work on plans to activate major port operations in France as quickly as possible after the initial invasion over the beaches of Normandy.

Operation Overlord, Phase Neptune, the amphibious invasion of Europe at Normandy, would be the largest amphibious operation in the history of warfare. Commander Walsh, thoroughly familiar with the plans, was assigned to form and command Naval Task Unit 127.2.8, to put details of those plans in operation. His unit would be attached to VII Corps of Gen. Omar Bradley's First U.S. Army. He organized a unit of fifty or so volunteers, most of them Seabees (Navy construction battalions, or CBs), trained in infantry combat and in the repair and construction of port facilities. They were to land over Utah Beach on 10 June, the fourth day of the invasion, and then enter and reconnoiter the vital port of Cherbourg and prepare it to receive Allied shipping as soon as possible. Walsh demanded and got the best in training and supplies for his men. He pushed them to undergo the rigors of infantry training for the Army, because he knew this naval unit would later operate alongside soldiers in the weeks following D-day.

Walsh's unit advanced westward toward Cherbourg. On 26 June they, with troops of the 79th Division, entered the city. Commander Walsh was the first U.S. naval officer to enter Cherbourg in 1944. His reconnaissance party comprised Lt. Frank Lauer, a Naval Reserve Seabee officer, and fifteen sailors armed with submachine guns, bazookas, and hand grenades. They fought their way to the harbor area along streets still defended by numerous pockets of enemy resistance; German machine-gun emplacements in corner buildings attempted to command the streets.

Advancing around the harbor to the well-guarded naval arsenal the following day, Walsh and his men captured an English-speaking German sailor to serve as their guide. Then they entered the arsenal, using their weapons as necessary. A German captain and some 400 men surrendered to Walsh's small band.

Later, using the Seabees' white scarf as a flag of truce, Walsh and his group approached nearby Fort du Homet for talks with the garrison commander. During negotiations, Walsh claimed he was backed by 800 men who would make their enemies' lives either miserable or short if they did not receive an unconditional surrender of the fort and its 350 defenders. The Germans fell for Walsh's bluff.

In the process, fifty-two U.S. paratroopers were freed and Commander Walsh obtained information from French Resistance forces concerning the location of German minefields, which he plotted on a chart of the harbor and delivered by special sailboat messenger to the British minesweepers off the harbor's entrance. Because of the large number of all types of mines, sailing was the only safe method of conveyance.

During their operations in Cherbourg, Walsh's unit suffered approximately 25 percent casualties while moving swiftly and courageously to occupy the vital elements for control of the port. On the third day, after occupation was complete, the task unit was dissolved. Commander Walsh was appointed assistant port director of Cherbourg, where massive amounts of men, equipment, materiel, and ammunition were landed. All were essential to sustain the invasion forces after their initial landing over the beaches.

After a month in this capacity, Walsh's old task unit was reformed with about 300 Seabees, and he was ordered to reconnoiter the coastal ports of Brittany, from St.-Malo west to Brest, with VIII Corps, 3rd Army.

They finished this task at the end of August and were then redeployed back east of Le Havre with the First Canadian Army, coming under fire again in this mission and entering Le Havre on 12 September. Within days Walsh was hospitalized with viral pneumonia and was ultimately sent back to the States.

For his heroism at Cherbourg, Commander Walsh was awarded the Navy Cross, the highest award for valor after the Medal of Honor. The citation concluded: "Commander Walsh's brilliant initiatives, inspiring leadership, and successful accomplishment of a difficult mission reflect great credit upon himself, his command, and the United States Naval Service." It also brought great credit and honor to the Coast Guard

Captain Walsh lived in Arizona on physical disability after World War II, but was recalled to active duty during the Korean War. He retired again on disability, as a captain, in 1960. He then settled in Maryland, where he died in May 2000 at age 90.

On 13 June 2008, Captain Walsh's heroic actions were celebrated in New Haven, Connecticut, as Coast Guard Sector Long Island Sound christened the Captain Quentin R. Walsh Sector Command Building.

Douglas A. Munro

Although Douglas Albert Munro was born in Vancouver, Canada (11 October 1919), his parents were American. Mr. and Mrs. James Munro raised their son in South Cle Elum, Washington, where he graduated from high school in 1937. He attended the Central Washington College of Education for a year, then left to enlist in the United States Coast Guard in 1939. He had an outstanding record as an enlisted man and was promoted rapidly through the ratings to signalman, first class.

By summer 1942, Munro was serving on board the USS *Hunter Liggett* (APA-14), a Coast Guard–manned personnel transport that was a passenger ship before the war. Munro's ship was ordered to take part in the first offensive U.S. operation in the Pacific, the occupation of Guadalcanal. After amphibious training and a rehearsal landing in the Koro Islands, on 31 July she sailed with other ships for the Solomons. The *Hunter Liggett* would be the only Coast Guard vessel taking part in this operation, although eighteen of the twenty-two other transports sailing with her had Coast Guardsmen in their Navy crews.

Munro's ship arrived off Guadalcanal the night of 6 August. In this assault, the first amphibious U.S. operation since 1898, the *Hunter Liggett* was assigned to a later wave but sent her boats to aid in the initial 7 August landings. Enemy air attacks began the day after the landing, sinking fellow transport *George F. Elliott* (AP-105). The *Hunter Liggett*'s gunners shot down several of the attackers as she remained off the beaches.

Early on the morning of 9 August, men in the transport area could see flashes of light from an engagement off Savo Island. As the Japanese attempted to reinforce their Solomons garrison and destroy the transports, they surprised an American task force and inflicted heavy losses. The *Hunter Liggett* and other vulnerable transports got under way, but soon returned to the transport area. After noon on 9 August, they began the grim job of rescuing survivors from the sunken cruisers *Vincennes* (CA-44), *Astoria* (CA-34), and *Quincy* (CA-39).

That afternoon the transport sailed with the wounded, in company with the damaged *Chicago* (CA-29), to Nouméa and arrived two days later. With the Guadalcanal campaign began the refinement of amphibious techniques that were to pay off so handsomely as the war progressed. Douglas Munro was among those who served as coxswains for the landing crafts carrying Marines to the beaches.

SM1/C Douglas Munro

On 27 September 1942, two weeks before his twenty-third birthday, Munro was in charge of ten craft that put ashore a small force of nearly 500 Marines in an attempt to encircle enemy troops in the Matanikau vicinity. Almost immediately upon his return, the officer in charge advised him that the Japanese forces were more numerous than anticipated, so the Marines had to be evacuated.

Douglas Munro, under constant strafing by enemy machine guns on the island and at great risk to his life, daringly led five of his small craft toward the shore. As he closed on the beach, he signaled the others to land. Then, to draw the enemy's fire and protect the heavily loaded boats, he valiantly placed his craft with its two small guns as a shield between the boats and the Japanese. When the perilous task of evacuation was nearly completed, Munro was mortally wounded. But his crew, two of whom were also wounded, carried on until the last boat had loaded and cleared the beach.

Munro remained conscious long enough to say four words: "Did they get off?" He died knowing his mission had succeeded and his final assignment had been carried out. Douglas Munro gave his life in one of the Coast Guard's finest traditions, while conducting a rescue operation.

He was awarded the Medal of Honor posthumously, the only Coast Guardsman on whom the nation's highest decoration for heroism in combat has ever been bestowed. He was also awarded the Purple Heart Medal and the American Defense Service Medal, the Asiatic–Pacific Area Campaign Medal, and the World War II Victory Medal. Douglas Munro, by his heroism and sacrifice, brought honor to every member of the Coast Guard. He epitomized the service's core values of honor, respect, and devotion to duty.

In 1944, the Navy commissioned one of its *John C. Butler* (DE-339)–class destroyer escorts as the USS *Douglas A. Munro* (DE-422). The 306-foot ship was decommissioned in 1960. One of the three 378-foot high-endurance cutters named for service heroes now bears Munro's name: the USCGC *Munro* (WHEC-724), commissioned in 1971.

Munro Hall was originally built in the early 1960s as the enlisted barracks and general mess at the Coast Guard Academy. Today it houses several administrative offices and guest quarters, a 70-room facility designed for use by personnel on temporary duty at the academy.

Since 1971 the U.S. Navy League has presented the Douglas A. Munro Award annually, for inspirational leadership. The honor goes to an enlisted service member who, by traditional performance of duty, has demonstrated outstanding leadership and the professional competence required by his or her rank.

At Coast Guard Recruit Training Center in Cape May, New Jersey, recruits live in another, newer Munro Hall, built in 1966 as one of three recruit barracks named after Coast Guard heroes. Douglas Munro's Medal of Honor is on display in this barracks. His statue, erected and dedicated in November 1989, graces the west end of the parade grounds, not far from the barracks bearing his name.

Coast Guard Training Center Cape May again honored SM1 Douglas A. Munro when it dedicated the USCGC *Spencer's* (WPG/WHEC-35) mast on the parade field near Munro's statue on 27 September 2008, the sixty-sixth anniversary of his heroic actions while protecting U.S. Marines at Guadalcanal. Munro served on board the *Spencer* before his service at Guadalcanal. In 2005, he became the first Coast Guardsman to be inducted into the Surface Navy Association's Hall of Fame.

2. RESPECT

We value our diverse work force. We treat each other with fairness, dignity, and compassion. We encourage individual opportunity and growth. We encourage creativity through empowerment. We work as a team.

OFFICIAL COAST GUARD STATEMENT OF THIS CORE VALUE

As Coast Guardsmen, we value the dignity of all people. Whether a stranded boater, an immigrant, or a fellow Coast Guard member; we honor, protect, and assist. This means we care for others, which means saying no to our own desires and yes to the needs of others. The Coast Guard is best known as a humanitarian service that protects and rescues others in need. Countless members of the service have given of themselves to help others. Some have even given their lives. Following are stories of some of those who have epitomized this core value of respect. All inspire us to do the same: care for the public and our fellow Coast Guard members.

William Ray "Billy" Flores

Flores joined the Coast Guard shortly after graduating from Western Hills High School in Benbrook, Texas, in 1979. After completing recruit training at Cape May, nineteen-year-old Flores, a brand new, proud seaman apprentice, was one of several other new members to report for duty on board the Galveston-based CGC *Blackthorn* (WLB-391), a 180-foot buoy tender that had been commissioned on 27 March 1944.

A few months later, on the evening of 28 January 1980, the *Blackthorn* was outbound from Tampa Bay, headed for her home port of Galveston, Texas. The weather was calm, with a visibility of nine miles. The *Capricorn*, a 580-foot tanker carrying 150,000 barrels of oil, was inbound . Shortly after eight o'clock, the two vessels collided nearly head-on about a half-mile west of the Skyway Bridge. This tragedy occurred a little more than a year after the sinking of the USCGC *Cuyahoga* (WIX-157) on 20 October 1978, following a

USCGC *Blackthorn* (WLB-391)

collision that took the lives of eleven of the twenty-nine Coast Guard person-nel on board.

The *Capricorn*'s port anchor tore into the hull plating of the *Blackthorn*'s port side. The tender became entangled in the freighter's anchor chain and cap-sized, sinking in less than a minute. Twenty-seven of Flores' shipmates did escape the sinking ship. He and another crew member, Larry Clutter, stayed on board to throw lifejackets to some of their shipmates who had jumped into the water.

When the *Blackthorn* began to sink, Clutter, along with most other crew members, abandoned ship. But Flores, who was less than a year out of boot camp, stayed put. He used his belt to tie open the lifejacket locker door so more jackets could float to the surface. He also assisted trapped shipmates and comforted those who were injured or disoriented. The young Coast Guardsman sacrificed his life to help shipmates in the frantic moments after their 180-foot cutter collided with the oil tanker. Despite Flores' efforts, twenty-three crew members died. Many survivors told the same story: They would not be alive had it not been for one of the new guys. They couldn't remember his name, though.

The actions of SA William Ray "Billy" Flores were somehow overlooked as officials investigated the worst peacetime disaster in Coast Guard history. But a few officers didn't forget. They pushed the service to formally recog-nize Flores' heroism. On the morning of 16 September 2000, Flores was hon-ored posthumously with the Coast Guard Medal, the service's highest award for heroism not involving combat. His parents, Robert and Julia Flores of

Benbrook, Texas, selected that date for the ceremony because it commemorates the beginning of Mexico's fight for independence from Spain.

The ceremony was held in Benbrook Cemetery, with their six surviving children and other relatives. About 100 people attended the ceremony near Flores' grave, among them Mayor Felix Hebert.

In presenting the medal to Mr. and Mrs. Flores, Rear Adm. Paul Pluta, the Coast Guard's Eighth District commander, said: "Seaman Apprentice Flores' exceptional fortitude, remarkable initiative and courage throughout this tragic incident were instrumental in saving many lives. . . . His example is all the more notable when one considers his youth and lack of experience. . . . He set the standard for us all and embodies the true spirit of what we stand for." Part of what every Coast Guardsman stands for is the core value of respect—for shipmates and all others. SA Billy Flores did indeed set the standard for all of us.

Fletcher W. Brown

A native of Brockton, Massachusetts, Fletcher W. Brown graduated in June 1913 from the Revenue Cutter Service's School of Instruction, which at that time was a three-year program at Fort Trumbull, New London, Connecticut. Over the next four years he served in the Atlantic and Caribbean on the cutters *Woodbury*, *Ossipee*, *Pamlico*, and *Algonquin*. As the Coast Guard entered the First World War, he was ordered to Newport, Rhode Island, to rejoin the *Ossipee*. The ship was soon ordered to Europe, arriving in late August 1917 with a mission to escort slow freighters in convoys between the British Isles and the Mediterranean. German submarines were active, and the *Ossipee* observed several torpedoings and was herself the target of one that she managed to evade. Of this incident, Lt. (jg) Fletcher Brown later wrote:

> On the morning of December 15, 1917, a merchantman, which fell behind her position alongside the *Ossipee*, was torpedoed. That evening at 4:30 a torpedo was discharged, presumably from the same submarine, just off our starboard bow. Viewed from [the] deck, its wake seared a white path that disappeared beneath our starboard quarter. As fast as her limited speed would permit the *Ossipee* reached the indicated locality of the enemy and dropped a bomb. You know the kind we had in those first days—the type in which the detonator was inserted before the bomb was thrown overboard by hand. The Hun did not renew the attack. The convoy of thirty-two ships scattered and but few returned to formation as that night the famous Biscay Gale came up, during which several vessels foundered. The *Ossipee*, though but one hundred and sixty feet in length, rode out the storm with but the loss of one lifeboat.

On Christmas day Brown was transferred to the USCGC *Seneca*, assigned the same type of convoy duty between Gibraltar and England. Shortly after he joined her, she also was attacked at night by a rapid succession of three torpedoes, this time while Brown had the conn. He successfully evaded the attack but never saw the enemy.

As convoys approached the Gibraltar danger zone, additional escorts joined them. Among them was the British 262-foot *Cowslip*. At 2:45 AM on 25 April 1918, a lookout on the *Cowslip* sighted a large, fully surfaced German cruiser submarine. Unfortunately, the U-boat had seen the British escort first and launched a torpedo that struck the ship just abaft the midship section. The explosion almost tore the ship apart. All the *Cowslip*'s officers—except the captain and officer of the deck, who were on the bridge—were killed instantly when the torpedo exploded under the wardroom.

The *Seneca*, which was nearby, dropped depth charges, but the U-boat escaped in the poor visibility. The *Seneca*'s depth charges awakened Lieutenant Brown. He wrote, "I jumped from my bunk, seized my binoculars and automatic, and clad only in pajamas, rushed on deck to the after battery which I commanded. As the *Seneca* circled close to the sinking ship, the hissing steam, mingling with the many cries, all cloaked in darkness, wrought into one's imagination a picture not soon forgotten."

The convoy, except the *Seneca*, proceeded. Naval orders of the time prohibited stopping a vessel for the rescue of survivors. But a Coast Guard cutter could not ignore the cries coming out of the night. The *Seneca* lowered a whaleboat (a six-oared pulling boat) commanded by Lieutenant Brown, still in his pajamas, and then resumed the search for the German sub.

Brown reached the *Cowslip* and moved the whaleboat close under the ship's port bow in a turbulent sea, while British sailors slid down a line into the boat. Brown signaled the *Seneca*, and the cutter stopped at 4:00 AM, pausing only long enough to transfer survivors. He headed back to the *Cowslip* in darkness, not knowing if he would find the ship still afloat. He reached it just before it made its final plunge. Brown reported:

> Our little boat was quickly filled, yet, though others remained aboard they did not attempt to gain this last chance to be saved. "Can you take more?" came from the darkness above. "How many are left?" I called. "Three!" "Come on." Wedged between my pajamered [*sic*] legs, so that I was fairly riding his back was one man. For once in handling a steering oar, my feet were firmly anchored. Under the thwarts and crouched in the bottom, in every possible space were jammed these uncomplaining British sailors. . . . The *Cowslip* gave us but scant time to get clear before she slid beneath the seas.

The three remaining sailors had been saved. The *Cowslip*'s captain was the last to leave the ship before it sunk.

Within two months Brown was again launched in a whaleboat to rescue survivors of the unfortunate steamship *Queen*, which an enemy submarine had torpedoed. But his biggest challenge came in September 1918.

The *Seneca* was again escorting a convoy to Gibraltar. Among the ships was the British collier *Wellington*. On 16 September the *Wellington* exploded after being torpedoed. When the torpedo struck, the crew panicked and immediately began abandoning ship. By the time the *Seneca* arrived, the *Wellington*'s boats were already heading toward her. Lieutenant Brown immediately requested permission to lead an expedition to salvage the *Wellington*. His skipper said he could take only volunteers, and when word of the salvage effort spread through the cutter, Brown had more than enough. They immediately headed for the *Wellington*. Brown later wrote:

> With twenty volunteers from the *Seneca* I took command of her and endeavored to work her into Brest, some 350 miles. Without protection, steam was raised on her boilers and the ship gotten underway, but a gale that night pounded through the weakened bulkheads and in the proverbial "darkest hour just before dawn," the *Wellington*, on September 17, 1918, sank. My men went off on rafts but I remained signaling a destroyer until the collier started her final plunge. Three hours and a half of cold, cramps, and chills, and limbs numb and aching from swimming—then unconsciousness. Rescued by daylight, I awoke at noon in the crew's quarters of the destroyer *Warrington*. Eleven of those twenty boys who had been through the whole show with me were lost. My immersion necessitated six months' hospital treatment.

Fletcher Brown and his volunteers risked their lives, more than half giving them, out of respect for the lives of mariners in distress and trying to save the vessels. He was awarded the Navy Cross for gallant conduct in volunteering and endeavoring to navigate the *Wellington* into port. At first he refused to accept the medal, feeling it derived from the bravery of his crew. But some forty years later, he finally did accept it in order to pass it on to his son and grandson.

Fletcher Brown served a long and distinguished career, including being recalled from retirement to serve five years during World War II. He resumed his retired status in 1946 and died in Orlando, Florida, in 1984, at age 95. Fletcher Brown serves as another fine example of the Coast Guard core value of respect, not only for those in peril on the sea, but also for his crew.

Billy R. Ryan

When the Japanese attacked Pearl Harbor on 7 December 1941, Billy R. Ryan was in the middle of his second-class year at the Coast Guard Academy. Within six months he and his classmates were commissioned and sent to war. Ryan was assigned to the USS *Leonard Wood* (APA-12), an attack transport manned by the Coast Guard. A 535-foot converted passenger ship, she now carried 2,000 troops with their vehicles, artillery, ammunition, supplies, and landing craft to get them to the beaches. When Ens. Billy Ryan reported to the ship, she was assigned to Operation Torch, the Allies' first major amphibious assault and the largest in the world up to that time. Ryan participated in landings at Fedhala in Morocco and Sicily in the Mediterranean, and later in the island-hopping campaign in the Pacific.

At Saipan, in the Marianas, some 3,000 miles west of Hawaii and 1,000 miles east of the Philippines, an American force made a bloody, hard-fought landing in June 1944. The invasion of Saipan would be the greatest challenge that Americans had yet thrown at Japan. The Japanese regarded that island as part of their homeland, as well as a link in their inner-defense perimeter. As a result, Saipan was not a one- or two-day battle but lasted for three weeks, delaying the assault on Guam. The 30,000 Japanese on the island put up a terrific resistance.

Saipan's narrow beach was backed by sand soil and low scrubby trees. Lieutenant Ryan was boat group commander during the landings, in charge of assembling the loaded craft, delivering them per schedule to the beaches, salvaging damaged boats, and expediting everything having to do with his craft. Saipan was a fifteen-mile-long tropical island with mountainous high ground in the interior and Japanese army defenses, including an airfield, all well installed. The landing beaches were obstructed by a coral reef a quarter-mile or so offshore, over which even the shallow draft landing craft, vehicle, personnel (LCVP) Higgins Boats could not operate. This necessitated transferring troops at the reef into tracked amphibious assault craft called alligators, landing vehicle tracked (LVTs), to be shuttled into the beaches. The best hope was for frogmen to blow a passage through the coral.

The landing operation had to be conducted under heavy fire from well-placed enemy artillery and mortars. When Ryan's boats were authorized to withdraw, one had been heavily damaged and was stranded on the exposed reef with her crew of five. Ryan, in the best Coast Guard tradition, turned back to rescue his crew. Having accomplished that, he remained two more hours to salvage the badly needed boat as well.

During the early stages of the landing, an urgent need became apparent to land tanks and ammunition as speedily as possible through a very narrow channel discovered in the reef. The spot, known to the Japanese, concealed shore batteries that had been placed to cover its length. The fire was so intense that the channel could not be used, and U.S. naval gunfire could not locate the enemy batteries that were denying it. Ryan again volunteered and took one of his boats into the channel to draw enemy fire, so the guns could be located and silenced. His action succeeded, and soon tanks were being landed through this coveted route.

Billy Ryan serves as another shining example of the core value of respect. For his heroism at Saipan Lt. Billy Ryan was awarded the Bronze Star Medal. He continued to serve for a full thirty years, retiring at the rank of captain in 1972.

Bernard C. Webber

Born on 9 May 1928, at age sixteen Bernard C. Webber joined the Merchant Marine Service. He trained at Sheepshead Bay Maritime School, New York. He enlisted in the Coast Guard in 1946 and attended boot camp at Curtis Bay, Maryland. He was transferred to Cape Cod to serve lighthouse duty at Highland Lighthouse, North Truro, and later went to the Gay Head Lighthouse on Martha's Vineyard. Webber was transferred to Chatham Coast Guard Station, Cape Cod, in 1949.

On 12 February 1952, the 503-foot, 10,448-ton tanker *Pendleton* departed Baton Rouge, Louisiana, for Boston, Massachusetts. She carried kerosene and heating oil and a crew of forty. The *Pendleton* arrived off Boston late on 17 February in very foul weather and decided not to enter the harbor. The weather soon became a severe New England nor'easter, with a fifty-five-mile-an-hour gale, a vicious sea, subfreezing temperatures, and swirling snow that reduced visibility to a few hundred yards. Capt. John Fitzgerald ordered the *Pendleton* into Massachusetts Bay at slow speed. By 4:00 the next morning, the *Pendleton* rounded Cape Cod. The storm had increased to the point that water washed over her stern as she slowly sailed on.

At approximately 5:50, the *Pendleton* suddenly broke in two. The bow, with Captain Fitzgerald and seven crewmen on board, drifted off. Machinery in the stern section continued to operate, providing lights for thirty-two survivors in that section.

Nearby Coast Guard cutters estimated the seas to be sixty feet high. No one on the *Pendleton* had time to get off a distress call, and both sections were drifting southerly. By mid-morning that day, the Coast Guard lifeboat station at Chatham, Massachusetts, was informed that the tanker *Fort Mercer* had broken in two. WO Daniel W. Cluff, the station's commanding officer, received orders from the First Coast Guard District office in Boston to send a 36-foot motor lifeboat out to the tanker, so he ordered Chief Boatswain's Mate Donald Bangs to select a crew and get under way in the lifeboat CG-36383.

BM1 Bernie Webber

Bangs chose EN1 Emory H. Hayes, BM3 Antinio F. Ballerini, and SN Richard J. Ciccone as his crew and started for the motor lifeboat.

Then Cluff ordered BM1 Bernard C. Webber to select a crew and take another boat, CG-36500, to help secure fishing vessels that had broken away from their moorings in Old Harbor. Webber and his men worked through most of the morning in heavy snow and wind. By the time they finished, there were exhausted and cold.

When he reported back to Cluff, Webber learned that two ships, not one, were broken in two off the coast. Cluff directed Webber to take his crew in a four-wheeled-drive truck and meet with the Nauset Lifeboat Station to check out the sighting of this second vessel. Upon arriving, Webber discovered that the aft section of the *Pendleton* was drifting toward Chatham. With no way to communicate with the Chatham Station, Webber leaped into his truck and drove his crew to the station to sound the alarm. By the time they reached the Chatham Station, it was early evening and near darkness. An experimental radar at the unit located the bow section of the *Pendleton* drifting out to sea, and the stern drifting toward the beach. Chief Bangs and his crew on board the other 36-foot motor lifeboat continued their battle to reach the bow section.

Warrant Officer Cluff instructed Webber to take the CG-36500 out across the bar to the stern section of the *Pendleton*. The weather was horrible. Winds were blowing at seventy knots, there was horizontal, sub-zero freezing rain and towering seas—the same weather that had split two tankers in half earlier.

Webber was twenty-four years old, eight days short of six years in the Coast Guard. He had no illusions of what awaited him and his men out there in the darkness. He selected EN2 Andrew J. Fitzgerald, SN Richard P. Livesey, and SN Ervin E. Maske for his crew. Maske, a crew member of the Stonehorse Lightship, was at the station waiting for the weather to clear so he could return to his lightship. Shortly before 6:00 that evening, CG-36500 got under way from Old Harbor and headed out into the terrible seas. Webber's crew suddenly started singing "Rock of Ages" and "Harbor Lights" as they approached the bar.

As the single-propeller, ninety-horsepower motor lifeboat headed across the bar, the first wave threw it into the air and landed it in the trough of the waves. Another wave struck the 36-footer, breaking its windshield and knocking Webber to the deck of the coxswain's platform. Another wave laid the boat on its beam. The extreme rolling caused the engine to lose its gasoline prime and it stopped. Engineman Fitzgerald repeatedly fought to keep the engine running.

They finally crossed the bar, but the open sea wasn't much kinder. Seventy-foot waves towered over the lifeboat. There was no radio communication. Four cold, wet Coast Guardsmen continued their battle. Amazingly, they found the stern section of the *Pendleton*. Webber carefully maneuvered his lifeboat around it and spotted the survivors. He thought the sailors might be safer where they were, but they disagreed. One put a rope ladder over the side, and the crew started down.

The Coast Guardsmen had no choice but to try to pick them off the ladder. Webber's crewmen made their way to the bow of the lifeboat and grabbed the lowest sailor on the ladder as he timed his approach with the seas. Twenty times Webber brought the boat alongside the *Pendleton*'s stern section, and each time his crew grabbed a survivor. The sailors were desperate and some leaped too soon, landing in the cold, churning sea. Webber's crewmen pulled them on board. Finally the stern section rose up and rolled over. Webber and his crew had been able to save thirty-two of the thirty-three survivors.

CG-36500 was now near capacity, with thirty-six men on board. Webber briefed the survivors and his crew that he intended to head toward land and ground the lifeboat on the nearest sheltered beach. Everyone agreed and the boat started toward the beach. But fortunately, Webber discovered that he could make it to the harbor after all. He maneuvered CG-36500 to the pier, where many men, women, and children waited to help the survivors.

Chief Bangs and his boat reached the bow of the *Pendleton*, which had only one survivor who jumped toward Bangs' boat—but did not make it. Sea conditions made it impossible for Bangs to get to him in time. Even though they spent more time in the storm than Webber's crew, Bangs and his men were unable to rescue anyone.

Webber initially refused the Gold Lifesaving Medal because his crew was only going to be awarded the Silver Lifesaving Medal. But the Coast Guard then agreed to grant the entire crew the gold medals for their heroic actions.

In all, Coast Guard vessels, aircraft, and lifeboat stations, working under severe winter conditions, rescued and removed sixty-two persons from the foundering ships or the water with a loss of only five lives. Five Coast Guardsmen earned the Gold Lifesaving Medal, four the Silver Lifesaving Medal, and fifteen the Coast Guard Commendation Medal.

Later in his career, Bernie Webber was assigned to UCGC *Point Banks* (WPB-82327) out of Woods Hole, Massachusetts. From there he and the ship were ordered to Vietnam, where they conducted interdiction patrols out of An Thoi. When he returned, he was assigned to the buoy tender *Hornbeam* (WLB-394) in Woods Hole. He retired 1 September 1966 as a senior chief petty officer, serving as a warrant boatswain. In May 2002, the Coast Guard reissued Bernie Webber's gold-medal crew their coveted medals, honoring their heroics fifty years earlier. In 2007, the service further honored Warrant Boatswain Webber and his crew by acknowledging theirs as among the top ten Coast Guard rescues ever.

By his willingness to risk his life to save those in peril on the sea, Bernie Webber personified the core value of respect. His bravery and seamanship are an inspiration, and he will always be a Coast Guard hero. Bernie Webber died in January 2009. On 9 May he would have turned eighty-one.

Richard H. Patterson

Ohio native Richard H. Patterson (born 6 November 1931) grew up in Florida and enlisted in the Coast Guard as a young man. He became a boatswain's mate, and by the mid-1960s he was a chief boatswain's mate and the officer in charge of Swansboro Lifeboat Station, on the western tip of Emerald Isle, North Carolina.

In 1966 Patterson was transferred to the cutter *Point Welcome* (WPB-82329) in South Vietnam. This was one of twenty-six patrol boats that formed Coast Guard Squadron One, sent to Vietnam in 1965. Under Navy control as a part of Operation Market Time, Coast Guardsmen cruised the coast of South

Vietnam and stopped vessels attempting to supply the Viet Cong ashore. The *Point Welcome*, commissioned in 1962, had been homeported in Everett, Washington, and was now assigned to Coast Guard Division Twelve, head-quartered at Da Nang.

Because these vessels were serving in combat, they were commanded by a lieutenant or lieutenant junior grade, with a lieutenant junior grade or ensign as the executive officer. Gunner's mates and electronics technicians had been added to their complement. Chief Patterson reported on board and met his commanding officer, twenty-five-year-old Lt. (jg) David C. Brostrom, a 1963 graduate of the Coast Guard Academy; and his executive officer, Lt. (jg) Ross Bell.

BMC Richard H. Patterson was on the *Point Welcome* in the early morning hours of 11 August 1966 when it came about and headed south, away from the line dividing North from South Vietnam. The cutter was on the second of a three-day patrol in the northernmost coastal area of South Vietnam. As was standard procedure she ran without lights, under way at about eight knots. At 3:30 AM, flares dropped by Air Force planes illuminated the cutter, which had been mistaken for a North Vietnamese vessel. The ship sprang into action. Patterson, up for the 4:00–8:00 AM watch, started for the bridge of the 82-foot patrol boat to relieve the officer of the deck and executive officer, Lieutenant (jg) Bell. But a U.S. Air Force B-57's 20-mm projectiles hit the vessel and Patterson, thrown down hard from the ladder, momentarily blacked out. Before toppling due to his wounds, Bell hit the general-quarters alarm.

The first attack exploded the five-gallon gasoline can on the stern, igniting a blazing fire on the fantail that threatened to engulf the entire after section of the vessel. Chief Patterson, displaying the finest qualities of bravery and leadership, took charge of the situation. Using a fire hose, he forced the flaming liquid over the side, thus extinguishing the fire. Then he and the rest of the crew stood amid the firefighting equipment to take a breather and try to figure out what had happened.

When the B-57 saw the fire on the stern go out, it was determined to take out the bridge of what was thought to be an enemy boat. The second attack killed Brostrom and EN2 Jerry Phillips and severely wounded several others. Unhesitatingly and with complete disregard for his personal safety, Chief Patterson got to his feet and ran up to the bridge of the patrol boat. Giving little mind to his dead skipper and wounded executive officer, he slammed the throttles ahead to get the idling boat from being a sitting target to a moving one. Patterson shouted orders to get the wounded below and stay off the main deck. He told BM1 Billy Russell to check on him after each pass, and if he was hit Russell was to assume command.

BMC Richard "Pat" Patterson on board USCGC *Point Welcome* (WPB-82329)

The B-57 made a third attack and then had to stop, because it was out of ammunition. Patterson ran an erratic southerly course, seeking refuge at the junk force base at Cua Viet. The second strafing had knocked out all the radios.

When Patterson saw two Air Force F-4C Phantom jet fighters arrive and climb into attack position, he drove the cutter hard, making reckless zigs and zags. To keep the attackers from anticipating his maneuvers, he at times pulled full back on the throttles, stopping the cutter before committing to a new direction. Because the rudder would not respond to the helm, Chief Patterson had to steer solely by throttle manipulation. His efforts avoided any major hits by the attacking fighters; at one point a 500-pound bomb missed the boat by just 150 feet, and another was close enough to lift the cutter completely out the water.

Knowing he could not outrun or continue evading the aircraft, and believing the *Point Welcome* was sinking, Chief Patterson decided to beach the patrol boat at the Cua Viet Junk Force Base.

The U.S. Navy adviser there had heard the *Point Welcome*'s radioed distress and contacted Capt. Richard P. Pierschala, the U.S. Marine Corps artillery adviser in Quang Tri city. Captain Pierschala switched to an aircraft frequency to notify the U.S. Air Force of the true identity of the vessel they had been trying sink.

Before running the boat aground, Chief Patterson told the men to gather the wounded and abandon ship, since immobility meant disaster. Under his composed leadership, the wounded were wrapped in lifejackets and paired with the able-bodied before going over the side. Patterson kept his crew calm and organized while they were in the water and until they were picked up by the nearby USCGC *Point Caution* (WPB-82301). Until that patrol boat arrived, however, skittish South Vietnamese sailors fired at them from the shore in another case of mistaken identity. In all, the *Point Welcome* crew's ordeal lasted more than an hour. The dead and wounded were taken ashore and flown by helicopter to the field hospitals at Hue and Phu Bai.

Soon thereafter, and with the Air Force now aware of their tragic mistake, men from another cutter joined Patterson and three of his crew who were not seriously wounded to take the *Point Welcome* back to Da Nang under her own power. It took three months to repair her, but she was returned to service. Without doubt, it was Chief Patterson's seamanship that kept the cutter from being hit, and his coolness under fire had a calming influence on the crew. He truly displayed respect for his shipmates, saving many of their lives at the risk of his own.

The Navy Department awarded him the Bronze Star with the combat V device for his actions. *Point Welcome* survivors believed he deserved no less than the Medal of Honor. In 2002, the BMC Richard H. Patterson Recreation Center was dedicated at Coast Guard Training Center, Petaluma, California. In 2007, Chief Patterson became the second Coast Guardsman to be inducted into the Surface Navy Association's Hall of Fame.

Mario L. Munoz

On 24 March 1978, a Coast Guard HH-52A helicopter deployed on board the USCGC *Steadfast* (WMEC-623) was preparing to launch on a law-enforcement patrol. AE3 Mario Munoz was serving as an aircrewman. The *Steadfast* was about fifteen miles east of Cat Island, Bahamas, in the Atlantic Ocean. Flight quarters were set around 9:00 AM. Cdr. Douglas Currier, the commanding officer of the *Steadfast*, was a cockpit passenger. He had requested to go along as an observer, since he had information there were "bad guys" in the area and did not want the helo to get too close to scare them off. AD3 William Billotta was a cabin passenger.

Petty Officer Munoz had a bad feeling that day, and so he told Petty Officer Billotta that in case something happened, he would take care of him. The aircraft was ready to go; the rotor head started turning, and the ship informed them of the winds and sea. The pilot, Lt. (jg) Robert C. Shearer, gave the order to take the tie-downs off. The left tie-down was the first one off. The ship was rolling quite a bit, and the pilot was trying to correct when the helicopter rolled off the flight deck and fell into the water.

As they were going in, Petty Officer Munoz screamed to Billotta to grab on. The helo filled with water almost immediately, and Munoz found himself trapped inside the aircraft, which was now upside down and sinking. He quickly released his seatbelt and floated upward, feeling his gunner's belt tighten itself. Without hesitation he located Billotta, who was struggling to free himself. After making sure the crewman was released from both his gunner's and seatbelts, Petty Officer Munoz mustered his strength and physically pushed the man out the cabin door to safety.

With complete disregard for his own safety, Munoz then tried to reach the cockpit crew to provide assistance. While feeling his way forward, he was temporarily snagged and realized he was still attached to the helicopter by his gunner's belt. Managing to release the buckle and now desperately needing air, Petty Officer Munoz found a small pocket of it—only to receive mouthfuls of seawater mixed with aircraft fuel.

Finally, instinctively knowing he had few precious seconds of air left, he felt his way out of the cabin to safety. At one point his helmet got caught, so he took it off. Reaching the surface, he saw that the entire crew was safely out of the helicopter, and the *Steadfast*'s motor surfboat was on scene.

AE3 Mario Munoz demonstrated remarkable initiative, exceptional fortitude and daring, despite imminent personal danger. He truly displayed respect for his shipmate, saving his life at the risk of his own. Munoz was awarded the Coast Guard Medal in April 1979 for his unselfish heroism.

3. DEVOTION TO DUTY

We are professionals, military and civilian, who seek responsibility, accept accountability, and are committed to the successful achievement of our organizational goals. We exist to serve. We serve with pride.

OFFICIAL COAST GUARD STATEMENT OF THIS CORE VALUE

Juliet Nichols

Juliet Fish was born in 1859, but her mother died young. She was raised by her aunt, Emily Fish, the longtime female keeper at Point Pinos Light Station on the central California coast. Juliet went on to marry Navy Lt. Cdr. Henry E. Nichols, a lighthouse inspector. He was sent to the Philippines in 1898, during the Spanish-American War, and died there. As the wife of a former Lighthouse Service officer, Juliet was offered the keeper's post at the Angel Island Light, San Francisco Bay, in 1902.

In that capacity she tended a fog bell and an uncovered fifth-order lens with a fixed red light, which was moved by pulley out of the bell house each evening and returned each morning. Because of the growing number of vessels traversing the bay, a fog bell had been established at Point Knox, on the west side of the island, in 1886. The light had been added fourteen years later. A one-story keeper's dwelling was built adjacent to the bell house. The station was accessed by a long wooden stairway down the face of a steep cliff facing the bay.

On the morning of 18 April 1906, Juliet Nichols was making a final check of her equipment when she heard a rumbling sound. She looked across the water toward San Francisco and was astonished to see buildings collapsing and fires breaking out. Juliet was experiencing firsthand one of the world's most devastating earthquakes. Her own building then began to shake and sway, while tinkling sounds of breaking glass came down from the tower. The shaking bent a connecting tube in the lantern and jarred the damper so that the flame burned much higher than it should. She fought to adjust it as the tremors continued.

When the earthquake finally ended, Juliet surveyed the damage. It was so great that it would become necessary to tear down and rebuild the tower with reinforced concrete. The earthquake had damaged every community within 100 miles of San Francisco.

Fog signals broke down frequently. The mechanical pounding of the bell produced strong vibrations, which caused the tension bars and hammer springs to break. Less than three months after the earthquake, on 2 July 1906, Angel Island's new signal, less than a year old, again broke down while Juliet was watching the fog roll in through the Golden Gate, as it does each evening. She heard the foghorns start up at lighthouses on both sides of the channel and rushed to start her own equipment, only to have the machinery cough into silence a few minutes later. She could see the tips of the mast of a sailing vessel approaching through the fog. With no time for repairs, Juliet grabbed a hammer and began pounding the bell, once every fifteen seconds, warning the ship away from her island. Twenty-four deafening hours later, the fog lifted and Juliet could rest.

But the Angel Island machinery failed again two days later, forcing Juliet to repeat her exhausting ordeal. When the weather cleared she summoned the lighthouse engineer to make repairs. Juliet Nichols received a letter of commendation from the Lighthouse Board for her dedication to duty.

Her entire career at Angel Island was a battle with fog; her log recorded periods as long as eighty hours at a time. During many of these she had to strike the bell by hand. Angel Island was one of the worst hazards in San Francisco Bay, and Juliet took her duties very seriously. Her devotion to duty is an example to all those who serve in the Coast Guard. She retired in 1914 and lived privately in the hills of Oakland, California, until her death in 1947. She is buried at Mountain View Cemetery, Oakland. A building is named in her honor at the Coast Guard Training Center, Petaluma, California.

John A. Pritchard Jr.

Born 12 January 1914 in Redfield, South Dakota, John A. Pritchard Jr. graduated from Beverly Hills High School, California, in 1931.

Searching for a career, he enlisted in the Navy from 1 March 1932 until 17 August 1934. While attending the Naval Academy Prep School, he was honorably discharged so that he could accept an appointment to the U.S. Coast Guard Academy on 20 August 1934. Pritchard graduated on 2 June 1938.

His first assignment as a commissioned officer was line officer on board the Coast Guard Cutter *Haida* (WPG-45) on the Bering Sea Patrol. In August 1940, Pritchard entered flight training at the Naval Air Training Center,

Pensacola, Florida. He graduated with the designation of Coast Guard aviator no. 82 on 15 February 1941, and reported for duty at Coast Guard Air Station Miami. On 2 June 1941 he was promoted to lieutenant (junior grade).

In February 1942, Pritchard was temporarily assigned as the aviation officer on board the CGC *Northland* (WPG-49) on the wartime Greenland Patrol. After returning to Air Station Miami for a brief period, he rejoined the *Northland*. He was promoted to lieutenant on 15 June 1942. While with the *Northland* only a short time, Pritchard performed his first heroic rescue on 23 November 1942, just a few days before another daring rescue was to take his life.

Pritchard volunteered to lead a rescue party for three members of the Royal Canadian Air Force who had been stranded on the Greenland ice cap for thirteen days. He led his party up a mountainside onto the glacier and, using flashlight signals and shouts, located the men in the arctic night. They were escorted across the heavily crevassed ice cap and returned safely to the *Northland*. Pritchard would be posthumously awarded the Navy and Marine Corps Medal for this rescue.

Five days later he volunteered to attempt the rescue of a B-17 crew that had crashed on the treacherous ice cap on the west side of Greenland, about forty miles from Comanche Bay. He used the *Northland*'s J2F-4, a single-engine Grumman amphibian. Accompanied by RM1 Benjamin A. Bottoms, he landed near the crash site without mishap, the first successful landing on the 2,000-foot ice cap.

While Bottoms stayed with the airplane to operate the radio, Pritchard tested the crevassed ice with a broomstick for the two-mile hike to the B-17. After recovering two injured survivors, Pritchard and Bottoms took off safely and returned to the *Northland*. The cutter had to use its searchlight to light the way for their plane to land. The following day, 29 November, they volunteered to fly out to the crash site again.

After again landing safely and recovering another survivor, they took off. As the dense fog and blowing snow closed in, the J2F-4's radio signals grew weaker until they were heard no more. Pritchard, Bottoms, and the B-17 crewman they rescued were never heard from again. The wreckage of their amphibian was later spotted from the air, but a rescue party could get no closer than six miles.

Lieutenant Pritchard was declared missing in action as of 29 November 1942 and declared dead as of 30 November 1943. For his heroism on this last rescue, he was posthumously awarded the Distinguished Flying Cross, although some believe he deserved the Congressional Medal of Honor. He also earned the Navy and Marine Corps Medal, the American Defense Service Medal with Sea Clasp, the American Campaign Medal, the European-African-

Lt. John A. Pritchard Jr. watches crew members secure his aircraft to the deck of the USCGC *Northland* (WPG-49)

Middle Eastern Campaign Medal, and the World War II Victory Medal. He left behind his mother and father. RM1 Bottoms was also posthumously awarded the Distinguished Fly Cross.

John Pritchard was the only war casualty of the Coast Guard Academy Class of 1938. His gallant exploits exemplify the unofficial Coast Guard motto: "You've got to go out, you don't have to come back." They also illustrate the Coast Guard's core value of devotion to duty.

At Coast Guard Aviation Training Center in Mobile, Alabama, a barracks and bachelor officers' quarters was dedicated as the Pritchard-Bottoms Hall in 1971. Lt. John Pritchard and RM1 Bottoms were kindred spirits, so the building, housing both enlisted men and officers, is aptly named.

Forrest O. Rednour

SC2 Forrest Orin Rednour, was born on 13 May 1923 in Cutler, Illinois. On 19 June 1941, he enlisted in the Coast Guard at Chicago. After becoming a ship's cook, Rednour was assigned to the USCGC *Escanaba* (WPG-77).

The *Escanaba*, together with the USCGC *Comanche* (WPG-76) and *Tampa* (WPG-48), departed St. John's, Newfoundland, on 29 January 1943, escorting the 5,252-ton U.S. Army transport *Dorchester*. The transport carried 751 soldiers, reinforcements for America's Greenland bases. The *Dorchester* also carried 1,000 tons of supplies, 130 crew members, and an armed guard unit of 23 men. She was in convoy with two other freighters.

Almost from the time they left Newfoundland, the *Escanaba* and the other five vessels in the convoy experienced heavy weather. The small Coast Guard escort ships, *Escanaba*, *Comanche*, and *Tampa*, were tossed around like corks in a bathtub by the rough seas. Due to heavy icing, the *"Esky"* and *Comanche* had trouble keeping up. They occasionally had to heave-to to de-ice using live steam, because the superficial icing had frozen the guns and depth charges, rendering them inoperable.

Early on 2 February the weather moderated, and the *Comanche* detected the presence of a U-boat. The *Tampa* commenced the chase but never located the German sub. Suddenly, not long after midnight that night, at 1:02 AM on 3 February, the *Dorchester* was torpedoed. She was within 150 miles of Cape Farewell, Greenland, and sinking rapidly. Hans Jorgen Danielson, the ship's master, ordered abandon ship on board the *Dorchester*. This was poorly executed, with only two of the fourteen lifeboats and a number of life rafts successfully launched.

The *Escanaba* and *Comanche* commenced searching for U-boats, but had no success. They proceeded back to the sinking *Dorchester* to search for survivors, while the *Tampa* escorted the two remaining freighters to Greenland. In the final moments before the *Dorchester* sank, four Army chaplains—Father John P. Washington, Rabbi Alexander D. Goode, and Protestant chaplains George Lansing Fox and Clark V. Poling—gave up their lifejackets so that others might live. They have since been immortalized as The Four Chaplains and have come to symbolize sacrificial devotion.

Most of those in the water were paralyzed by cold when the cutters reached them, so Coast Guardsmen introduced a new retriever rescue technique: clad in rubber suits, they swam to survivors and tied lines to them so they could be

Painting of *Dorchester* rescue

hauled on board. Among the three volunteers who entered the frigid, dark, stormy sea and went to work helping rescue survivors was SC Forrest Rednour. The water temperature was 34 degrees, with an air temperature of 36 degrees.

The *Escanaba* had spotted one lifeboat, which appeared to be in fair condition. But it had picked up other survivors and was getting overcrowded. While the *Escanaba* maneuvered to pick up survivors, Rednour was in the water, working heroically to prevent floating survivors from getting caught in the suction of the *Escanaba*'s propeller. As he secured lines to rafts and individuals afloat, Rednour was himself in danger of being crushed between the rafts and the side of *Escanaba*. At one point he bravely swam under the cutter's stern, running the risk of being struck by a propeller blade, to rescue men loaded on a raft that had drifted dangerously close.

The rescue operations continued until 9:30 in the morning. After that, the *Escanaba* and *Comanche* could find no more survivors. The *Escanaba* saved 133 men, 1 of whom later died, while the *Comanche* was credited with 97. More than 600 of those on board the *Dorchester* were lost, including 16 Coast Guardsmen.

The *Dorchester* rescue was the last for Ship's Cook Rednour and the *Escanaba*. A little more than four months later, the cutter was torpedoed in the waters between Labrador and Greenland, sinking within three minutes. Rednour was not one of the only two enlisted survivors. Ship's Cook Rednour, who risked his life numerous times during the rescue of the *Dorchester* survivors, received the Navy and Marine Corps Medal for his heroic efforts in August 1943—posthumously. His body was never recovered.

In 1944 the USS *Rednour* (APD-102), a high-speed transport, was commissioned in honor of this Coast Guard hero. The ship's sponsor was Mrs. Forrest O. Rednour, his widow. The *Rednour* saw service in the Pacific and was decommissioned in July 1946.

In 2009 the Coast Guard renamed one of its honors the Forrest O. Rednour Excellence in Food Service Awards, in memory of the most heroic cook in the Coast Guard's history.

Jack Rittichier

Akron, Ohio, native Jack Columbus Rittichier (born 17 August 1933) graduated from Coventry High School in 1951. He then attended Kent State University, where he played college football and was the team's captain. He graduated with a bachelor of fine arts degree in March 1957.

He joined the Air Force in August of that year, and went through flight training at Bainbridge Air Base, Georgia, and Loredo Air Force Base, Texas, earning his wings in December 1958. Trained to fly the Boeing B-47 *Stratojet*, Rittichier was assigned to Strategic Air Command's 340th Bomb Wing, based at Whiteman Air Force Base, Missouri. During his Air Force career, he was promoted to the rank of captain.

After being discharged in November 1962, Rittichier accepted a commission in the Coast Guard Reserve as a lieutenant (junior grade), in September 1963. While assigned to his first tour of duty at Coast Guard Air Station Elizabeth City, North Carolina, he served as a search and rescue pilot and had collateral duties as the unit's legal affairs officer and public information officer. He was promoted to lieutenant in the regular Coast Guard on 28 March 1966. The Coast Guard awarded Rittichier and his unit the Coast Guard Unit Commendation for their rescue work during Hurricane Betsy.

In May 1966, he was assigned to Air Station Detroit, based out of Selfridge Air Force Base, where he again flew search and rescue missions, and he also served as the assistant operations officer and the unit's public information officer. On 29 November of that year, Rittichier and his crew responded to a distress call from the West German merchant vessel *Nordmeer*, which had run aground on Thunder Bay Island Shoal in Lake Huron.

The cutter *Mackinaw* (WAGB-83) also responded to the distress call, but prevailing weather conditions and the location of the stranded vessel prohibited her crew from effecting a rescue, and they awaited the assistance of a Coast Guard helicopter. Rittichier navigated the helicopter for 150 miles from Detroit, with the "final 80 miles flown through snow showers at 200 feet over the lake utilizing the shoreline for navigation." After locating the vessel, Rittichier established contact with her crew by radio. They indicated that they were stranded on the forward deck, exposed to the elements, had no power, and were in imminent danger. Rittichier assisted the pilot in maneuvering the helicopter and accomplishing the hoist of the eight crewmen from the *Nordmeer* to the decks of the *Mackinaw* safely. The rescue was completed in a mere twenty-two minutes. Soon after, the *Nordmeer* broke apart and sank. In June 1967, the Coast Guard awarded Lieutenant Rittichier the Air Medal for his role in this dangerous rescue.

While at Detroit, he laid the groundwork for a public information campaign on the activities of Coast Guard aviators flying as exchange officers with the U.S. Air Force Rescue Service. The program allowed Coast Guard officers the opportunity to serve a tour of duty with an Air Force unit and vice versa. It was designed to give officers experience in the other service's rescue operations and procedures.

Soon after this, Rittichier volunteered for the program himself. He became one of the first three Coast Guard exchange pilots to volunteer to fly combat search and rescue missions with the Air Force's 37th Aerospace Rescue and Recovery Squadron, based at Da Nang in the Republic of Vietnam. He and the other rotary wing pilots underwent extensive training for this. After instruction in the H-3 helicopter, they went to combat crew survival and mountain flying training. Before deployment they also completed combat rescue crew training, which included instruction in air-to-air refueling from the HP model of the C-130 and in combat search and rescue tactics with escort aircraft.

Arriving at Da Nang on 10 April 1968, Rittichier began flying large Sikorsky HH-3E "Jolly Green Giant" combat rescue helicopters. He was literally thrown into the fire as soon as he arrived in Vietnam. Within three weeks he demonstrated his courage and devotion to duty above and beyond the call of duty.

Rittichier started as a copilot on rescue missions but soon became an aircraft commander himself. His first Distinguished Flying Cross citation noted: "Lieutenant Jack C. Rittichier distinguished himself by heroism while participating in aerial flight as Rescue Crew Copilot of an HH-3E helicopter in Southeast Asia on 21 April 1968. On that date, Lieutenant Rittichier was instrumental in the rescue of four crew members of two United States Army helicopter gunships shot down by hostile ground fire. With great determination and superior airmanship, Lieutenant Rittichier effected the rescue in the face of hostile ground fire."

On 2 May 1968, again as a copilot, he made another combat rescue for which he was awarded his second Distinguished Flying Cross: "Lieutenant Jack C. Rittichier distinguished himself by extraordinary achievement while participating in aerial flight as Rescue Crew Copilot of an HH-3E helicopter in Southeast Asia on 2 May 1968. On that date, Lieutenant Rittichier penetrated the extremely hostile, heavily defended A Shau Valley to investigate an aircraft crash site for possible survivors or confirmation of an aircrew fatality.

Lt. Jack Rittichier, on left, at Coast Guard Air Station Detroit, before departure for Vietnam

With great determination and superior airmanship, Lieutenant Rittichier braved numerous thunderstorms and hostile antiaircraft positions to complete this mission."

Flying on another rescue mission, this time as the commanding officer (aircraft commander/rescue crew commander) on 12 May 1968, he earned his third Distinguished Flying Cross, with a citation that read:

Lieutenant Jack C. Rittichier distinguished himself by heroism while participating in aerial flight as an HH-3E Rescue Crew Commander near Da Nang, Republic of Vietnam, on 12 May 1968. On that date, Lieutenant Rittichier twice entered an extremely hostile area to effect the rescue of four survivors of a downed helicopter and five seriously wounded personnel. The survivors were located on an extremely small landing zone, surrounded by tall trees, on the side of a steep mountain slope. With great determination and superior airmanship, Lieutenant Rittichier executed the second approach and departure at night by flarelight even though the distress site was obscured by smoke and clouds.

On 9 June 1968, 37 miles west of Hue, Rittichier, along with his crew, attempted to rescue a downed Marine Corps fighter pilot. He was injured, so the crew would need to deploy their pararescue jumper (PJ). This was a dangerous procedure under any conditions, as the helicopter would need to remain hovering while the PJ deployed—making a large, stationary target for enemy fire.

Adding to the danger was the possibility that enemy forces had captured the Marine pilot and were using him as bait to bring in Jolly Green Giants as close to their guns as possible. These rescue missions into hostile territory were some of the most dangerous flights undertaken during the war, and it took a special breed of serviceman to volunteer for this type of duty.

Helicopter gunships first fired their ordnance around the area where the pilot lay, to suppress enemy fire. Then Jolly Green 22 made the first attempt to rescue the injured pilot, but heavy enemy fire repeatedly drove it off. After trying three times and running low on fuel, Jolly Green 22 flew off to refuel. The gunships and fighter-bombers then once again pummeled the surrounding area with ordnance, but the enemy appeared to be well dug in and therefore resistant to suppression. The control officer, orbiting the area while he orchestrated the rescue and ground suppression missions, asked if Jolly Green 23 would make an attempt. Rittichier, as the command pilot, answered in the affirmative.

After heavy enemy fire forced him to pull away during his first attempt to hover over the injured pilot, Rittichier came around after attack aircraft had swept the area yet again. He hovered over the downed pilot and his PJ began to deploy, but enemy bullets riddled the HH-3E Jolly Green just above and aft of the cockpit, causing a fire. Rittichier pulled up and attempted to fly to a nearby clearing to put his helicopter down.

As he cleared a line of trees, witnesses saw his rotor slow and the helicopter lose altitude. It exploded as it impacted the ground. An official report of the crash noted "that at an altitude of approximately 50' JG 23's rotor very noticeably slowed down and it looked like he was attempting to set the helicopter down on a small knoll. Upon crashing the entire aircraft burst into a fire ball and within 30 seconds the entire structure was nothing but smoking ashes. The aircraft had melted out of sight."

Subsequent attempts to rescue the Marine proved unsuccessful, and he remains missing in action to this day. Lieutenant Rittichier and his crew on board Jolly Green 23 were listed as "killed in action/bodies not recovered." Their names appear on the Vietnam Veterans Memorial in Washington, D.C. Rittichier was the only Coast Guard MIA from the conflict. He was awarded, posthumously, the Distinguished Flying Cross with two oak leaf clusters, the Air Medal with three oak leaf clusters, the Silver Star, a Purple Heart, and a Coast Guard Unit Commendation.

On 16 June 1969, the hangar at Coast Guard Air Station Detroit, Selfridge Air Force Base—Lieutenant Rittichier's last duty station—was dedicated in his honor. On 10 November 1998, the Coast Guard Integrated Support Command at Portsmouth, Virginia, dedicated one of their buildings in his honor as well. In 2002, a Joint Task Force Full Accounting investigation team located the crash site inside Laos and recovered the remains of the crew. Lieutenant Rittichier's remains were laid to rest in Arlington National Cemetery with full military honors on 6 October 2003.

During his distinguished career, Coast Guard pilot Jack Rittichier demonstrated a fearless determination to save lives at the risk of his own. He was not only the first Coast Guard casualty due to enemy action in South Vietnam, but he gave his life for the proudest service mission of all: trying to rescue someone in need. He epitomized devotion to duty.

Kelly Mogk

Born in Minnesota and raised in Seattle, Kelly Mogk became interested in the military at an early age. Talking with recruiters, she discovered that the Coast Guard, unlike the other services, did not restrict women from certain jobs and duties. The missions of the Coast Guard appealed to her, and so, as a teenager, she enlisted in 1984. An attractive, athletic woman, she was five feet seven and weighed 120 pounds. Initially she wanted to be a yeoman, a gunner's mate, or even a quartermaster.

During a Christmas assignment at Air Station Cape Cod, she got a chance to work with the aviation survivalmen. As a result she changed her career request to join that rate, even knowing it would be a two-year wait to start the training. During that time, the Coast Guard changed the rating to include rescue swimmers. That changed decreased the waiting period considerably. Being a great swimmer, Mogk was not discouraged.

She reported to the Coast Guard Aviation Survivalman school at Elizabeth City, North Carolina. Training included classroom work, pool lessons,

Kelly Mogk

equipment familiarization, and fitness drills. Mogk then attended the Navy's Aviation Rescue Swimmer School in Pensacola, Florida. Instructors there had already watched a Navy woman try to succeed but in the end resign.

Mogk believed she could make it despite their efforts to eliminate both her and her male classmates. She became the first woman to complete the difficult course. Returning to Elizabeth City, she became the first woman to qualify as a rescue swimmer in the Coast Guard.

Two and a half years later, Kelly Mogk was put to the test while assigned to Coast Guard Air Station Astoria, Oregon. On the rainy, foggy morning of 3 January 1989, an Oregon Air National Guard F-4 ditched thirty-five miles west of Tillamook Bay, off the coast. The ready helicopter was launched with a rescue swimmer, but because there were two pilots in the F-4, it was decided to send a second helicopter as backup.

Mogk answered the telephone when it rang in the Aviation Survivalman shop and eagerly agreed to join the second crew on the mission. In accordance with standard procedures, the air station also launched a Falcon fixed-wing jet to provide overhead communications support for the rescue effort.

While still on the runway, Mogk learned that the duty helicopter, which had just taken off, was forced to return to the hangar with engine problems and torque splits. The helos at Astoria were the relatively new HH-65 Dolphins and were experiencing a few problems transitioning from the older HH-3F Pelicans. Mogk and the rest of her crew took off minutes later, now not only the primary search and rescue helicopter, but the only capable one. All the other helos at Astoria were in "Charlie," or repair status. A second one was launched from the nearest unit to the south, Air Facility Newport, Oregon.

As soon as Mogk's aircraft reached the Pacific Ocean, the pilot descended to 100 feet to keep below the ceiling of clouds. He headed toward the last reported location of the downed F-4. After thirty minutes of flying, they were on scene searching for the two pilots. They soon spotted a life raft with one pilot clinging to it with one arm. They dropped a data marker buoy to mark his position and located the second raft, empty and adrift, about 200 yards away.

The sea conditions were terrible. There were sixteen-foot waves with a six-foot wind-driven chop. Rescue Swimmer Mogk entered the water to assess the situation. She soon discovered that the pilot's leg was broken and he was tangled in his parachute. Mogk knew she needed to release the harness connecting the injured pilot to his chute. However, when the suspension lines came loose, he was still caught. Mogk had to dive under repeatedly to free the shrouds from the disabled pilot. She put her own life at risk when she removed her gloves to expedite the removal of the shrouds, exposing herself to hypothermic effects of the water seeping into her wetsuit. When she finally got him loose, the parachute slowly floated down and faded from sight.

Mogk's next challenge was to get the injured pilot to let go of his raft. When at length he did, she held him in a cross-chest carry and began to swim with him and hold him in position in preparation for the hoist to the hovering helicopter. Because of his injuries and size—more than six feet tall and 200 pounds, a rescue sling looped under his armpits was necessary. Ending a twenty-five-minute operation, Mogk snapped the sling in place, and the injured pilot was hoisted on board and immediately flown to the nearest hospital.

Before departing, the helicopter signaled to Mogk that a second aircraft was going to pick her up. She bobbed in the ocean while she waited. The helo eventually arrived and hovered above her, lowering a harness. But the rescue swimmer program was still relatively new, and not all units had swimmers attached, nor were all flight mechanics familiar with hoisting swimmers. Mogk's hoist was a rough one, wrenching her back. By this time she was also experiencing symptoms of hypothermia, but she arrived safely back at the Astoria Air Station.

The mission-helicopter's pilot, copilot, and flight mechanic received Coast Guard Commendation Medals, while Kelly Mogk was awarded the Coast Guard Air Medal. In April 1989, Major General Rees of the Oregon National Guard presented Mogk and the rest of her crew with Meritorious Service Medals. The injured Air Guard pilot, in a wheelchair, attended the ceremony.

Understandably, AS3 Kelly Mogk became the Coast Guard's role model. She met with President George H. W. Bush, who congratulated her, and Secretary of Transportation Sam Skinner, who presented her the Air Medal in a formal ceremony. She epitomized the service's core value of devotion to duty in saving a downed pilot from certain death in the North Pacific Ocean.

Mogk went on to serve as a rescue swimmer at Air Station Sitka, Alaska, and as a Coast Guard recruiter in Seattle, Washington. She later married, taking her husband's last name of Larson, and in 1993 graduated from the Coast Guard's Officer Candidate School in Yorktown, Virginia. Ten years after becoming the first female Coast Guard rescue swimmer, Kelly Mogk Larson attended the Navy's Flight Training Command in Pensacola, earning her second set of aviation wings and becoming a Coast Guard rescue helicopter pilot. She retired from the service in December 2009.

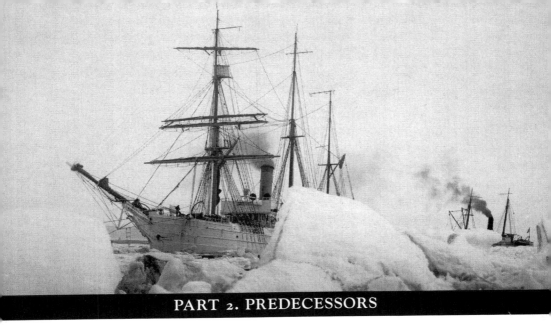

PART 2. PREDECESSORS

The United States Coast Guard is unique among the nation's armed forces, not only because of its humanitarian mission, but also in its background. It comprises several predecessor federal agencies born at different times in history.

The service became known as the Coast Guard in 1915, when Congress joined the existing Revenue Cutter Service (established in 1790) with the Life-Saving Service (launched in 1848). In 1939 the Lighthouse Service, the origins of which preceded the Revenue Cutter Service by one year (1789), also became part of the Coast Guard. Then in 1942, the Bureau of Navigation and Steamship Inspection was absorbed as well into the Coast Guard. That agency had itself been formed by the 1932 merger of the Steamboat Inspection Service and the Bureau of Navigation.

These mergers have made the Coast Guard a true multi-mission service. A look at some significant individuals in each of the predecessor services illustrates their heritage and history.

4. REVENUE CUTTER SERVICE

One of the challenges facing the new United States of America was ensuring revenue collection from incoming vessels. In April 1790 Alexander Hamilton, first secretary of the treasury, asked Congress to create a revenue marine service with a fleet of ten small cutters "to be employed for the protection of the revenue." On 4 August 1790 Congress passed Hamilton's Revenue Cutter Bill, and what became known as the Revenue Cutter Service was born. The Continental Navy had been disbanded, and the sole maritime defense of the new nation for several years would be this service. In the same act that established the Navy in 1797, Congress authorized the president to augment it with revenue cutters when needed.

For many decades the service had no official title, though Revenue Marine or Revenue Service seems to have been the most common appellations in the 1880s. Not until 1863 did Congress actually call the service by name, using United States Revenue Cutter Service.

Hopley Yeaton

Born in 1739, Hopley Yeaton served as a lieutenant in the Continental Navy on board the frigates *Raleigh* and *Deane*. He would later play an important role in this new service. Knowing that the new revenue cutters would need masters, Yeaton took the initiative to contact President George Washington, whom he had earlier met through their connection as Masons, requesting such a position. On 21 March 1791, Hopley Yeaton received the first commission given to a seagoing officer. It was signed by both George Washington and his secretary of state, Thomas Jefferson.

Yeaton was assigned to command the cutter *Scammel*, home-ported in Portsmouth, New Hampshire. There were some problems with its construction, and it was not launched until 24 August 1791, a month after the launching of the *Massachusetts*. Securing officers and crew for these new cutters was not easy. Intially Yeaton had to sail without a full complement of mates. The person appointed as his first mate refused the appointment to accept command of a merchant ship. The *Scammel's* second mate resigned in July 1791, also to command a merchant vessel, and Yeaton's third mate resigned in July 1792 after the *Scammel's* first cruise.

It was not until December 1792 that Yeaton had a full complement of mates. Concerned for his people, he led the fight for increased pay and an increase in the ration allowance for Revenue Cutter Service personnel. As did other early revenue vessels, the *Scammel* patrolled the coasts and harbors for vessels seeking to avoid paying the necessary tariffs. Ships were boarded, inspected, and sometimes seized.

Hopley Yeaton resigned from the Revenue Cutter Service and in 1809, at age seventy, settled on a farm in North Lubec, Maine. He was active in community affairs, including the incorporation of the town of Lubec. He died on 12 May 1812 at age seventy-three, and was buried in a small cemetery behind a private dwelling.

The USCGC *Yeaton* (WSC-156)—a 125-foot steel-hulled, diesel-powered cutter—was commissioned in 1927. Sometime in 1942, the ship was classified as a patrol craft and given the hull number WPC-156. After World War II, the *Yeaton* resumed operation with the Coast Guard out of New London, Connecticut. In the 1960s, the service reclassified the ship as a medium-endurance cutter and gave her the hull number WMEC-156. The *Yeaton* was eventually decommissioned and laid up in 1970.

When the Coast Guard Academy was relocated to its present site in the 1930s, one of the original buildings, Yeaton Hall, served as the enlisted barracks. It later was used as classrooms and offices for the academy's nautical science and mathematics departments. It now houses the Leadership and Development Center, established in 1998.

In the early 1970s, Coast Guard officials decided that Yeaton's remains should be taken from the remote grave in North Lubec and removed to a special monument on the grounds of the Coast Guard Academy in New London, Connecticut. On 1 November 1974, five cadets armed with shovels, spades, and a pickaxe began to dig on a straight line behind the gravestone. A few officers, a Lubec undertaker and one from New London, and several onlookers watched the process. As the excavation reached a four-foot depth, the son of the Lubec undertaker probed the dirt with an iron bar and struck what seemed to be wood. Using a spade, he removed enough dirt to enable the anxious watchers to see what appeared to be the top of a wooden box.

The cadets continued to dig until the whole shape of the box was exposed. The two undertakers decided it would not be feasible to remove the casket in one piece. So the cover, which was laid over it and not nailed down, was handed to the cadets. It was in excellent condition, thought to be made of pine. The inner side resembled a smooth, beautifully grained countertop recently finished. The undertakers removed the human bones visible in the water-filled casket, and placed them in a plastic bag to be preserved. The remains of the coffin were then taken up in pieces.

Late that afternoon, the remains of Captain Yeaton were placed in a concrete vault and buried in a grave at West Quoddy Lighthouse, Maine, where they would remain until a suitable monument could be established at the Coast Guard Academy.

On 18 August 1975, the Coast Guard training ship *Eagle* (WIX-327) arrived in Lubec and anchored in Johnson's Bay. In preparation for the ship's arrival, the remains of Hopley Yeaton had been brought to the site of his original grave in North Lubec in a flag-draped casket. The Coast Guard had placed there a new stone plaque. The following morning about 200 people, including 75 cadets from the *Eagle* and Coast Guard officials from the academy and the First District, attended a brief ceremony.

It opened with a prayer by Chaplain Frederick K. Brink of the Coast Guard Academy, who also spoke of the important role that Captain Yeaton had played during his years of service in patrolling the coast against smugglers. Rear Adm. James P. Steward, U.S. Coast Guard, commander of the First Coast Guard District in Boston, read aloud the story of the life of Hopley Yeaton. Following the closing prayer, six cadets lifted the casket and carried it along the dirt road to the pier. There it was placed on board the Coast Guard cutter *Point Hannon* (WPB-82355) from West Jonesport, Maine, to be transferred to the *Eagle*. Two platoons of cadets followed the casket bearers, accompanied by drumbeats. Later that afternoon, the *Eagle* sailed for the academy.

On Sunday 19 October 1975, an impressive service was held in Memorial Chapel at the Coast Guard Academy, with speakers representing the armed forces, the Masonic Lodge, and friends and relatives from his home state of New Hampshire. Immediately following the service, outside on the north side of the chapel, the monument marking Capt. Hopley Yeaton's final resting place was dedicated.

William Cooke

A serious international problem developed during President George Washington's first term. The French Revolution precipitated war in Europe and, during the first years of this conflict, the French and Spanish attempted to use American ports as bases for privateering. Protecting commerce also meant suppressing piracy.

The revenue cutter *Diligence*, like the *Scammel*, was one of the first ten built for the service. It was sent to Wilmington, North Carolina, to enforce revenue laws and deter illegal acts. Capt. William Cooke commanded the cutter and attempted to enforce the laws without any visible symbol of authority. The cutter service at this time had no ensign, and the men had no special uniform. Many early officers wore their Revolutionary War Continental Navy uniforms.

The privateers considered southern ports to be desirable bases, and in May 1793 the Frenchman François Henri Hervieux appeared off Cape Fear, North Carolina, with the British prize *Providence*. Hervieux, with the help of some residents of Wilmington, converted the sloop to the privateer *Vainqueur de la Bastille*. Sailing under the French tricolor, Hervieux captured the Spanish brig *San Jose* off the coast of Cuba in September. She had been en route from Cartagena, South America, to Cadiz, Spain. The brig proved a valuable prize, with more than $35,000 worth of gold on board. To minimize his chance of being caught, Hervieux immediately sailed for Wilmington and anchored off Smithville at the mouth of the Cape Fear River.

Hearing of this seizure, President Washington instructed Governor Richard Dobbs Spaight to take the proper action. With no local or state law enforcement agency immediately available, Spaight turned to Capt. William Cooke. Captain Cook could not use the *Diligence*, because he had discharged his entire crew due to illness. He asked Governor Spaight for twenty-five militiamen but only received four men from the New Hanover County Militia.

While Cooke gathered his force, the prize *San Jose* escaped. Cooke, however, learned that a pilot boat had taken a trunk off the *Vainqueur de la Bastille*. Hervieux and two of his crew offloaded it near Brunswick, North Carolina, under cover of darkness. There Cooke and the four militiamen confronted the French privateer, and they confiscated the trunk full of gold on the grounds that it was a "breach of the laws of the United States to land goods at night."

Captain Cooke forced the men to carry the trunk to a local house, and the next day he turned the gold over to the local deputy marshal. Even at this early date, the Revenue Cutter Service cooperated with law enforcement agencies. Respect for and adherence to the law has been a major Coast Guard mission throughout its history.

A federal investigation concluded that Hervieux had legally entered the Cape Fear River to make necessary repairs to his ship, but that the *Vainqueur de la Bastille* had been seized illegally. It was returned to its owners—and the gold was returned to the Spanish government, much to the dismay of Hervieux.

The war in Europe that brought privateers to U.S. shores also brought increasing tensions between France and the young nation. The French expected the United States to be their ally, since France had helped the United States during its war for independence from Great Britain. But we maintained neutrality.

French ships despoiled American commerce, and French captains mistreated American seamen to the point to torture. President Washington and his successor, John Adams, urged Congress to act in the national defense.

At last in 1797, Congress, in "An Act Providing a Naval Armament," increased the complements of cutters and empowered the president to "cause the said revenue cutters to be employed to defend the seacoast and to repel any hostility to their vessels and commerce, within their jurisdiction, having due regard to the duty of said cutters in the protection of the revenue."

The deteriorating relations eventually forced Congress to create a navy. Several frigates were built in 1798, and the Navy Department was established that same year. In March 1799, Congress stated the general rule that until 1915 was to govern relations between the Revenue Cutter Service and the new Navy Department. At the president's discretion, the cutters were to cooperate with the Navy, during which time they would be under the direction of the Secretary of the Navy.

Thus, at this early date the service's military role was established. However, at the same time the fundamental difference between the Navy and Revenue Cutter Service was recognized. Clearly the Navy had been created solely for military operations and the Cutter Service for the enforcement of maritime law. It was obvious that the cutters' availability as naval reinforcements during wartime, however valuable, was a secondary, collateral design. Yet they would contribute significantly to the nation's naval forces in the Quasi-War with France (1798–99), the War of 1812, and the Mexican-American War (1846–48).

Thomas M. Dungan

Among the Revenue Cutter Service personnel who served during the American Civil War was Thomas M. Dungan, who was commissioned as a 3rd lieutenant on 19 September 1859. By 1862, he had been promoted to the rank of captain and given command of the relatively new 100-foot steam tug *Reliance*, home-ported in Baltimore. The *Reliance* carried a 12-pounder rifle gun as well as twelve Minnie muskets, twelve pistols, twelve boarding pikes, and twelve cutlasses.

Captain Dungan and the *Reliance* usually cruised in the lower Chesapeake Bay, where goods were constantly being smuggled to Confederate forces defending Richmond. He had seized a number of small craft carrying contraband and dispatches. On one occasion, Dungan sent his men ashore on Mill Creek to investigate rumors that rebel cavalry were "prowling around the neighborhood." He also seized several vessels loaded with coal for enemy steamers. Many of the *Reliance's* missions were charitable. Dungan rescued several people, both white and black, fleeing from Southern-held territory, including stranded slaves escaping from masters.

On 11 August 1864, while under way Captain Dungan had his crew practice firing the rifled gun and small arms. That evening Dungan anchored the *Reliance* off Point Lookout, where the Potomac River meets the Chesapeake. This was also the home of the Union's largest prisoner-of-war camp.

On the morning of 12 August, Capt. Thomas M. Dungan headed the *Reliance* for the Great Wicomico River, on an errand of mercy. A Mr. Appleby had asked Dungan to pick up his children on the banks of Tibbots Creek and take them to northern territory, out of the hotbed of rebels along the Wicomico.

Captain Dungan stopped at the lightship off Smith's Point so he could communicate with its men. At noon they traveled up the Great Wicomico and anchored off Tibbot's Creek. Dungan sent a boat ashore with Lieutenant Hall to search for the Appleby children and bring them back to the cutter. The boat returned without the children. While Dungan was waiting to see if they could be found, he noticed a number of unfriendly people congregating on the shore near a fleet of three canoes. Concerned that these might be used by the growing group, he sent another boat ashore to get them. Coxswain G. W. Agus and four ordinary seamen—Sam Lewis, Peter Cooper, Eli Cantley, and David Smithers—went ashore. Two canoes were brought to the cutter, but when the men went back for the third, guerrilla soldiers in the woods fired on and immediately captured them.

Captain Dungan opened fire on the shore, using the *Reliance*'s small pivot gun and small arms. This brought more rebels to the shore. Concerned about the growing number of Confederate sympathizers, Dungan ordered the *Reliance* to slip anchor and escape. As soon as he gave the order, a bullet struck and mortally wounded him. At the same time Thomas Roberts, in charge of the pivot gun, was wounded.

Dungan's men continued to fire as they turned the cutter in the river and headed downstream. They took Roberts to Point Lookout to have his wound dressed and then made their way back to Baltimore "with the remains of our gallant captain." Captain Dungan is believed to be the only man in the Revenue Cutter Service to lose his life in combat during the Civil War.

Michael A. Healy

Born near Macon, Georgia (1839), Michael A. Healy's father, Michael Morris Healy, was a white planter of Irish ancestry. His mother, Eliza Clark, was variously reported to be either a slave or former slave. His father sent him and his nine siblings north to be educated and escape slavery. Michael repeatedly ran away from the schools to which he was sent. Finally he ran away to sea in 1855, as a mate on board the clipper ship *Jumna*, bound for Calcutta from Boston. He sailed on merchant vessels for the next ten years, until in 1864 he applied for an appointment as an officer in the U.S. Revenue Marine.

Because Healy's skin was quite light, he was never publicly known as a black man during his lifetime. The closest he seems to have come to encountering social epithets was in Unalaska in 1890, when an unruly sailor who had

Michael A. Healy on board the USRC *Bear*

been disciplined publicly termed Healy "the bucko captain," a reference to his Irish ancestry and name.

After serving successfully on several cutters along the East Coast, he began his lengthy service in Alaskan waters in 1875, as the second officer on the cutter *Rush*. Healy was given command of the revenue cutter *Chandler* in 1877, and the cutter *Thomas Corwin* in 1880. In March 1883 he was promoted to the rank of captain.

In 1886, Healy took command of the cutter *Bear*. Although already held in high regard as a seaman and navigator in the waters of Alaska, Healy truly made his mark in history as commanding officer of the *Bear*. During that nine-year period, from 1886 to 1895, he became known throughout the Arctic as "Hell-Roaring Mike Healy."

He was a strong and complex man who considered himself to be the best mariner and shiphandler in northern waters. He prided himself on the high standards of performance he set for himself and his ship. Captain Healy gained the unlimited respect and unstinting praise of the whaler captains and crews who relied upon him for protection and rescue. He and the *Bear* served as guardians for the lives of those who sailed in the whaling ships.

Healy also had deep-seated sympathy for those in need, whether missionaries, distressed seamen, or Alaskan natives. He was particularly concerned about the natives, whose lives were being disrupted and whose survival was being threatened by the advent in the Arctic of seal hunters and whaling ships.

Perhaps as a result of his own parentage, he showed great humanitarian interest in the future of the natives, and he initiated a major social experiment for the benefit of tribes whose lives were being changed. In response to the reduction in the seal and whale populations, in 1890 Healy launched the successful program that transferred herds of reindeer from Siberia to Alaska to help feed the native population.

During the last two decades of the nineteenth century, Captain Healy was the de facto U.S. government in most of Alaska. In twenty years of service between San Francisco and Point Barrow, he acted as judge, doctor, and policeman to Alaskan natives, merchant seamen, and whaling crews. Woe to any mutineer, seal poacher, or liquor trader who fell to Healy's tender mercies. In law enforcement he preferred the instant and strong correctives of the frontier to the legal niceties of less harsh climates.

Healy operated in an eerie echo of what would become the mission of his Coast Guard successors a century later: protection of the natural resources of the region, suppression of illegal trade, resupply of remote outposts, enforcement of the law, and search and rescue. Even in the early days of Arctic operations, science was an important part of the mission. Renowned naturalist John Muir made a number of voyages with Healy during the 1880s, as part of an ambitious scientific program.

As Healy's reputation grew, the number of his enemies also grew. Every criminal he apprehended became a foe and a source of slander against him. Every grafting petty official he exposed joined the ranks. Healy was direct and uncompromising. Influential people who sought to use the *Bear* for pleasure cruises were bluntly refused. Those who were granted transport were required to pay for the food they consumed. In such circumstances, Captain Healy was no diplomat. He despised those who pulled strings to achieve their ends.

Among his most formidable enemies were seamen from whaling ships whom he had punished for mutiny. As the sole representative of government in the far north, Healy was required to deal with mutiny. With no court and no jail at his disposal, he acted with characteristic directness—he triced 'em up. Tricing up was a punishment Healy knew from his early days at sea, before the reforms of disciplinary practices. A man was handcuffed behind his back, and a line passed through a ring bolt was attached to the cuffs. The mutineer was then hoisted upward until only his toes touched the deck. While painful, this punishment was never fatal and a very effective deterrent.

But to the genteel folk of San Francisco, it sounded cruel and barbarous. Union officials—eager to organize seamen—joined the chorus of protest. Temperance organizations became convinced that Healy's cruelty was traceable to his use of alcoholic beverages. His methods also created enemies among his officers. In 1895 three of them charged Healy with drunkenness, abusive treatment of his officers, and endangering the *Bear* while drunk.

Healy was convicted and placed "on the beach," suspended from rank and command. For four years he was kept ashore on waiting orders. But in 1902 a new administration came to power in Washington, and the case against Healy was reviewed. It was determined that he had been treated too harshly. Much of the testimony at his trial had been perjured, with favorable testimony given too little weight. Healy was given a new command, this time the *Thetis*, a steam bark that had been acquired for the Greely Relief expedition in 1883, along with the *Bear*. Restored to dignity and self-respect, Captain Healy successfully completed cruises to Alaska in the *Thetis* during 1902 and 1903. He retired in 1903 at the mandatory age of sixty-four and died of heart failure less than a year later, his life's work completed.

His career may best be summed up in his own words, which he spoke during his 1896 court-martial: "When I am in charge of a vessel, I always command; nobody commands but me. I take all the responsibility, all the risks, all the hardships that my office would call upon me to take. I do not steer by any man's compass but my own."

Healy Hall, one of three recruit barracks at Coast Guard Training Center in Cape May, was built in 1962. It is named for Coast Guard hero Capt. Michael Healy, U.S. Revenue Cutter Service. In 2000 the Coast Guard's newest Polar icebreaker, USCGC *Healy* (WAGB-20), was commissioned in honor of the Arctic hero.

David H. Jarvis, Ellsworth P. Bertholf, and Samuel J. Call

In November 1897 the USRC *Bear*, now under the command of Capt. Francis Tuttle, returned from the Bering Sea to its home port of Seattle to find that eight Arctic whaling vessels had been caught in the ice at Point Barrow. Nearly three hundred officers and crewmen in the whaling fleet would probably perish from hunger unless relief could reach them. Three weeks after arriving back in Seattle, the *Bear*, carrying an all-volunteer crew, steamed north. It was fully understood that the cutter could not, even under the most favorable conditions, reach Point Barrow before July or August, which would be too late. The *Bear* would steam as far north as possible, then put ashore a rescue party to drive reindeer herds overland to the trapped whalers. The reindeer would supply enough food to keep everyone alive.

By 14 December 1897, the *Bear* was able to get to about eighty-five miles south of Nome, Alaska. Captain Tuttle asked for volunteers from among his officers, to lead the overland rescue expedition. First Lt. David H. Jarvis, 2nd Lt. Ellsworth P. Bertholf, and Dr. Samuel J. Call of the U.S. Public Health Service and the *Bear*'s surgeon volunteered. The three were hastily landed

Heroes of the Overland Expedition. From left: 2nd Lt. E. P. Bertholf, Surgeon S. J. Call, and Lt. D. H. Jarvis.

with their supplies on Nelson Island, near Cape Vancouver, on 16 December. The *Bear* then turned south toward Dutch Harbor, Unalaska, its home base for the winter of 1897–98.

The expedition members had to procure dogsleds and dog teams, then travel while assembling a large herd of reindeer from various stations. On the very first day, the party had to cross a range of mountains more than 1,500 feet in height. On 29 March 1898, the expedition reached Point Barrow after a journey of ninety-nine days. The herd of four hundred reindeer arrived a few days later, bringing the stranded whalers the first square meal they had seen for several months.

On 28 July 1898, the *Bear* reached the whalers and their eleven-month ordeal came to an end. The cutter steamed into Seattle on 13 September, receiving an international ovation for its rescue of the whalers. The overland relief expedition was hailed as and is still considered one of the greatest Arctic rescues of all time. The U.S. Congress later awarded Jarvis, Bertholf, and Call special gold medals of honor "commemorative of their heroic struggles in aid of suffering fellow-man." They completed the longest rescue mission ever undertaken in Coast Guard history.

The Revenue Cutter Service officers who participated in that overland expedition personified the humanitarian nature of the service and its successor, the U.S. Coast Guard. Today they serve as an excellent example of the core value of respect for others.

The U.S. Navy League annually presents the Captain David H. Jarvis Award, named for this Arctic hero of the Coast Guard. Presented since 1971, this inspirational-leadership recognition is conferred upon a Coast Guard officer who has made an outstanding contribution. The USCGC *Jarvis* (WHEC-725) was commissioned on 4 August 1972. The USGC *Bertholf* (WMSL-750) was commissioned on 4 August 2008, and the Call Medical Clinic at Training Center Cape May honors Dr. Samuel Call.

Frank H. Newcomb

Boston, Massachusetts, native Frank H. Newcomb (born 10 November 1846) served in the Navy as acting master's mate during the Civil War and was commissioned an officer in the Revenue Cutter Service in 1873. By 1898 he had become the commanding officer of the revenue cutter *Hudson*, a 96-foot tugboat commissioned in 1893. The *Hudson* was the service's first vessel with a steel hull and triple-expansion plating, and she had an interracial crew. She was assigned to the harbor of New York City.

In 1898, when the United States declared war on Spain, the Revenue Cutter Service was again placed under the Navy Department. It fought proudly in both the Atlantic and Pacific theaters of this brief war known as the Spanish-American War. Eight revenue cutters served in Adm. William T. Sampson's fleet and helped to blockade Cuban harbors. Among those was Frank Newcomb's *Hudson*, now a Navy auxiliary and retrofitted with two rapid-fire guns and a Colt automatic machine gun. Even so, the *Hudson* was still more of a tugboat than a combat vessel.

On 11 May the revenue cutter *Hudson*, along with the Navy gunboat *Wilmington* (PG-8) and torpedo boat *Winslow* (TB-5), were sent on a reconnaissance mission near Cardenas, Cuba. The *Winslow*, far inshore of the other

USRC *Hudson* at Cardenas Bay

two warships, came under heavy enemy fire. The *Hudson* and *Wilmington* arrived shortly thereafter.

Newcomb directed the *Hudson* into action, firing on the enemy battery with his two 6-pounder guns. The enemy guns concentrated their fire on the *Winslow*. Two hits destroyed her steering gear and damaged a boiler; another hit put the emergency (hand gear) steering out of commission, as well as hitting an engine. The *Winslow*, without power and steering, became a target for the Spanish gunners. Nature too began to conspire against the *Winslow*, and a rising eastward wind began pushing her toward the enemy batteries. Lieutenant Newcomb offered assistance to the apparently disabled *Winslow*, but the Navy vessel declined. Fifteen minutes later the *Winslow's* officers, realizing their ship could no longer be controlled and was drifting toward the Spanish battery, requested Newcomb's help.

He found that getting a towline to the *Winslow* was a difficult task due to the shallow water and continuing enemy bombardment. Deeper hulled than the *Winslow*, the *Hudson* was soon practically aground, grooving the muddy bottom. Newcomb backed and filled and carefully ploughed his way through unknown waters toward the *Winslow*. During this time he had his crew keep up an intense fire on the enemy shore battery. Newcomb later singled out Moses Jones, the black steward, for his gallant service at the after gun of the *Hudson*.

It took thirty minutes to pass a line to the *Winslow*. Meanwhile shells continued to strike the torpedo boat and passed just overhead and near the *Hudson*. Finally the towline was secured, and the *Winslow* was pulled to safety.

The engagement had lasted three hours. The *Hudson* had fired some 135 rounds and, in the midst of the battle, escaped with only minor structural damage.

Lieutenant Newcomb's quick decisions and service saved the *Winslow* and its survivors. He had not received orders before the expedition as to what part the *Hudson* was to play, so he used his initiative and leadership to develop a role for his command while the action was ongoing. After the battle, Newcomb also had the unpleasant responsibility of transporting the dead and wounded to Key West.

Navy Secretary John D. Long said the rescue of the *Winslow* deserved the "warmest" commendation. Three members of the torpedo boat's crew received Medals of Honor for their actions. However, because of the Revenue Cutter Service's status at the time, President William McKinley felt that Newcomb could not be nominated for a Medal of Honor. Instead he recommended him for a special congressional medal. The president noted:

> In the face of a most galling fire from the enemy's guns, the revenue cutter *Hudson*, commanded by First Lieutenant Frank H. Newcomb, United States Revenue Cutter Service, rescued the disabled *Winslow*, her wounded commander and remaining crew. The commander of the *Hudson* kept his vessel in the very hottest fire of the action, although in constant danger of going ashore on account of the shallow water, until he finally got a line fast to the *Winslow* and towed that vessel out of range of the enemy's guns, a deed of special gallantry.

Numerous revenue cutters served honorably throughout this war, but few distinguished themselves as much as the *Hudson*. On 3 May 1900, Congress instructed that a special gold medal be struck for 1st Lt. Frank H. Newcomb. At the time, it was thought to be an honor equivalent to the Medal of Honor. Congress also recognized the gallantry of Lieutenant Newcomb's crew with special medals. The *Hudson* officers received silver medals, while the crew received bronze medals for their heroism. These were the only such medals specially created and awarded for bravery during the Spanish-American War.

After the war, Newcomb was appointed inspector general of the Life-Saving Service, the number three man in the organization. Frank Newcomb retired from the Revenue Cutter Service in November 1910 and died at age eighty-seven in Los Angeles, on 20 February 1934. He is buried in Arlington National Cemetery. The Navy *Fletcher* (DD-445)-class destroyer USS *Newcomb* (DD-586) was named in his honor in 1943. After seeing considerable combat action in the Pacific, the *Newcomb* was decommissioned in 1945.

These are but a few of many heroes of the Revenue Cutter Service, which was merged with the Life-Saving Service in 1915 to become the United States Coast Guard. The Revenue Cutter seal and ensign were slightly modified to become those of the Coast Guard, and all named Coast Guard vessels are referred to as cutters to this day, in recognition of this predecessor service. From it the Coast Guard gets its military, law enforcement, and seagoing traditions and identity.

5. LIFE-SAVING SERVICE

Established in 1848, the Life-Saving Service traces its roots to the 1785 Massachusetts Humane Society, which built stations along its coast. The movement then spread to New York and New Jersey, then along the Atlantic and Pacific coasts and the Great Lakes.

Joshua James

Volunteers manned Life-Saving Service stations until 1856. One, Joshua James, became probably the most celebrated lifesaver in the world. Born 22 November 1826, Joshua was the ninth of twelve children. His brothers and sisters called him a "great caretaker." His older sister Catherine tended him from infancy and took over the family care upon the death of their mother, who, along with Joshua's baby sister, perished in the sinking of the schooner *Hepzibah* only a half-mile from safe harbor. Joshua was ten at the time, and this first tragedy of his life would be influential in shaping him as a lifesaver.

Joshua James joined a Massachusetts Humane Society volunteer crew at Hull in 1842, at age fifteen. That same year he participated in a rescue from the wreck at Harding's Ledge in one of the society's lifeboats. He went into the profession of hauling, lightering, and freight-carrying, like his father and brothers, at age twenty-five, all the while continuing as a volunteer lifesaver.

James was awarded a bronze medal on 1 April 1850 for the rescue of the crew of the *Delaware* on Toddy Rocks. In 1864 he helped rescue the crew of the *Swordfish*, and in 1871 he helped in the rescue of a schooner. Two years later he helped with the rescue of the crew of the *Helene*.

In 1876, James became keeper of the society's volunteer stations along the Massachusetts coastline at Stony Beach, Point Allerton, and Nantasket Beach. On 1 February 1882, he and his crew of volunteers launched a boat in a very heavy gale and thick snowstorm to rescue the crew of the *Bucephalus*, and on the same day they also rescued the crew of the *Nellie Walker*.

One of Joshua James' most exciting rescues was that of the crew of the *Anita Owen* on 1 December 1885. It was midnight and dark, with a northeast gale blowing a thick snow. Joshua and his crew got to the wrecked vessel

Joshua James, legendary lifesaver, died on active duty at age seventy-four.

under hazardous conditions and found ten people on board. They could only take five at a time. The captain's wife was taken off first, then four others in the first trip. On the way back to the beach, a huge wave hit the boat and filled it, but everyone reached shore. The second trip was more dangerous. The steering oar was lost, and wreckage was all about. Nevertheless they managed to get the remaining five crewmen ashore.

On 9 January 1886, Joshua and his men rescued the captain of the three-masted schooner *Millie Trim* but were unable to save the rest of the crew. The Humane Society struck a special silver medal for Joshua in 1886, for "brave and faithful service of more than 40 years." The report said, "During this time he assisted in saving over 100 lives."

On 25–26 November 1888, James and his crew rescued twenty-nine people from five different ships during a great storm. This would be the most famous exploit of his career, for which he received the Humane Society's gold medal as well as the Gold Life-Saving Medal from the U.S. government.

The storm of this event was the greatest ever known in Hull, sweeping the Atlantic coast from the Carolinas to Maine. Early in the morning of the 25th, Captain James and a few of his beachmen climbed to the top of Telegraph Hill for observation. They saw several schooners through the blinding snow. James knew they could not withstand the storm, so he alerted his crews and ordered a beach patrol starting at two in the afternoon. Hardly had it begun when the three-masted *Cox and Green* was found broadside on the beach. They used a breeches buoy to remove nine men.

The second three-masted schooner, the *Gertrude Abbott*, was found an eighth of a mile farther up the beach, just as the first rescue was completed. It was dark now, and this vessel was too far from shore to use the breeches buoy. Rescue by lifeboat was so dangerous that Joshua asked for volunteers (even though they were all volunteers), warning that chances were they would never return from the attempt. All were willing to go with him.

People gathered and built a great bonfire on Souther's Hill, assisting the crew. The boat was filled by every wave, and two men were kept busy just bailing. They got to the vessel, and the eight stranded sailors dropped one by one into the rescuers' outstretched arms. Getting back to shore was the hardest part. The large crowd on shore watched the desperate struggle, cheering one moment and gasping the next.

Two hundred yards from shore the boat struck a boulder and rolled under water—but the crew shifted weight and saved it. Then a monster wave lifted it high and smashed it on the rocks. All the men managed to reach the hands of the crowd, which rushed into the surf to assist them. At nine o'clock, all were safe ashore. Joshua James and his men resumed their patrol of the beach on foot.

At three in the morning they found the third three-masted schooner, the *Bertha F. Walker*. They had to walk four miles for a boat to replace the one lost. The new one was untested, designed by Joshua James' brother Samuel. With it they rescued the seven survivors without mishap.

While the third rescue was still in progress, a messenger arrived on horseback with news of two more wrecks at Atlantic Hill. Two other lifesaving crews were already on the scene, and they had handled one of the cases. They had tried unsuccessfully for the other, the *H.C. Higginson*, with five men in the rigging. James and his men launched their boat and struggled desperately for forty-five minutes, only to be washed back ashore with two holes in the new boat. They patched it and tried again, this time reaching the vessel.

With difficult maneuvers and great suspense, they got the five men into the boat. The body of the steward had all the time been bound to the topmast and they could not remove him, so it remained overlooking the scene. Having completed this fourth rescue, Captain James and his men then got their first rest in twenty-four hours.

The damage resulting from this storm emphasized the need for additional government lifesaving stations along the coast, with full equipment and drilled and paid crews. It was natural that a station should be established in the vicinity of Hull. In 1889 this occurred at Stony Beach, and the station was named Point Allerton. When it came to the selection of a keeper, there was no doubt who was to be the man. On 22 October 1889, Joshua James took the oath of office as keeper of the U.S. Life-Saving Station at Point Allerton. He was sixty-two years old, seventeen past the maximum age limit for a federal appointment with the new service, but an extraordinary exception was made and the requirement waived. At sixty-two, and again eleven years later at seventy-three, Joshua James passed all the physical examinations without difficulty.

The crowning achievement of his career was the rescue work in the storm of 1898, even worse than the one in 1888. On the morning of 27 November 1898, James and his men rescued two survivors of thirteen men in two vessels dashed on Toddy Rocks. Then they took in a family whose home was threatened by the storm. Next, by breeches buoy, they removed seven men from a three-masted schooner. After that they fought their way to a barge in the surf and rescued five men. All that night they kept a constant patrol.

The second day they rescued three men from a schooner, then three men from Black Rock. For forty-eight hours they were engaged in continuous rescue work. James said of the storm, "We succeeded in getting every man that was alive at the time we started for him, and we started at the earliest moment in each case."

On 17 March 1902, the entire crew, save one, of the Monomoy Point Life-Saving Station perished in a rescue attempt. The tragedy affected Joshua deeply and convinced him of the need for even more rigid training of his own crew. So at seven o'clock in the morning of 19 March, with a northeast gale blowing, he called them for a drill. For more than an hour, the seventy-five-year-old man maneuvered the boat through the boisterous sea. He was pleased with it, and with the crew. Upon grounding the boat he sprang onto the wet sand, glanced at the sea and stated, "The tide is ebbing," and dropped dead on the beach.

With a lifeboat for a coffin, Joshua was buried; another lifeboat made of flowers was placed on his grave. His tombstone shows the Massachusetts Humane Society seal and bears the inscription "Greater love hath no man than this—that a man lay down his life for his friends."

Joshua James is the most celebrated lifesaver in Coast Guard history, with 626 lives saved. His attitude—"We succeeded in getting every man that was alive at the time we started for him, and we started at the earliest moment in each case"—remains at the heart of any search and rescue endeavor to this day.

James Hall, one of three recruit barracks at Coast Guard Training Center, Cape May, is named after Coast Guard hero Capt. Joshua James, U.S. Life-Saving Service. It was dedicated in 1962. In 2003, the service created the Joshua James Ancient Keeper Award to honor the Coast Guard person with the most seniority in rescue work and the highest record of achievement. It is based on both longevity and outstanding performance in boat-forces operations. The recipient must also have served as the commanding officer or officer in charge of a boat-forces unit.

Richard Etheridge

Born a slave on the beaches north of Pea Island, North Carolina (16 January 1842), Richard Etheridge grew up knowing the tides and currents, channels and shoals. He also knew the savage power of storms that struck the region. On 28 August 1863, during the Civil War and with Union troops occupying the area, twenty-one-year-old Etheridge escaped and joined the Union Army. He was among the first blacks to serve as guards of Confederate prisoners of war at Point Lookout, Maryland, and take part in a number of attacks, including one on Richmond, Virginia.

His enlistment expired and he was discharged in September 1866. Etheridge returned to the Outer Banks of North Carolina. By 1875 he had become a surfman in the Life-Saving Service at its Bodie Island station.

On 24 January 1880, the service appointed him keeper of the Pea Island Life-Saving Station near Cape Hatteras, North Carolina. He was the first African-American to command a U.S. Life-Saving station. The Pea Island station had been established in 1878 along one of the most dangerous stretches of the Atlantic coast.

The Revenue Cutter Service officer who recommended his appointment, 1st Lt. Charles F. Shoemaker, noted that Etheridge was "one of the best surfmen on this part of the coast of North Carolina." Shoemaker described him as "thirty-eight years of age, [of] strong robust physique, intelligent, and able to read and write sufficiently well to keep the journal of the station." Aware of the difficulties that would then have been inherent in a black man commanding a white crew, Shoemaker also recommended that the crew be entirely black. The white men were transferred to another unit, and blacks from another station were ordered in.

There had been a few black surfmen before, and by deciding on an all-black crew, the service provided additional jobs to highly qualified

Pea Island Life-Saving Station, North Carolina, the only unit in the history of the service to be crewed solely by African Americans; Richard Etheridge, first African American keeper, is at far left. (Courtesy National Park Service Collection, Outer Banks History Center, Manteo, North Carolina)

personnel. It also avoided placing Etheridge in command of potentially racist white surfmen.

Local reaction to his appointment or the employment of his crew was never recorded. However, four months after his arrival the station burned down. On the last day of April 1880, Etheridge dismissed his surfmen for the season. Like all keepers, periodically he returned to the locked station to assure all was well. On Saturday 29 May, three days after one such trip, the building caught fire and, with a light ocean breeze stoking the flames, burned to the ground. An investigation cited arson as the cause, but no one was ever charged with the crime.

Determined to execute his duties with expert commitment, Etheridge supervised the construction of a new station on the original site and developed rigorous lifesaving drills that enabled his crew to hone their skills. Before Etheridge's crew, blacks were mostly used to tend horses, stables, corrals, and boat trailers. He was determined to overcome this image.

The Pea Island Station quickly earned the reputation of "one of the tautest on the Carolina Coast," with Etheridge known as one of the most courageous and ingenious lifesavers in the service. He demanded swift obedience, insisted on constant drills, and required strict adherence to standards of appearance.

Keeper Etheridge urged his men to keep a watchful eye for distressed vessels, especially during storms. This vigilance often resulted in his surfmen being on the scene quickly enough to lend a helping hand to other lifesaving crews. Such was the case, in the early morning hours of 5 October 1881, when an alert Pea Island surfman discovered the schooner *Thomas J. Lancaster* grounded and wrecked off Loggerhead Inlet. Although the crew of the adjoining Chicamacomico Station had already begun a rescue attempt, the Pea Island crew skipped breakfast and rushed to help.

It was to be a long, hard day filled with frustration and futility, and their noble sacrifice of skipping breakfast would prove an important factor. Fighting a wind in excess of sixty miles per hour, the crew hauled their boat-wagon through the sand and surf to the wreck, and "upon their arrival were nearly worn out with their exertions." The men were suffering from hunger, and then failure to establish communication with the wreck added depression to their problems. By sundown, every attempt to rescue the thirteen stranded on the wreck had failed. Keeper Etheridge and the combined crews of both stations had been unable to haul the heavy surfboat to the scene. It was not until more than twenty-eight hours after the grounding that six survivors could be brought to shore.

But most of the assistance that other crews provided brought happier results to the Pea Island surfmen, as evidenced by a letter to the general superintendent from the master and crew of the schooner *Charles C. Lister, Jr.*:

> We came ashore in the morning of the 22nd [December 1888] in a heavy north-by-northwest gale, and we want to inform you of the timely heroic service that was rendered us by the crews of the Oregon Inlet and Pea Island Stations. They bravely did their work in saving our lives, landing everyone safe, and we join in sincere thanks to the crews for the kindness and care we have received since we have been here. . . . If they had not been on hand we should likely all have been lost.

Perhaps the Pea Island surfmen's most dramatic rescue occurred on 11 October 1896. The three-masted schooner *E. S. Newman* was caught in a hurricane while en route from Providence, Rhode Island, to Norfolk, Virginia. The ship lost all sails and was blown 100 miles south off course before she ran aground near Pea Island. The lifesaving station had discontinued its routine patrols that night, due to the high water that had inundated the island.

Surfman Theodore Meekins, who was watching the ocean, saw what he thought was a distress signal and lit a Coston flare. He also called station keeper Etheridge to help spot a return signal. Both strained to look through the storm-tossed waves. Etheridge ordered Meekins to bring up a red rocket. When Meekins returned with the cylindrical missile, Etheridge fired it in the direction Meekins had pointed out. Moments later the men saw a faint signal that meant a vessel was in distress.

Etheridge knew the surfboat would be extremely dangerous in the hurricane-force winds and heavy surf, so he told his crew to leave it behind. Instead they quickly began hitching mules to the beach cart, and headed toward the vessel that was aground two miles south of them. The beach cart weighed a half-ton, literally. It contained projectiles and shot, the breeches buoy, hawser, and other valuable rescue items. The brass Lyle gun alone weighed 250 pounds. The beach cart's wheels sank into the sand and made it a great effort to move quickly. Arriving on scene, they found the vessel's captain and eight others clinging to the wreckage. "The voices of gladdened hearts" on the grounded schooner greeted them. It had taken the Pea Island crew two hours to cover two miles.

High water prevented them from firing a line to the schooner with a Lyle gun, and, as keeper Etheridge later noted in his log, "It seemed impossible under such circumstances to render any assistance." But Etheridge, now a seasoned veteran of sixteen years as keeper, refused to admit defeat. He believed firmly in the service's unofficial credo regarding the mandate to go out—but not necessarily to return. Etheridge relied on the courage and loyalty of his crew to save the *Newman*'s survivors.

He directed two surfmen to bind themselves together with a line. Grasping a second line, the pair fought through the breakers while the remaining surfmen secured the other end on shore. The first wave caught the leading surfman and knocked the air out of him, and would have carried him away if he hadn't been tied to the other man. The two reached the wreck and, using a heaving stick, got the line on board. Once a line was tied around a survivor, the crew on the beach pulled that person and the two surfmen back through the waves.

The first survivor pulled from the sea was the three-year-old child of the captain, and the second was the captain's wife. After each trip, two different surfmen replaced those who had just returned. The seemingly inexhaustible Pea Island lifesavers journeyed through the perilous waters a total of ten times that day, rescuing the entire crew of the *E. S. Newman*.

Once everyone was safely ashore, Etheridge had his crew check each of them for signs of hypothermia, tend to significant cuts and scrapes, and load those least able to walk onto the cart for the trek back to the station. By 1:00 AM, the cold, wet, exhausted crew and survivors were warming themselves back at the station. There was plenty of doctoring to be done. Etheridge spent the night tending wounds, bandaging bruises, and treating cuts with alcohol. It had taken six hours in pitch darkness, compounded by driving rains and fierce winds, to effect the rescue.

It was a truly remarkable feat. For the crew of Pea Island Station, though, there would be no medals, no rewards—it was simply all in a day's work. The attitude of the surfmen was best summed up by William Simmons, who served at Pea Island during the 1920s: "We knew we were colored and, if you know what I mean, felt we had to do better whether anybody said so or not." Etheridge and his men proved that race had nothing to do with being a great surfman.

Not four years after the famous rescue of the *E. S. Newman*, Richard Etheridge fell ill at the station. Too weak to walk, he had to be carried home for medical treatment. He returned four days later but suffered a relapse. On Tuesday, 8 May 1900, keeper Richard Etheridge died at the Pea Island Life-Saving Station.

He had put in twenty years of creditable service as keeper, becoming a legend in the process. North Carolina historian David Stick called Richard Etheridge "one of the most experienced, able and daring lifesavers in the entire service." The Pea Island Station was disestablished in 1947, when improvements in technology allowed consolidation of its duties with those of other stations.

On 29 February 1992, the Coast Guard honored the memory of Richard Etheridge and all the other African American lifesavers of Pea Island by christening the forty-seventh Island-class 110-foot cutter the USCGC *Pea Island* (WPB-1347). Many years later, on 5 March 1996, the all-African-American crew of the Life-Saving Station—Richard Etheridge, Benjamin Bowser, Dorman Pugh, Theodore Meekins, Lewis Wescott, Stanley Wise, and William Irving—were posthumously awarded Gold Life-Saving Medals for their heroic rescue almost a hundred years earlier.

Rasmus S. Midgett

One of the most dramatic rescues in the history of the Life-Saving Service was accomplished by a single surfman, Rasmus S. Midgett. Born in 1850, Midgett came from a small family with no brothers and only one sister.

On the night of 17 August 1899, the 643-ton barkentine *Priscilla* ran aground in a hurricane off Cape Hatteras, North Carolina. Winds whipped at more than 100 miles an hour. Fourteen people were aboard. The ship was hard aground, and the waves began breaking over the hull. A huge wave swept overboard the captain's wife and their two sons, as well as the cabin boy. Fifteen minutes later the hull split in two. Survivors managed to remain on the after deck, calling vainly and desperately for assistance.

At 3:00 AM on 18 August 1899, surfman Rasmus S. Midgett of the Gull Shoal Station, North Carolina, set out on horseback to make the regular south patrol. When he reached a point about three-fourths of a mile from the station, he discovered buckets, barrels, boxes, and other articles washing ashore. This indicated a wreck somewhere in the neighborhood. The night was so dark that Midgett could scarcely tell where he was going. Nevertheless, he knew the patrol must be made at all hazards.

Rapidly multiplying evidences of a disaster urged him on. When he had traveled a little more than two miles farther, he thought he detected the sound of voices. Midgett paused to listen and caught the outcries of the shipwrecked men. He could see nothing of them or of the wreck, but he dismounted and proceeded toward the edge of the bank. Soon he made out part of a vessel, with the forms of several people crouching on it, about a hundred yards away.

Realizing that if he went back to the station it would take hours to return with help, Midgett decided he would have to take action immediately. Timing the waves as they pounded the shore, he ran into the surf and came as close to the wreck as he could. He urged the survivors to jump overboard, one at a time, promising to take care of each of them. Midgett then ran back to the beach.

One by one, the first seven sailors jumped into the sea and Midgett rushed forward, grabbed them, and dragged them ashore. The last three were so badly bruised and exhausted that they were unable to move. Midgett plunged again into the surf and made his way to the side of the wreck, seized on the lines, and pulled himself hand over hand to the deck. After catching his breath, he put one of the survivors over his shoulder, slid down the line, and fought his way back through the pounding surf to the shore. Twice more he made this grueling trip.

Finally all ten survivors of the *Priscilla* lay panting and shivering on the beach. Midgett directed the seven who could walk toward Gull Shoal Station and set out for help. As soon as he arrived at the station, Midgett sent surfmen to harness horses to their carts and bring up the disabled survivors. He directed other surfmen to set up a stove in the sitting room and prepare for the survivors. It was the end of a splendid day's work, well worthy of the entire country's admiration. Midgett, who carried out the noblest part, was subsequently awarded a Gold Life-Saving Medal by the secretary of the treasury. With the award, the secretary transmitted a highly commendatory letter reciting the story of the brave man's heroism.

Rasmus Midgett died in 1926 at age seventy-five. The USCGC *Midgett* (WHEC-726), commissioned in 1972, was not named for him but for another member of his family, Chief Warrant Officer John Allen Midgett. This keeper at the Chicamacomico Lifeboat Station, North Carolina, received the Gold Life-Saving Medal for his 1918 rescue of the crew of the torpedoed British tanker *Mirlo*.

Lawrence Oscar Lawson

Not all Life-Saving Service stations were located on the seacoasts of the United States. Some were on the Great Lakes. The one at Evanston, Illinois, also had an unusual crew of university students.

Northwestern University, in Evanston along the shores of Lake Michigan, received the gift of a lifeboat in 1871. In 1876 the university built a red-brick lifesaving station to house it. Students were selected for the crew, who selected their own captain. Eventually the Life-Saving Service felt the station needed a seasoned mariner to oversee the operation.

Lawrence Oscar Lawson, a Swedish immigrant who had fished and sailed on the Great Lakes for many years and lived in Evanston, was the obvious choice for the new position. He was appointed in 1880. There were fears that an outsider and seasoned sailor would not be able to get the cooperation of his student crew. But those fears proved unfounded, as Lawson quickly won the love and respect of all the students. His crew did provide him with some unusual challenges, however.

In 1900 the *Chicago Tribune* reported that Lawson was concerned that his surfmen were not keeping their minds completely on their duties: Both before and following afternoon drills, the lakeshore was filled with young Ladies talking to his crew. But under Lawson's guidance, they would become some of the best and bravest surfmen in the Life-Saving Service, as demonstrated by the wreck of the steamer *Calumet*.

On Thanksgiving Day 1889 at 10:30 PM, the 1,500-ton steamer *Calumet* ran aground to prevent its sinking, about twelve miles from the Evanston Life-Saving Station. A local resident discovered the wreck and telephoned the station, "There is a large vessel ashore off Fort Sheridan. Come!"

Fort Sheridan was an Army installation more than ten miles up the lakeshore at Highland Park, Illinois. The thermometer was at 22° below zero, and the strong gale made the wind-chill factor much colder. Upon notification keeper Lawson, with no freight train available to carry his boat to the site, rented teams of horses from a livery stable. The horses pulled the boat, beach equipment, and some of the crew to the wrecked vessel. Lawson and the remainder of the crew boarded a passenger train and arrived first to survey the situation.

Overlooking the site were seventy-to-eighty-foot bluffs. A fire was built atop the hill for warmth, and to encourage those on the *Calumet*. They crashed into the bluffs. Keeper Lawson wanted to reach the vessel by breeches buoy

The men of the Evanston, Illinois, Life-Saving Station

rather than risking the lives of his student surfmen, as well as the destruction of their boat. The Lyle gun was aimed and fired twice from the hill to attempt a breeches-buoy rescue, but the ship was too far offshore: both times the projectile fell short.

Keeper Lawson now had no alternative; he was forced to use his boat. Aided by fifty soldiers from nearby Fort Sheridan, along with some civilians, they wrestled the boat down the cliff and to the beach. They had to cut a pathway through the thick brush. Everyone helped with the cutting, but Lawson's surfmen did the most dangerous work.

Working waist-deep in the icy water, the soldiers and civilians got the boat into position. As a wave lifted the boat they gave a mighty push, while the surfmen sprang to their oars. Facing the full brunt of one of Lake Michigan's fall storms, Lawson and his crew soon found their clothing, oars, and oarlocks covered with ice.

These college students were not weather-hardened fishermen, yet they performed in professional Life-Saving Service manner. They had grown up in the area, and Artic conditions were nothing new to them. Eventually they reached the steamer, took about half a dozen survivors on board, and returned to the beach. They continued boat trips until all eighteen sailors on the *Calumet* were safely ashore.

For their heroism in extremely adverse circumstances, the entire crew of Evanston Station was awarded the Gold Life-Saving Medal. By 1903, failing vision forced sixty-one-year-old Lawson to retire. He had been responsible for the rescue of more than 500 people from the stormy waters of Lake Michigan during his time as keeper. He died on 29 October 1912.

Alfred Rimer and Oscar S. Wicklund

On 4 January 1913 the Associated Oil Company's tanker *Rosecrans* left Monterey, California, with 19,000 barrels of crude oil bound for Portland, Oregon. As the *Rosecrans* approached the mouth of the Columbia River, she encountered sixty-to-seventy-mile-an-hour winds, heavy seas, and heavy rain. The ship's officers became confused after passing Tillamook Rock lighthouse and in the early morning hours of 7 January, the *Rosecrans* ran aground on Peacock Spit, off the Washington side of the entrance to the Columbia.

The surf was extremely heavy and began smashing the tanker, breaking her up and ripping away all her lifeboats. The captain was able to send out one wireless distress message. Someone who heard it telephoned the Life-Saving Service stations at Point Adams, Oregon, and Cape Disappointment, Washington. The lines were out of order to Cape Disappointment, but the message reached Point Adams. Three and a half hours after the tanker had grounded, the lookout tower watch at Cape Disappointment spotted her. Even though no distress flags were visible, keeper Alfred Rimer decided to go out in his station's power lifeboat *Tenacious*. Rimer and his crew had no way of knowing that thirty-two of the thirty-six crew members had already drowned, swept off the tanker shortly after she went aground.

The lifeboat hit the full fury of the forty-foot-high surf and was forced back. Keeper Rimer tried another tack and was forced back again. He tried a third time, only to be driven back yet again.

Meanwhile, keeper Oscar S. Wicklund and the crew of the Point Adams Station set out to find the grounded tanker in their motor lifeboat *Dreadnaught*. Unable to locate the ship, Wicklund decided to cross the Columbia River to confer with Rimer. Once the two keepers got together, Wicklund decided he would try to reach the ship. By now, three men could be seen clinging to the rigging of the *Rosecrans*. Wicklund and his crew made two attempts, but each time were forced back. In the best tradition of the Life-Saving Service, keepers Rimer and Wicklund decided they "would not quit trying as long as there was anyone in the rigging."

Both boats made the next attempt, with Rimer's leading the way. But it capsized, damaging its motor. His crew broke out the oars. Wicklund's boat continued on and finally circled the *Rosecrans*, urging survivors to jump into the water so they could be picked up. During its fifth circle around the grounded tanker, Wicklund's boat also capsized, throwing him and his men into the sea. When the boat righted, the crew scrambled back in—then realized that Rimer's boat was signaling for help. Wicklund pulled it safely back to its moorings.

Keeper Wicklund and his crew then headed back into the towering seas toward the *Rosecrans*. This time two of the survivors leaped into the water and were picked up. The lifeboat also recovered the dead body of another crew member who had been washed over the side. Wicklund did not think he could get back safely across the river bar, so he set his course for the Columbia River lightship, in the open sea. Everyone boarded the lightship, but Wicklund's boat could not be hoisted on board. During the night it broke its line and was lost. Miraculously, a third *Rosecrans* survivor managed to reach shore by clinging to a piece of driftwood.

The Point Adams and Cape Disappointment surfmen had lost both of their new power lifeboats, faced forty-foot-high waves, and repeatedly risked their lives. The Life-Saving Service report stated that "rarely have crews of the service worked against more distressing odds or exhibited more indomitable spirit."

Although most of the *Rosecrans* crew were lost, the lifesavers' efforts were indeed commendable. The Oregon State Legislature adopted a resolution commending Rimer, Wicklund, and their crews. The personnel of both stations also received the Gold Life-Saving Medal for their efforts.

These heroes are only a few of the many who served in the U.S. Life-Saving Service, which was merged with the U.S. Revenue Cutter Service to form the United States Coast Guard in 1915. For more than fifty years, the Life-Saving Service, as a separate federal agency, earned a worldwide reputation for assisting those in distress at sea. Perhaps more than any other, this agency represents the contemporary Coast Guard's most recognized mission—search and rescue. The bravery and spirit of its personnel endure in today's service.

6. LIGHTHOUSE SERVICE

In August 1789, the new federal government assumed responsibility for all aids to navigation. It took over existing lighthouses as well as those under construction, placing them under the authority of the secretary of the Treasury. The Lighthouse Establishment, commonly called the Lighthouse Service, was created in 1789 and charged with constructing, maintaining, and operating the nation's lighthouses. This was the oldest of the predecessors that eventually became part of the Coast Guard.

The organization was put under the direction of the Lighthouse Board in 1852. In 1903 the service was transferred to the new Department of Commerce and Labor. Renamed the Bureau of Lighthouses in 1910 and placed in the Commerce Department, it was merged with the Coast Guard in 1939.

Ida Lewis

Idawalley Zorada Lewis, called Ida, was born in Newport, Rhode Island, in 1842. In summer 1858, at age fifteen, she moved with her father, mother, and three younger siblings to nearby Lime Rock, a tiny island one-third of a mile from the shores of Newport. Ida's father, Captain Hosea Lewis, served as the first keeper of Lime Rock Beacon. He was incapacitated by a stroke a year later, so Ida and her mother took over the responsibilities of tending the light. When her mother died in 1879, Ida was appointed the light keeper.

With water completely surrounding Lime Rock, the only way to reach the mainland was by boat. In the mid-nineteenth century most women didn't row boats, but Ida rowed her siblings to school every weekday and fetched needed supplies from town. As a result, she became a very skilled boat-handler. Her ability was quickly put to the test.

She made her first rescue at age fifteen, during her first year at the lighthouse. Ida single-handedly saved four young men who had capsized their sailboat in rough waters and were clinging to their overturned craft.

Several other rescues quickly followed. Throughout her time at Lime Rock, Ida sandwiched rescues between her lighthouse duties year after year. She became well known and received numerous medals and awards. By 1869

Ida Lewis

she had already saved eleven lives and the Benevolent Society of New York awarded her a silver medal and a hundred dollars. *Harper's* and *Leslie's* magazines ran stories and pictures describing her feats. Mail from all over the country came by the bagful. President Ulysses S. Grant even visited Ida.

She served as the keeper of Lime Rock Light for thirty-nine years and is credited with saving eighteen lives, but it may have been as many as twenty-four. Her last recorded exploit occurred when she was sixty-five years old. She pulled a drowning woman out of the harbor. Four years later, Ida died of a stroke.

After her death, the lighthouse was renamed the Ida Lewis Lighthouse, the only such honor ever accorded a keeper. In 1996 the Coast Guard commissioned the first of its new 175-foot Keeper-class coastal buoy tenders and named it *Ida Lewis* (WLM-551).

She serves as a wonderful example of those who served in the Lighthouse Service. It was not uncommon for women to be appointed as keepers when their fathers or husbands became incapacitated or died. As Ida Lewis' life shows, lighthouse keepers did far more than tend their lights. The location of the beacons made them ideally suited for helping those in distress. Lewis was a keeper who was also a lifesaver.

Kate Walker

While serving as an assistant keeper at Sandy Hook Light Station, John Walker took his meals at a boarding house where a German immigrant woman named Kate served the tables. She had a child named Jacob, but no husband. Walker decided to teach her English, married her, took her to Sandy Hook, and taught her to tend the light.

In 1885 he received the keeper's appointment to Robbins Reef, located on the west side of the main channel into New York City's inner harbor, a mile from Staten Island. Kate was appointed his assistant keeper. Two years earlier, the Lighthouse Board had replaced the old stone tower with a four-tiered conical iron lighthouse on the hidden ridge of rock. The keeper's quarters fit around the base of the tower like a donut. The kitchen and dining room were on the main floor, with two bedrooms on the smaller floor above. The area of rock ledge was hardly larger than the lighthouse itself, providing no mooring for boats. The keeper's skiff hung in davits from the lighhouse's platform. Access to the keeper's quarters was by a 30-foot steel ladder that rose out of the water up to the kitchen door.

When Kate first saw their new home on this tiny foothold in the channel, she threatened to leave her husband and refused to unpack her trunks. But gradually she did unpack and stay on. They had a daughter, Mamie, who would later board with a family on Staten Island when she was old enough to go to school. A year after their arrival, Jacob rowed John Walker, ill with pneumonia, to the mainland in the skiff. Kate stayed to tend the light. His last words to his wife were, "Mind the light, Kate." John died ten days later. A substitute was sent so Kate could attend his funeral, but she was back on duty before the day ended.

Kate was forty years old with two children to care for. She applied for the keeper's appointment, but objections were raised because she was only four feet, ten inches tall and weighed barely 100 pounds. It was thought she would not be able to withstand the rigors of the job. While Kate continued

Kate Walker

to mind the light, several men were offered the position but turned it down, considering it too lonely, or perhaps they did not want to deprive Kate of her job. Finally, eight years after John died, she received the appointment in June 1894. Jacob, now seventeen, was appointed as the assistant keeper, a position for which Kate trained him. He would later become keeper of the light, when his mother retired.

Their life on Robbins Reef was focused: the light was everything. But Kate did not neglect her children. Every school day she rowed them a mile to and from Staten Island, weather permitting, until Mamie was old enough to board there during the week. This meant Kate often had to lower and raise the heavy boat several times a day, using a winch. Once a year a lighthouse tender brought six tons of coal, a few barrels of oil, and a pay envelope to Kate Walker. Other than an occasional inspector's visit, she received little official attention unless the fog signal broke down. A *New York Times* reporter in 1906 emphasized the limits of her horizons: "All that she knows from personal experience of the great land to which she came as a girl immigrant from Germany is compromised within the limits of Staten Island, New York City, and Brooklyn."

Like Ida Lewis in Newport, Kate not only kept her light burning brightly, she also rescued mariners nearby who were in distress. She saved as many as fifty people by her own count, mostly fishermen whose boats were blown onto the reef by sudden storms. One noteworthy incident was the wreck of a schooner that struck the reef. Kate launched her dinghy and took on board the five crewmen and a small Scottie dog, whose survival pleased her greatly. She noted, "He crouched, shivering, against my ankles. I'll never forget the look in his big brown eyes as he raised them to mine."

Upon reaching the lighthouse with the survivors, Kate carried the dog inside her cloak to the kitchen, where she placed it on the floor. It promptly fell over as if dead. Reaching to the stove, Kate poured some coffee from the pot she always kept warm in stormy weather, and fed a little down the dog's throat. "Then his eyes opened, and there was that same thankful look he had given me in the boat." The next day, she rowed the crewmen ashore.

A week later the captain returned and took the dog. As he was being carried down the ladder, the Scottie looked up and whined. "It was then I realized that dogs really weep, for there were tears in Scottie's eyes. It is strange that one of the most pleasant memories I have of my more than thirty years in the lighthouse should be of the loving gratitude of a dog."

Kate was well known in the New York maritime community. Captains often called Robbins Reef "Kate's Light." When the fog obscured the light, as it frequently did in winter, she went down into the deep basement and started the engine that sent out siren blasts from a foghorn at intervals of three seconds. When the machinery broke down, Kate climbed to the top of the tower and banged a huge bell.

With Jacob's assistance, Kate tended the Robbins Reef Light until her retirement in 1919 at age seventy-three. She then moved to a small frame cottage in Tompkinsville, Staten Island, where she remained until her death in 1931. Her obituary was carried in the *New York Evening Post*: "A great city's waterfront is rich in romance . . . there are queenly liners, the grim battle craft, the countless carriers of commerce that pass in endless procession. And amid all this and in sight of the city of towers and the torch of liberty lived this sturdy little woman, proud of her work and content in it, keeping her lamp alight and her windows clean, so that New York Harbor might be safe for ships that pass in the night."

In 1996 the Coast Guard commissioned its second 175-foot Keeper-class coastal buoy tender and named it the *Kate Walker* (WLM-552).

Marcus Hanna

Born in Bristol, Maine (3 November 1842), Marcus Hanna was the son of the Franklin Island Light keeper. He spent his early years at the station before going off to sea at age ten. By eighteen he had risen to the position of ship's steward. When the American Civil War began Hanna enlisted, serving in the Navy for one year before being mustered out. He later joined the Army and saw action in 1863 at Port Hudson, Louisiana, while serving as a sergeant with the 50th Massachusetts Infantry. For his courage under fire in that battle he was later awarded the nation's highest military medal, the Congressional Medal of Honor, in 1895. In the years following the Civil War, Hanna piloted a small vessel supplying a fish market.

In July 1869, Hanna was appointed keeper of the Pemaquid Point Light, at the entrance to Johns Bay, Maine. In 1873 he was transferred to Cape Elizabeth Light, south of the entrance to Portland Harbor, where he served as the head keeper. It was here, on 28 January 1885, that Hanna saved two sailors from the schooner *Australia*, which had wrecked on the rocks below the station. For this rescue he was awarded the Gold Life-Saving Medal, the nation's highest civilian award for lifesaving.

On 27 January 1885, the *Australia* had departed Booth Bay en route to Boston. A winter storm hit off Halfway Rock Light at 11:00 PM, and the captain decided to seek shelter at Portland, Maine. One of the two crew members suggested they stand off Portland instead of trying to enter the harbor. But the mainsail blew to pieces, and the captain decided to sail back and forth (or jog) off the harbor entrance under a reduced (reefed) foresail until morning.

With the temperature at 4° above zero, the schooner had iced heavily, and the crew had jettisoned the deck load to keep the *Australia* afloat. At 8:00 PM the Cape Elizabeth Light was sighted, and they hoisted the peak of the damaged mainsail in an attempt to get past the cape. But the wind and sea drove them onto the rocks. Huge waves buffeted the now grounded ship. The captain was swept off the ship to his death, leaving two sailors hanging on to the rigging in sub-zero temperatures and a snowstorm.

Marcus Hanna, learning of this disaster, grabbed his coat and ran to the shore, signaling his assistant, Hiram Staples, to follow. Hanna knew it would be impossible for the two men to launch a boat. The two surviving sailors were half frozen and unable to move, and the vessel was perched at a 45-degree angle, being swept by angry seas from the stern. Hanna returned to the fog

Marcus Hanna

signal for an axe, then hastened to a boathouse three hundred yards away for a line with which to rescue the men.

Finding the door blocked by a great mass of snow, he ran back to the fog signal and shouted to one of his assistants to bring a shovel. An entrance was soon cleared, and with the axe they obtained a suitable line. Hanna grabbed a line, weighted one end of it with a piece of metal, and carefully worked his way down the slippery, ice-covered rocks almost to the edge of the surf. At this dangerous location, he took the weighted line and heaved it toward the *Australia*. Repeated attempts were unable to reach the desperate sailors.

Then the sea tipped the ship over on its beam, and Hanna threw the line once again and this time it reached the *Australia*. One sailor tied the line around himself and leaped into the breakers. Hanna pulled him single-handedly to safety, untied the line, and then threw it back to the second sailor. By now Hanna was nearly exhausted, but his assistant soon appeared with two neighbors, and they hauled in the second sailor.

The frozen clothing was cut from the sailors' bodies and everything was done to try to warm them. Hanna and his wife tenderly nursed them until the roads could be opened. A few days later they had recovered enough to be carried to a hospital in Portland. That these men survived because of the self-sacrificing devotion of the brave keeper is beyond doubt.

Marcus Hanna retired later that year, after manually working the fog signal throughout another storm. He died on 12 December 1921 and is buried in Mount Pleasant Cemetery in South Portland, Maine. He was seventy-nine years old. As for Ida Lewis and Kate Walker, the Coast Guard named a coastal buoy tender in his honor in 1997, the USCGC *Marcus Hanna* (WLM-554).

Sometimes lighthouse keepers rescued mariners in distress, as those discussed above. Usually, however, it was monotonous, tedious work, contending with loneliness and isolation as well as storms, fog, and ice. The sea was a ceaseless enemy. Dozens of lighthouses were crushed and washed away. During the great gale of April 1851, the newly constructed Minots Ledge Light was washed into the sea and its two keepers drowned. In 1893, three lighthouses in the Chesapeake—Wolf Trap, Smiths Point, and Solomons Lamp—were swept away by ice. The hurricane of 1906 destroyed twenty-three lighthouses along the Gulf Coast. And on one rare occasion, some keepers had to contend with an armed attack.

John W. B. Thompson and Aaron Carter

The Seminole Indians of Florida refused to go along with President Andrew Jackson's Indian Removal Act of 1830. On 28 December 1835, Indian agent Wiley Thompson and a junior officer were shot to death while walking outside the stockade of Fort King. The fort sat on the edge of the Everglades into which Seminoles who refused to move west had retreated. That same day, Major Francis Dade's detachment of 108 men was also annihilated.

These events began the undeclared Second Seminole War. The relatively new keeper of Cape Florida Light, located at the southern end of Key Biscayne, was a Mr. Dubose who was unwilling to risk the safety of his family at the lighthouse and left them in Key West. But Dubose was a family man, and he missed them. Soon he made arrangements to visit them regularly. He hired help—a white man named John W. B. Thompson to act as assistant keeper, and an elderly black man named Aaron Carter. On the afternoon of 23 July 1836, Dubose left Cape Florida to visit his family in Key West.

To the Indians, the 65-foot light was an eye-catching symbol of the hated white intrusion on their territory. The same afternoon that Dubose left, assistant keeper John Thompson was walking from the dwelling at Cape Florida to the outside kitchen when he saw a group of some forty Indians, barely sixty feet away, carrying rifles and coming through a stand of palms behind the kitchen. He immediately ran to the keeper's dwelling and got Aaron Carter.

The Indians chased them, firing their rifles as they pursued. Thompson and Carter made it to the door of the light tower and locked it. The Indians surrounded the tower and began firing at every window. They then set the wooden door afire, which ignited the spilled lantern oil and turned the interior of the light into a furnace. Thompson and Carter retreated upstairs and took refuge on the platform around the light. With fire consuming the wood stairs, the two thought their Indian attackers could never reach them. But the flames burned through the trapdoor and reached the inside of the lantern, causing it to burst and fly in every direction.

Thompson's clothes, earlier doused with whale oil, now caught fire and he had to tear them off. The two men crawled to the two-foot iron rim and railing, on the outer edge of the platform, to survive. The Indians below continued to fire at their targets, now sharply silhouetted. The shots penetrated one of Thompson's feet; another shattered the ankle of his other leg. Carter was hit and killed. Wounded and suffering under the sun's rays, Thompson watched the Indians loot the wooden keeper's dwelling before setting it ablaze. With the stolen goods, they departed.

Thompson had no way to get down from the platform and was losing hope of surviving. A night breeze gave him some relief, but he knew it would not last long. With the rising of the hot morning sun, his nearly naked body would be given another baking. He had no food or water.

Later that day (24 July), a party of U.S. Marines came ashore from the transport schooner *Motto* to investigate the flames they had seen. They spotted Thompson, wounded at the top of the light tower. But the seamen and Marines could not devise a way of reaching him to bring him down. They tried various means throughout the remainder of the day and into the night, while Thompson fell into a state of despair. The men below kept yelling encouragement.

The following day a Marine came up with the idea of firing a ramrod from his musket with a tail of twine. He tried it, and Thompson had enough strength left to catch the ramrod when it passed over the rail. He summoned the further strength to haul up the block they then tied to the twine and hang it on the rail. With the tackle in place, those on the ground were able to hoist two men up to the platform. They carried down a barely living Thompson, buried Carter, and took Thompson on board the *Motto* to Key West.

Cape Florida Light was restored and heightened to 95 feet in 1867, but is no longer an aid to navigation. It was replaced by a new lighthouse on Fowey Rocks. It stands today as a tourist attraction and reminder of the price sometimes paid by those who guard our nation's coasts.

Indians set afire the original Cape Florida Light during the Seminole War. This tower replaced the original in 1846 and remained in service until 1878.

Walter L. Barnett

Besides lighthouses, the Lighthouse Service also operated fog signals, an extensive buoy system, a fleet of tenders, and numerous lightships. An important aid to navigation, lightships were special vessels moored in shallow water or near shoals where, because of a difficult location, it was impossible to build a lighthouse. Service on board lightships consisted of a strange mixture of danger, uncomfortable living conditions, boredom, and loneliness. Lightship duty was arguably the most dangerous in the Lighthouse Service.

Real danger generally came from two sources. The first was weather. In November 1913, for example, Lightship No. 82, on station thirteen miles southwest of Buffalo, New York, disappeared in a storm with a crew of six. Divers located the submerged wreck six months later, two miles from her station. Only one body was ever found, a year later, some thirteen miles from the wreck site.

The second greatest danger was collision. Ships would steer toward the light, and later radio beacon, on the lightship and then forget to change course in time to avoid a collision, especially during restricted visibility. Occasionally, as happened to John Thompson and Aaron Carter at Cape Florida Light, sailors faced armed attack. Such was the case of the Diamond Shoals Lightship during World War I.

Lightship No. 71 was 124 feet in length, with a beam of 29 feet and a draft of 13 feet. The ship had a composite hull—a steel frame with wood bottom and steel-plated topside—and two masts with lantern galleries on each. She was steam-powered and could make 8.5 knots under way.

In August 1918, Germany's newest and largest cruiser submarine, the U-140, was deployed to American waters. It carried 35 torpedoes and 4,000 rounds of ammunition for its two deck guns—a 6-inch forward and a 4-inch after. Lightship No. 71 was assigned to Diamond Shoal near Cape Hatteras, North Carolina, on 6 August 1918 when the U-140 surfaced nearby. The day was calm, with a moderate southwest breeze and a hazy sky.

The German submarine's target was the 3,024-ton steamship *Merak*, sailing under a U.S. flag and carrying a load of coal. The U-140 opened fire on the freighter with its deck guns, and the *Merak* zigzagged down the coast at full speed. More than thirty rounds were fired at the *Merak* without a hit. However, the shifting sands of Diamond Shoals would prove more fatal. The *Merak* ran hard aground on the fringe of the shoals, and the crew abandoned the ship, taking to their lifeboats.

It was 2:50 PM when the crew of the lightship first heard gunfire to the northeast and saw the U-140 on the surface a half-mile away. First Mate Walter L. Barnett, born and raised in the tiny fishing village of Buxton, near Cape Hatteras, had joined the U.S. Lighthouse Service in 1901 at age thirty. Recently assigned to Lightship No. 71, he was mate-in-charge while the lightship's master was ashore on liberty. Two Navy radiomen were assigned to the ship during the war.

As soon as Barnett heard the shots and sighted the submarine, he hurried to the wireless shack and ordered the Navy men to begin transmitting a warning to all shipping in the area. The brief message read: "Enemy submarine shelling unknown ship E.N.E. ¼ mile off lightship." This message may have

Diamond Shoal lightship

spelled doom, because only after it was sent did the *U-140* turn its guns on the Diamond Shoals Lightship.

The submarine opened fire at 3:25 PM, six shots from a distance of two miles. The first one took away the wireless, but the other five missed the lightship. Barnett realized the ship was a sitting duck, held in place by 185 fathoms of heavy chains firmly attached to a 5,000-pound mushroom anchor imbedded in the sandy shoal. Getting up steam and at the same time hauling in the huge anchor and chains could not be done quickly. Normally it took the lightship five hours to get under way.

But even if it could have been done in five minutes, Barnett realized they stood no chance of eluding the U-boat in the tub-shaped vessel. At 3:30 PM he ordered his crew to abandon the lightship. Within ten minutes the whaleboat was lowered, and all twelve crew members rowed as fast as they could for about five miles.

The German sub broke off its attack on the lightship when it sighted another merchant ship to the north. That ship escaped, so the *U-140* returned to the lightship and fired seven rounds into her hull, sending her to the bottom. Barnett and the crew were safely ashore five miles away when they saw Lightship No. 71 go down.

Later reports indicated that the radio warnings had enabled twenty-five vessels to take shelter in Lookout Bight, thus avoiding possible attack. Barnett reported details of the *U-140*'s attack to naval headquarters from the wireless station at Cape Hatteras.

With the sinking of the Diamond Shoal Lightship, the dangerous waters were temporarily marked by a gas and whistling buoy. Relief Lightship No. 72

was established on Diamond Shoal on 30 March 1919. In 1967, Diamond Shoals Light Tower was erected thirteen miles off the coast, eliminating the need for the lightship.

The last lightship, *Nantucket I*, was decommissioned on 29 March 1985. Today these vessels have been replaced by offshore platforms or large navigational buoys.

Frank T. Warriner

The main mission of the Lighthouse Service's fleet of tenders was to service lighthouses and buoys. Capt. Frank T. Warriner served as the commanding officer of one of these tenders, the *Columbine*. Having been built in 1892, it was one of the older tenders in the fleet and a single-screw steamer. The steel vessel was 155 feet in length, with a beam of 27 feet.

On 17 January 1916, during a terrible storm that swept through the Hawaiian Islands, the bark *British Yeoman* wallowed deep in the raging seas just off Port Allen, on the southern coast of Kauai Island. With a heavy load, she was in danger of running aground on the nearby beach. The bark's radio distress call was intercepted by the nearby lighthouse tender *Columbine*, which managed to find her during the stormy night—only to discover that she had no anchors, the rudder had been carried away, and her stern was drifting toward the breakers near the beach.

In the blustery darkness Captain Warriner gave the order, "Prepare to pass the *Yeoman* a line." Captain Warriner personally took charge of the tender's whaleboat, bringing it and its crew into the "boiling breakers four times" as he attempted to pass a heavy towing hawser to the stricken vessel. But each time a strain was put on the hawser, it parted. Undeterred by a heavy sea and this repeated breaking, Captain Warriner continued his efforts to save the *British Yeoman* under the most dangerous and difficult conditions.

Skipper Frank T. Warriner knew there was little chance that his tiny lighthouse tender could tow the 1,900-ton sailing bark to Oahu. The *Yeoman* was four times the size of the 424-gross-ton *Columbine*. He radioed for assistance the next morning and was told Navy tug *Navajo* (AT-52) was en route. The *Columbine's* officers and crew stood by, prepared to render assistance in case of an emergency until the *Navajo* arrived the next morning and took over the tow. The *Columbine's* untiring efforts had kept the *British Yeoman* from imminent disaster on a lee shore, which would have meant the loss of that vessel and everyone on board.

The *Columbine* escorted both ships more than sixty miles to Honolulu. Captain Warriner, in his modest report, spoke highly of the conduct of his officers and crew in "most trying and dangerous conditions." All hands went without sleep for fifty-six hours, and the wireless operator, although sick, stuck

Lighthouse tender *Columbine*

to his post until his apparatus would no longer function. It was he who called the Navy tug.

Secretary of Commerce William C. Redfield noted that despite darkness and storm, and undismayed by the heavy seas or by the repeated breaking of hawsers, the courageous tender crew stood steady at their tasks without letup until the bark was safe. In a letter of commendation to Captain Warriner, he wrote:

> From accounts of this rescue it appears that had it not been for the courage, resourcefulness, and persistence displayed by you, and the hearty cooperation of the officers and crew and other employees of the Lighthouse Service on board *Columbine* at the time, the *British Yeoman* would have been wrecked on the beach.
>
> I take special pleasure in commending you for your gratifying exhibition of seamanship in connection with this rescue, also desire to express my high appreciation for the services rendered by all during the rescue, in which the best traditions of the Lighthouse Service have been upheld so well. It is my wish that you cause the enclosed copy of this letter to be brought to the attention of all those persons who assisted in the service rendered.

On 1 July 1939, President Franklin D. Roosevelt signed a congressional resolution consolidating the Lighthouse Service and the Coast Guard. Merging the two services saved the government about $1 million per year, while increasing the personnel of the Coast Guard by nearly 50 percent.

At the time, the Lighthouse Service's members numbered 5,355, ranging from lighthouse keepers and tender captains to part-time janitors and carpenters. Most were offered the option of enlisting in the Coast Guard or continuing as civilian employees. Former district superintendents and other senior administrators became Coast Guard officers; captains and officers of the tenders were offered appointments as warrant officers.

The Coast Guard continued the color scheme of the Lighthouse Service tenders: black hull with a white superstructure. It was not until 1947 that lighthouse tenders were called buoy tenders. The proud legacy of the Lighthouse Service lives on today in all the aids-to-navigation duties of today's Coast Guard.

7. BUREAU OF MARINE INSPECTION AND NAVIGATION

E arly steamboats were so dangerous that 14 percent of them had exploded by 1832, with the loss of more than a thousand lives. As disasters continued, Congress decided to begin the regulation of private marine enterprises. By 1838 it had provided for the inspection of steamboats, which led to the creation of the Steamboat Inspection Service. In 1884 Congress created another organization, the Bureau of Navigation, to supervise the collection of tonnage dues and regulate the hiring and discharge of seamen as well as protecting them from abuses. This bureau also documented commercial vessels and administered details of the navigation laws. In 1932 these agencies were merged to form the Bureau of Navigation and Marine Inspection.

Eugene Tyler Chamberlain

Born 28 September 1856 in Albany, New York, Eugene Tyler Chamberlain was a member of a prominent New England family that included Joshua Lawrence Chamberlain, the hero of the Civil War battle at Gettysburg and later governor of Maine and president of Bowdoin College. While Eugene Chamberlain was at Harvard University three future presidents—Theodore Roosevelt, William Howard Taft, and Woodrow Wilson—were also students there.

After graduating in 1878, Chamberlain served as an instructor at Albany Academy for a year. In 1888 he sailed on the Erie Canal for two weeks, on the cruiser *Thomas Jefferson*. This was a promotional voyage to bolster Grover Cleveland and tariff reduction. Chamberlain later worked for the Albany *Journal* and in 1891 became editor of the Albany *Argus*. He also became friends with Theodore Roosevelt, who served in the New York state legislature from 1882 to 1884.

In 1893 Chamberlain was appointed commissioner of navigation. Over the following years, Congress and the secretary of the treasury assigned additional duties to the commissioner and the Bureau of Navigation. An act of 21 December 1898 contained a sweeping revision of the law with respect to governmental supervision over shipping and the discharge of merchant seamen. Chamberlain, in his annual report for 1899, described this act as "the most comprehensive measure ever passed in this country for the benefit of seamen. It is probably within bounds to assert that no parliamentary body ever adopted legislation which has worked so radical a change in the historical relations between the seaman and the master or owner."

President Theodore Roosevelt transferred the Bureau of Navigation to the newly created Department of Commerce and Labor in 1903. Under the new department, the bureau found its duties further increased.

In the nineteenth century, ships and land telegraph stations adopted call signs to aid in signaling, a practice that continued when ships and the shore stations serving them began to use radio. At first users picked their own signs, but that led to duplication. In an effort to organize all this, the 1906 Berlin International Wireless Telegraph Convention declared that ship and shore stations should have unique call signs consisting of three letters. The United States, no doubt bridling at the thought of being told what to do by a bunch of foreigners, declined to ratify the convention until 1912, with the result that we had stations with two- or even one-letter call signs, plus many duplicates.

Fed up with this, the head of the federal Bureau of Navigation, Eugene Tyler Chamberlain, decided that an 1884 statute that gave it the right to assign signal-flag codes to ships could be used as a basis to assign radio call signs as well. Ships on the Atlantic and Gulf coasts were assigned calls beginning with K, and those on the Pacific coast and Great Lakes were assigned calls beginning with W. Under Chamberlain's leadership, the Bureau of Navigation adopted a system of examining and licensing radio operators similar to that used by the Steamboat Inspection Service in testing and certifying pilots and officers. The Wireless Ship Act of 24 June 1910 gave the bureau the enforcement duties it desired.

Eugene Chamberlain had been the commissioner for more than nineteen years when the nation and the world suffered one of its greatest maritime tragedies. On the night of 14 April 1912, during her maiden voyage, the *Titanic* hit an iceberg and sank two hours and forty minutes later, early on 15 April. The sinking resulted in the deaths of 1,517 people, making it one of the most deadly peacetime maritime disasters in history. The high casualty rate was due in part to the fact that, although complying with the regulations of the time, the ship did not carry enough lifeboats for everyone on board. Chamberlain was instrumental in organizing the International Conference on Safety of Life at Sea, in response, in part, to the loss of the *Titanic*, and he attended that conference at London from 12 November 1913 to 21 January 1914 as one of the U.S. delegates.

With the creation of the new Department of Labor in March 1913, the Bureau of Navigation remained in the Department of Commerce. When the bureau and the Steamboat Inspection Service became the Bureau of

Navigation and Steamboat Inspection in 1932, the supervisory positions were also merged into one: director of the new bureau.

Liberty Ships during World War II were named for famous Americans. The SS *Eugene T. Chamberlain* (hull no. 2368) was launched in August 1944 at the J. A. Jones Construction Company in Brunswick, Georgia.

George Uhler

Virginia native George Uhler (born January 1850) made his home in Philadelphia, where he was soon recognized as a practical marine engineer of great ability. He was serving as the president of the Marine Engineer's Association of the United States in 1903, when he was appointed to replace the retiring General James A. Dumont as supervising inspector general of the Steamboat Inspection Service. Dumont was seventy-nine years old, and the government authorities wanted a younger man. Uhler assumed the office on 1 April. The following July, the service came under the jurisdiction of the newly formed Department of Commerce and Labor.

Early steamboats had so many disasters that in 1838 Congress stepped in and required the owners and masters of steam vessels to employ an adequate number of experienced engineers and carry specified safety equipment, and to have their boilers and hulls inspected regularly. The Treasury Department appointed competent individuals to carry out these inspections. This action marked the beginning of the Steamboat Inspection Service, although it did not become a separate government service until August 1852.

George Uhler had been the supervising inspector general of the Steamboat Inspection only for about a year when a major steamboat disaster occurred. On the morning of 15 June 1904, the excursion steamer *General Slocum* departed the Third Street Pier on the East River for excursion to Long Island Sound and to return the same day. Only six weeks earlier, the *Slocum* had passed federal inspection and obtained a renewal of its sailing permit. The 1,358 passengers on board, mostly women and children, members of St. Mark's Evangelical Lutheran Church on East Sixth Street on the Lower East Side neighborhood called Little Germany, were looking forward to a pleasant day's voyage away from the city.

Soon after the vessel passed through Hell Gate, a crew member discovered a fire in the forward cabin space and immediately notified the first mate. Notifying the master in the pilothouse, the first mate then took charge of the firefighting efforts. The hoses burst, making it impossible to douse the flames with water. With the fire beginning to burn out of control, the master decided to beach his vessel on nearby North Brother Island. After grounding, the master and pilot jumped overboard. The fire spread unchecked, and the passengers were faced with either burning to death or jumping overboard into the swift current. Most of those who jumped had no life preservers and, unable to swim, drowned. This accounted for most of the 1,021 deaths. It was New York's deadliest tragedy until 11 September 2001.

The *General Slocum* disaster shocked New York and dominated the press for weeks, as bodies were fished from the East River. The day after the disaster, secretary of commerce and labor George B. Cortelyou ordered a federal inquiry to be headed by George Uhler, supervising inspector general of the Steamboat Inspection Service.

Uhler learned that William Van Schaick, master of the *General Slocum*, was an experienced seaman, having been a sailor for decades, and a trusted employee of the Knickerbocker Steamboat Company, which owned the *General Slocum*. The investigation also revealed that as the fire spread quickly, hundreds of passengers panicked. They rushed to the lifeboats and life preservers, only to find that the boats were lashed to the ship with wires and could not be freed. The life preservers, made of cork, were so old and shoddy that they crumbled in the passengers' hands. The ship's crew could not put out the fire because the pumps were old and the hoses leaked. Desperate to escape the flames, more than a thousand people jumped overboard.

Uhler submitted his committee's report on 8 October 1904, placing most responsibility on certain officers of the Steamboat Inspection Service. President Theodore Roosevelt approved the report and ordered the dismissal of all officers connected with the disaster. Bronx coroner Joseph Berry ordered an inquest, which was to be the precursor to a criminal trial of the *General Slocum's* master.

Stirred by this report, in 1905 Congress markedly increased the authority of supervising inspectors. In the years following, Congress passed a number of acts that imposed new duties on the Steamboat Inspection Service and extended the scope of its work. The Liberty Ship SS *George Uhler* (hull no. 1785) was launched in 1943 by the Bethlehem-Fairfield Shipyard in Baltimore, Maryland.

In 1942, Executive Order 9083 transferred the Bureau of Marine Inspection and Navigation to the Coast Guard on a temporary basis. This was a period of intense shipbuilding, and the new construction had to be inspected. A large number of regular Coast Guard personnel were assigned to this duty. In 1946, after World War II, the transfer of Marine Inspection and Navigation into the Coast Guard was made permanent. Functions relating to merchant-vessel inspection, safety of life at sea, merchant-vessel personnel, and merchant-vessel documentation functions have been a part of the Coast Guard ever since.

From these two predecessor agencies have come all the merchant marine responsibilities of today's Coast Guard. Service experts examine ships beginning with the plan on the drawing board, and including the soundness of the actual construction, hull, wiring, boilers, and engines, watertight compartments, signaling devices, firefighting apparatuses, life preservers, lifeboats and their equipment, and the ability of seamen to launch and use them.

Members of the Coast Guard set merchant marine standards for personnel and issue licenses and certificates. They investigate all cases of collision and violations of the laws of navigation in U.S. waters and press the prosecutions. Out of this heritage also comes the Coast Guard's enforcement of laws against the pollution of harbors.

PART 3. TEAM COAST GUARD

The term "Team Coast Guard" has been used for several decades to refer to the active duty service, the Reserve, the Auxiliary, and civilian employees working together to accomplish the many missions of the Coast Guard.

But it was not until August 1994 that Adm. Robert E. Kramek, commandant of the Coast Guard, formally defined the term in a general message that spoke primarily of the relationship between the active duty and Reserve services, marking dramatic changes for the latter. The message disestablished all Coast Guard Reserve units except Harbor Defense Command and Port Security Units and sought to eliminate Reserve-only workspaces where active duty ones were more efficient. It shifted administrative support of Reservists from Reserve-only administration offices to integrated personnel support units. The majority of Reservists were from then on to be assigned to active duty commands.

The commandant's desire was for Team Coast Guard to have one set of missions, one command structure, and one administrating structure, and to fully integrate Reserve forces. The goal was the functional integration of the service. However, Team Coast Guard has now come to refer to all the elements listed earlier. Working together, these different team members enable the Coast Guard to accomplish much more than it could if acting with only the active duty service. The Coast Guard Reserve and the Auxiliary have come to be seen as force multipliers. The entire team has acted together in responding to major disasters or operations. What follows are a few examples of that teamwork.

Mariel Boat Lift: 1980

In April 1980 the Cuban government permitted numerous citizens to embark at Mariel for passage to the United States. It quickly became apparent that this would be a major exodus, with the potential for loss of life. Privately owned vessels were flocking to Mariel, where they embarked passengers with little regard for capacity or seaworthiness. Not surprisingly, many found themselves in difficulty when they stood into the turbulent waters of the Florida Straits.

The Coast Guard responded with what they named "Operation Key Ring." Cutters had to abandon their quest for drug smugglers to become lifesavers. Eleven cutters and eight aircraft began patrolling the waters between the United States and Cuba to prevent loss of life. Ships from Maine to Texas were ordered into the area, as were aircraft and helicopters from five different air stations. Two Navy ships—the USS *Saipan* (LHA-2) and *Boulder* (LST-1190)—joined the Coast Guard in the first week of May. Cdr. Clinton H. Smoke, commanding officer of the 210-foot Coast Guard cutter *Dauntless* (WMEC-624), said, "We are not doing anything that we don't normally do, it's just that the caseload is extremely heavy because of the Cuban boatlift."

Larger cutters patrolled open waters and directed escort vessels to the refugee boats, while helicopters and fixed-wing aircraft patrolled the Straits night and day in search of disabled craft and those going the wrong way. If they couldn't help from the air, the crews radioed for surface units to assist. Coast Guard cutters frequently took six or seven refugee boats in tow.

By 15 May, Coast Guard forces in the Cuban Straits included seventeen cutters, seventeen aircraft, and approximately 2,000 personnel. There were not nearly enough to meet the need, so President James E. Carter diverted twelve more naval vessels to assist. Other Coast Guard districts on the Atlantic coast, sending forces to help out, left themselves extremely short-handed as recreational boating activity increased with the coming of summer.

Coast Guard Auxiliarists began standing watches at shore stations that the regulars had left unattended. They contributed 25,000 man hours, conducted 400 patrols, and handled 75 search and rescue cases.

On 4 June, President Jimmy Carter authorized the commandant to order 900 Coast Guard Reservists to active duty for six weeks. This call-up was initiated by a request from the commander, Atlantic Area, Vice Adm. Robert Price, U.S. Coast Guard. Three hundred Reservists would serve for two-week periods over the next six weeks, supporting active service units in the Seventh District and in those districts that had supplied personnel to support the Cuban boatlift operation. It was the first time Reservists had been called to active duty since April 1973, when they were called in response to emergency flooding in the Mississippi River basin. On 16 July 1980, the president authorized the extension of involuntary call-ups until 30 September.

By 17 June the crisis had subsided and Operation Key Ring ended. Some 115,000 Cubans had been ferried to Florida. Never before in peacetime history had the collective Coast Guard forces undertaken a mission of mercy of such magnitude. Coast Guard, Navy, and Auxiliary vessels had rendered assistance to 1,419 boats, and the Coast Guard had interdicted 199 American boats trying to enter Cuban waters illegally. The success of the Coast Guard operation was due to the contributions of active duty service members, Reservists and Auxiliarists and serves as an excellent example of Team Coast Guard in action.

Cocaine Bust: 1987

One of the biggest cocaine busts in history was made on 8 May 1987, due to Team Coast Guard action. That day an Auxiliarist, searching for a missing diver off the northwest coast of St. Croix, spotted a 28-foot fishing boat in a deserted cove. *La Toto* was anchored 50 feet from shore in the abandoned Cala Bola Cove, a shallow reef area where boats had run aground. When the Auxiliarist approached and offered help, the boat's skipper appeared very jittery and said he had injector problems. But the Auxiliarist knew this was impossible with a gasoline engine, and he became suspicious. He thought the skipper of *La Toto* was smuggling illegal immigrants.

He reported the situation to an H-65 Coast Guard helicopter from Air Station Borinquen that was also searching for the diver. The H-65, with crew members Lt. Dave Neal, Lt. (jg) Tom McBeth, and AM2 John Lawrence, flew over *La Toto*. They confirmed the vessel's position and passed their report to the Greater Antilles Section operations center. The vessel's description matched that of one targeted for lookout by Lt. (jg) Paul Steward, Greater Antilles Section law enforcement and intelligence officer. A Borinquen HC-130 was diverted to establish a watch, while the 110-foot patrol boat *Ocracoke* (WPB-1307) sped to the location.

Lt. (jg) James Rendon, executive officer, navigated the *Ocracoke* to within surveillance range and launched a small boat, crewed by BM1 Patrick Domy and SA Steve Michels. The boarding party from the *Ocracoke*, including BM1 Paul Pratt, GM3 Enrique Avila, MK3 Steve Abbot, and SA Gary Mattos, noted that a fuel tank had been tampered with. Inside, they found the first batch of cocaine.

Steward and the operations center staff quickly coordinated a statement of no objection to seize the vessel as stateless. *La Toto*'s captain had claimed Dominican registry but could produce no proof. The *Ocracoke* seized the vessel and arrested the five Colombians on board.

While escorting *La Toto* to San Juan, the custody crew made note of likely locations of additional concealed compartments, which were investigated upon mooring. After taking out interior bulkheads and panels, a total of 3,771 pounds of pure cocaine was offloaded, leaving the boat a foot higher in the water. The cocaine had an estimated street value of $250 million. The crew was jailed.

It was the actions of an alert Auxiliarist, a Team Coast Guard member, that led to the biggest cocaine bust in the service's history to that date and the second largest ever.

Jupiter Fire: 1990

Sunday morning, 16 September 1990, was quiet in Bay City, Michigan, misty with low clouds hovering overhead. The 394-foot gasoline tanker *Jupiter* was moored at the Total Petroleum fuel storage dock on the Saginaw River, offloading 2.3 million gallons of unleaded gasoline. But the quiet would soon be shattered by the sounds of one of worst disasters on the Great Lakes in recent history.

At about 8:30 AM the inbound motor ship *Buffalo* passed close by the *Jupiter*. The suction of the *Buffalo*'s propellers caused the *Jupiter*, which was facing upriver, to pull away from the dock. As a result, the aft pilings broke off and the fuel lines parted, which caused a spark and ignited the spilled gas. At the time, 22,000 barrels of a total of 54,000 barrels were still on board. In an instant, more than a million gallons of unleaded gas was burning out of control at the fuel storage dock and on the tanker. Flames catapulted higher than 100 feet, filling the air with smoke that could be seen for 50 miles.

With minimal firefighting equipment on the tanker, it was obvious to the *Jupiter*'s captain that attempts to extinguish the blaze would be futile. It was rapidly spreading across the decks and even the pilings to which the ship was moored. The captain gave the order to abandon ship and at that moment also heard the siren of an approaching Coast Guard patrol boat. Everyone jumped over the side. But not all crew members had lifejackets on, and some yelled, "I can't swim! I can't swim!" (Merchant seamen are not required to pass a swimming test and, indeed, some do not know how.)

Robert and Jean Colby, Coast Guard Auxiliarists who lived on their 42-foot trawler on the Saginaw River, heard the *Jupiter*'s mayday over their marine radio. The Colbys donned their survival suits and were under way within two minutes. They were the first rescuers to arrive on the scene, just moments after the *Jupiter* exploded. A Coast Guard 41-foot utility boat was right behind them.

Undaunted by the smoke and intense heat, Robert Colby maneuvered his small boat toward the exploded gasoline tanker. "We were close enough to touch the *Jupiter*," Colby said, "and we could hear the fire crackling." They took five crew members on their boat, administered treatment for shock and hypothermia, and delivered the men to an ambulance at the pier. The Colbys then returned to the burning ship to help transfer two more men to a Coast Guard utility boat, and came back a third time to set up a safety zone.

According to the citation that accompanied the Colbys' Gold Life-Saving Medals, their "determined efforts, outstanding initiative, and fortitude during this rescue while jeopardizing their own safety were instrumental in saving the lives of eight people." Both Robert and Jean Colby also received the Auxiliary Plaque of Merit.

Moments after the Colbys pulled alongside the *Jupiter*, a 41-foot Coast Guard utility boat from Station Saginaw River arrived on the scene. EM1 Mike Klaczkiewicz, a member of Reserve Unit Saginaw, was boat coxswain of the 41-footer. MST2 Leo Trahan, another Reservist, was also on board. The boat engineer was regular fireman (FN) Bill Martin. "I kept telling Mike to go faster," Trahan said. "He kept telling me that he was giving it all it had."

Seaman Jim Huffman, another Reservist who was part of the 41-footer crew, added, "As we came upon the scene, we saw people on the fantail waving their arms, screaming and jumping into the water." The utility boat transferred the rescued victims to safety on the station's nearby 22-footer, manned by regulars MK2 Nathaniel White, MK1 Greg Bergeon, and BM3 Jed Stene. One by one, the sailors were pulled from the water until all but one had been accounted for. Sixteen were rescued, but forty-six-year-old Tom Sexton drowned while trying to swim ashore. His body was recovered three days later. These rescues were carried out at great personal risk, right next to a burning ship with the potential for more explosions.

Huffman, Trahan, and Klaczkiewicz received the Coast Guard Medal for their heroic actions. Sea Cadet Lynn Kulinec, also on board, was awarded the Meritorious Service Medal. Kulinec later enlisted and served on active duty in the Coast Guard.

All traffic on the Saginaw River was shut down. By noon a call had gone out for more Reserve help. A few hours later, eleven more members of Reserve Unit Saginaw were on scene, and within twelve hours, the total number of Reservists had swelled to eighteen. BMC Herb Mann, officer in charge at Coast Guard Station Saginaw River, said, "If you didn't know any of these guys, you wouldn't have known the regulars from the Reservists."

With the *Jupiter*'s crew accounted for, thoughts and actions turned toward securing the burning ship to the dock. Marine Safety Office Detroit and Toledo crews were en route by both car and helicopter. The Detroit-homeported 140-foot icebreaking tug *Bristol Bay* (WTGB-102) was upbound in the Detroit River, with an estimated arrival time about midnight. The crew of the Coast Guard's 180-foot buoy tender *Bramble* (WLB-392) was likewise recalled. Helicopters from Air Stations Detroit and Traverse City, Michigan, flew toward the scene. Several fire departments near Bay City responded to the emergency. The dock at the storage area was on fire and in danger of spreading to the monster storage tanks.

Fire chief Jerry Ball of the Bangor County Fire Department immediately took charge of the effort. In less than an hour the dockside blaze was out. However, all but one of the mooring lines that held the vessel to the fuel dock had parted in the explosion. If the fire broke the remaining line, the flaming *Jupiter* would become a potential danger floating down the Saginaw River. With only one line holding to the fuel dock, the bow of the vessel had drifted toward the shipping channel in the middle of the the river.

A team of Coast Guard regulars, Reservists, and Bangor Township firemen worked together to prevent a major disaster. Reservists MK2 Daniel Cummings and BM2 Paul Cormier earned Meritorious Service Medals for climbing on board the burning tanker and securing a cable to the *Jupiter*'s anchor so that it would not drift farther out into the shipping channel. Station Saginaw Coast Guard personnel also deployed containment booms downriver, minimizing an environmental impact from floating debris and contaminants.

Cdr. Tom Daley, commanding officer of Marine Safety Office Detroit, arrived in Bay City Sunday afternoon and assumed the duties of federal on-scene coordinator. The tanker was still aflame, lighting the sky. Dozens of firefighting units, some from as far away as Detroit, were soon also on scene, seeking to keep the flames from spreading to the thirty fuel storage tanks located near the burning *Jupiter*.

The tanker's owners hired a Texas-based marine firefighting company. A Coast Guard C-130 from Air Station Clearwater, Florida, flew to Houston to pick up the civilian firefighters' equipment for transport to Bay City. Shortly after midnight, the USCGC *Bramble* (WLB-392) and USCGC *Bristol Bay* (WTGB-102) arrived and tied up just downstream. As soon as it arrived, the Texas firefighting equipment was quickly loaded on board the *Bramble*. The cutter would take the firemen into the intense flames and smoke so they could blanket the *Jupiter* with A-Triple-F foam. The *Bristol Bay* would remain close by, just in case.

While the *Bramble* worked its way along the starboard side of the *Jupiter* at a distance of less than 10 feet, the firefighting equipment was used to knock down the flames. The fire that was visible above deck was extinguished within an hour. As the *Bramble* moved to safe water, the *Jupiter* once again reflashed and burst into flames, igniting gasoline on the river. Returning the next day with a fresh supply of foam, the *Bramble* again extinguished the fire, then remained in position through the night, checking the *Jupiter* with a thermal imager for possible hotspots.

After three days of hard work under harsh conditions, the fire was out for good. The *Jupiter* had been totally destroyed, but hardly any gas had leaked into the river. More important, not even a minor injury was reported during the dangerous mission.

In addition to the individual awards mentioned earlier, Coast Guard Marine Safety Office Detroit, Coast Guard Station Saginaw, Michigan, and the cutter *Bramble* were awarded Coast Guard Unit Commendations with Operational Distinguishing Devices.

The response to the *Jupiter* fire serves as another excellent example of Team Coast Guard's work. Petty Officer Mike Klaczkiewicz, U.S. Coast Guard Reserve and coxswain of the 41-footer, reinforced this thought in a personal letter to Rear Adm. Gregory A. Pennington, commander of the Ninth Coast Guard District. He stated: "It is my sincere desire that the *Jupiter* fire incident will be a reminder to everyone of the great team the Coast Guard becomes when all its elements work together."

Red River Flood Relief: 1997

In April 1997, flood waters of the Red River engulfed Grand Forks, North Dakota, and the surrounding area. It was the most severe flooding of the river since 1826, topping the 52-foot levees. Eventually it reached 26 feet above flood stage. When the dikes in Grand Forks could no longer keep out the water, Mayor Pat Owens ordered the evacuation of more than 50,000 people on 18 April. It was the largest U.S. civilian evacuation since Atlanta, Georgia, in the Civil War. Tens of thousands of people were forced from their homes, and seventeen downtown buildings burned amid the water.

The Coast Guard set up a 1,200-mile relief pipeline from St. Louis, Missouri, where Coast Guard Forces Command at the Marine Safety Office managed relief operations. Coast Guard crews would enter a cold, wet, wind-swept region with no Coast Guard radio stations or bases and little food, water, or electrical power. Search and rescue helicopters from Coast Guard Air Stations Traverse City, Michigan, and New Orleans were stationed at Grand Forks to conduct emergency rescues resulting from the flooding and fires that burned out of control.

Eight Coast Guard Disaster Response Units (DRUs), teams of shallow-draft boat operators seasoned by the floods of 1993 and 1995 farther south, were dispatched to Grand Forks, on both sides of the river. Their mission was to help emergency operations response centers in Breckenridge, Minnesota and Fargo, North Dakota. These teams consisted of active duty personnel from Omaha, Peoria, Quad Cities, Dubuque, and St. Louis, as well as Reservists from throughout the Midwest. Other help came from units in Duluth, Minnesota, and Sault Ste. Marie, Michigan. "The DRUs are a tribute to the success of the Coast Guard's integration plan and its members' ability to adapt to any challenge," noted BMC Paul Scholesser of Marine Safety Detachment St. Paul,

Minnesota. "Each DRU is made up of both active and Reserve, and they function like a team."

Regional Auxiliarists provided vital links and logistics to these personnel. The Coast Guard commander described the response: "We had no VHF communications until the Auxiliary provided it. We had no means of getting the on-scene-commander on scene until the Auxiliary provided it." At Wahpeton, North Dakota, the Coast Guard for the first time turned over two small boats to the Auxiliary so it could maintain its own disaster response unit. Nine other relief units were deployed along the Red River. Auxiliary members ferried utility crews and home owners. They marked obstructions in flooded roads and conducted rescues. Operating with personnel from the Fargo Fire Department, the Coast Guard also located three 14-foot boats for possible use during flood emergency response. Four Auxiliary planes conducted levee surveys and rotated personnel in and out of the region. This allowed Coast Guard helicopter aircrews to concentrate on search and rescue operations.

Not until 30 May did the river recede below flood stage everywhere in North Dakota. In forty days, 200 Coast Guard active duty, Reserve, and Auxiliary personnel had conducted more than 900 boat and helicopter missions and rescued 916 people. Among the Team Coast Guard members were 29 Coast Guard Reservists who had assisted as needed, and 60 Auxiliarists from nine states, constituting 30 percent of the service's forces participating in the effort.

Hurricane Katrina: 2005

On 29 August 2005, Hurricane Katrina made landfall in southern Louisiana. The most severe loss of life and property damage occurred in New Orleans, which flooded as the levee system catastrophically failed, in many cases hours after the storm had moved inland. Nearly every levee in metro New Orleans was breached as Hurricane Katrina passed just east of the city limits.

Eventually 80 percent of the city became flooded, as well as large tracts of neighboring parishes. The floodwaters lingered for weeks. At least 1,836 people lost their lives in the hurricane and subsequent floods. On 3 September, Homeland Security Secretary Michael Chertoff described Katrina and its aftermath as "probably the worst catastrophe, or set of catastrophes" in the history of the United States.

In the aftermath of this devastating national tragedy, the Coast Guard saved more than 24,000 people and evacuated nearly 9,500 hospital patients to safety. In addition, the service responded to more than 3,800 marine pollution cases, and in most areas reopened affected waterways to resume commerce in less than a week. The rescue and response efforts were some of the largest in Coast Guard history, involving units from every district and a total of 5,600 service personnel.

How did the Coast Guard accomplish so much in so little time? The answer is simple: by leveraging the power of its diverse workforce and using every part of Team Coast Guard. Active duty, Reserve, and Auxiliary components stepped forward and offered a sense of pride and hope.

Rescue operations commenced as the hurricane moved inland. Cutters had trailed it as closely as they could and began rescuing those offshore. The helicopters—HH-65 Dolphins and HH-60 Jayhawks—were launched as the eye of the storm passed over New Orleans. The tempo increased as everyone realized the levees had given way, creating an urban nightmare. Dispensing with peacetime regulations on the time needed to rest between flights, aircrews worked around the clock to pluck survivors from rooftops, while maintenance crews kept the aircraft in service.

There were many challenges, but the Coast Guard is known for and prides itself on its ability to improvise. When rescue swimmers found victims trapped in their attics with no way to escape rising waters, axes were used to chop through rooftops. When it was found that not enough were available, a trip to Home Depot solved that. Urban search and rescue techniques were developed on the fly, since few aircrews had experience with night sorties through a flooded city where high winds and hanging power lines added to the danger. Coast Guard cutters and small craft too entered the disaster area, rescuing people from small islands of dry land, flooded overpasses, inundated homes and buildings, and transporting them to safety.

CWO3 Robert D. Lewald commanded the CGC *Pamlico* (WLIC-800) and the small fleet of vessels that safely evacuated thousands from New Orleans in what was called Operation Dunkirk. He dealt with armed gangs, desperate survivors, and local law enforcement officials.

Disaster area response teams paddled and operated their small boats through flooded streets searching for survivors at water level. Many of these Coast Guardsmen, including 800 Reservists, came from as far away as Alaska and Maine. Master Chief Petty Officer Ann Tubbs, a Reservist stationed at Coast Guard Headquarters, was recalled on 7 September and headed to the Disaster Recovery Center in Ocean Springs, Mississippi. Working from dawn to dusk, Tubbs said she lost all track of time. "We were set up in an old K-Mart and had all kinds of federal and state agencies working there assisting people," she said. "We had FEMA, USDA, emergency child care, counseling, the Red Cross, Mississippi state agencies, Customs and Border Protection, other DHS agencies, you name it."

Lt. Cdr. Brad Wallace, U.S. Coast Guard Reserve, served as the operational commander of what was to become a 167-member Coast Guard unit, with almost fifty flood relief punt boats and a complete sector model organization. His unit was affectionately dubbed Coast Guard Hurricane Task Force One. Other members of the service representing Port Security Units, Marine Safety and Security Teams, and Tactical Law Enforcement Detachments provided boat crews and force protection. For days on end these forces departed early in the morning and returned later in the afternoon to tell tales of the rescues and other events of the days—some of which had happy endings, many of which did not. At the height of operations, more than 5,500 Coast Guard volunteers performed rescue and recovery operations.

When key Coast Guard assets were damaged during and after Katrina, Auxiliary members responded with radio and boat assets, and their trained personnel to make the difference. When the Coast Guard Aviation Training Center Mobile, Alabama, lost its roof and communication capabilities from the hurricane winds on Monday, 29 August, a call was made to Auxiliarist Rene Stiegler. He was also the owner of ShipCom LLC, a large marine communications service provider. Stiegler prepared and provided ATC Mobile with a VHF radio, power supply, and emergency antenna, establishing a link with ShipCom. Within the hour Auxiliarist Stiegler and his engineer Mike Ramage had two ShipCom VHF receivers tuned to Coast Guard working frequencies. They communicated with Coast Guard aircraft traveling to ATC Mobile and from there to the areas affected by Katrina. Additionally, ShipCom tuned two transmitters to frequencies used by Communications Area Master Station Atlantic.

Stiegler and Ramage relayed hundreds of messages. Coordinates of victims stranded on rooftops were communicated to rescue aircraft, and reports of their rescue were relayed back to the ATC Mobile command center. For three days Stiegler and Ramage stood radio watch twenty-four hours a day, alternately taking short naps. Until late in the week, Stiegler said, the Auxiliarists—including John LaPointe, Palmore "Duke" Dupree, and Jim Patterson and staff at ShipCom—were the only communications available to the Coast Guard assets.

The day after the hurricane struck, Coast Guard Station Dauphin Island, on a barrier island in southwest Alabama, was the only operational facility on the western part of the Gulf. They found themselves with no immediately available boats at the station to provide for search and rescue, so they asked members of Auxiliary Flotilla 3-9, Mobile, Alabama, to bring one, Auxiliary vessel 9580, the Merry Sue, to Station Dauphin Island for search and rescue standby until the station was able to launch its own boat.

On 3 September, Coast Guard communications in the Biloxi, Mississippi area were still limited, with no ground facilities available from Houston to Mobile. They called on members of local flotillas to send a boat to provide communications relay for the service's active component. Again Flotilla 3-9 responded, this time with Auxiliary vessel *Argo*, which made its way on site in six hours. Station Dauphin Island, just two hours away by water, launched daily patrols of the Biloxi area using Coast Guard 25-foot fast boats. The *Argo* provided assistance to these patrols by means of facilities, meals, rest, and water, and was also available with emergency fuel for the Coast Guard assets if necessary.

The Bay of Biloxi was closed to all pleasure boating, and local law enforcement tasked the *Argo* with being watchful for boaters and reporting them. The *Argo* remained on station until 6 September. Auxiliary aircraft transported personnel and photographers, as well as making aerial surveys of aids to navigation on the southern part of the Mississippi River.

On 25 May 2006, at the commandant's change of command ceremony, President George Bush presented the Presidential Unit Citation to the entire Coast Guard for meritorious achievement and outstanding performance from 29 August to 13 September 2005, in preparation for, response to, and recovery from the devastation wrought by Hurricane Katrina. Since this was an all-hands effort, all Coast Guard active duty, Reserve, Auxiliary and civilian personnel affiliated with the service during this period were eligible for the award. It was, in every sense of the word, a recognition of Team Coast Guard.

8. COAST GUARD AUXILIARY

The U.S. Coast Guard Auxiliary is the uniformed civilian component of the Coast Guard. An organization of vetted and trained volunteers, the Auxiliary provides a broad inventory of vital skills, assets, and experience for Coast Guard units across the nation. It is an essential component of Team Coast Guard and directly supports the service in all missions except military and direct law enforcement actions.

Established in 1939 to involve experienced recreational boaters in promoting boating safety, the Auxiliary is now also a valuable force multiplier for the active duty service, which is tasked with new homeland security missions and is chronically underfunded by Congress. Overall, the Auxiliary accounts for some 12 percent of the Coast Guard's total search and rescue caseload. Auxiliarists teach public courses in seamanship, navigation, and other specialties. They provide free courtesy vessel safety checks of recreational boats to make sure they meet federal and state requirements. Besides conducting safety patrols in their own vessels, the Auxiliary also has a small aviation arm that flies surveillance and search and rescue patrols over coastal areas.

Auxiliary members are legally civilians not subject to the Uniform Code of Military Justice. They perform tasks that in the Coast Guard are usually carried out by enlisted personnel, and although they have no rank, they wear officers' uniforms and insignia (with a capital "A" embossed on them) to denote the most important elected or appointed position they've held in the Auxiliary.

Malcolm Boylan

A well-known Hollywood screenwriter and avid yachtsman, Malcolm Boylan was elected in 1934 as the first commodore of the Pacific Writers Yacht Club, headquartered in Los Angeles. One of the first outings the new yacht club planned was a twenty-six-mile cruise to Catalina Island. It was to start at Watchorn Basin in Los Angeles harbor, where most members kept their boats. Boylan was proud of the ways he maintained his own boat, the *Chula*, but was worried that some of the other members' craft might not be in shape to make such a long cruise.

Also at anchor in the basin were two 165-foot Coast Guard cutters, the *Aurora* (WPC-103) and the *Hermes* (WPC-109). Boylan paid a call on the commanding officer of the *Hermes*, who was also the senior Coast Guard officer present, and persuaded him to inspect the club's boats. He also invited the officer to go along on their cruise to Catalina. The *Hermes* skipper could not accept the invitation, but agreed to send the commanding officer of the *Aurora*, Lt. Francis W. Pollard, on board Boylan's boat for the trip.

During the cruise, Boylan and Pollard developed a close relationship and had several lengthy conversations. Pollard discussed the Coast Guard's history and traditions, including its lack of a reserve force. After the cruise, Boylan sent a letter to Lieutenant Pollard, dated 23 August 1934, stating: "The thought has come to me that the Coast Guard, alone of all the armed services, has no organized reserve. . . . A Coast Guard Reserve would be an excellent thing to perpetuate its traditions, preserve its entity and, more particularly, to place at the disposal of the Coast Guard officers, auxiliary flotillas of small craft, for the frequent emergencies incident to your prescribed twenty-two [defined duties], and countless unexpected duties."

Boylan's letter later became known as the "Founder's Letter," which crystallized the idea of what would become today's Coast Guard Auxiliary. Lieutenant Pollard forwarded Boylan's letter through the chain of command to the office of Rear Adm. Harry G. Hamlet, the commandant of the Coast Guard. Boylan's suggestion held little interest for the commandant, but it did make an impression on Admiral Hamlet's aide, Cdr. Russell R. Waesche.

In 1936 Hamlet retired and Waesche, at age fifty, was promoted to rear admiral and appointed commandant. Waesche recognized that manpower was one of the service's most serious concerns, especially with the explosion in the popularity of pleasure boating. One way to solve the problem would be to create a reservoir of manpower that could be called upon in emergencies without increasing the Coast Guard's budget. As Waesche contemplated this possible solution, he remembered Boylan's letter.

Early in 1939, he assigned Lt. Cdr. Alfred C. Richmond, along with Lt. Cdr. Merlin O'Neill and a civilian from the Life-Saving Service, to draft a bill to create such an organization. A Coast Guard Reserve bill was forwarded to Congress, with the support of the Treasury and Commerce Departments. Waesche assured Congress that this new reserve would not cost the government any money and would be run by volunteers, loosely supervised by Coast Guard officers.

On 23 June 1939, President Franklin Roosevelt signed into law "An Act to establish a Coast Guard Reserve to be composed of owners of motorboats and yachts." This Reserve was to (1) assist the Coast Guard; (2) promote efficiency in the operation of motorboats and yachts; (3) foster a wider knowledge of and better compliance with the laws, rules, and regulations governing the operation of motorboats; and (4) promote safety and effect rescues on and over the high seas and navigable waters. Large numbers of U.S. boat owners became members of this voluntary nonmilitary Reserve. Groups of boat owners were organized into flotillas, and these into divisions within Coast Guard districts around the country.

The Coast Guard Reserve Act of 1939 was the key legislation in the founding of what became the Coast Guard Auxiliary. On 19 February 1941, Congress amended the original Reserve Act as the Coast Guard Auxiliary and Reserve Act, creating a new military Reserve and renaming the original Reserve the Coast Guard Auxiliary.

Malcolm Boylan later became commodore of the Eleventh Coast Guard District Auxiliary. He played a key role in the founding of organization. He died in 1967 in Hollywood.

Charles R. Zeller

At about 4:00 PM on 13 August 1961, Coast Guard Auxiliarist Charles R. Zeller of Brooklyn, New York was, standing on the dock of Happy's Yacht Basin in Brooklyn. Suddenly a terrific explosion occurred next to the fuel dock on board the moored 45-foot yacht *Jolly Roger*, immediately engulfing the vessel in flames.

Disregarding his personal safety, Zeller approached the yacht, and a teenage girl, aflame from head to foot, jumped into his arms. He immersed her in water to extinguish the flames and pulled her back on the dock. A second person leaped from the burning vessel and ran up and down the dock, screaming. Zeller grabbed him and tore off his flaming clothes. A third passenger had jumped unnoticed from the *Jolly Roger* and was in the water, clinging to one of the fuel dock pilings in too great a state of shock to call for help. Zeller pulled this man onto the dock.

Although seriously burned himself, and while would-be helpers were standing around too dazed to assist, Zeller instructed onlookers to call an ambulance and the fire department. With the possibility of a second explosion occurring, Zeller had the gasoline pumps turned off at the main valve. By this time the fire had burned the mooring lines, and the *Jolly Roger* was drifting toward the Brooklyn Yacht Club. Under Auxiliarist Zeller's direction, the vessel was retrieved and held off until the fire department arrived and extinguished the flames. In the cabin of the *Jolly Roger* was the body of a four-year-old who had perished in the fire.

Auxiliarist Charles Zeller's prompt and efficient actions that day resulted in the saving of lives and property. Later at his Auxiliary district's annual rendezvous at the Coast Guard Academy in New London, Connecticut, Rear Adm. R. M. Ross, commander of the Third Coast Guard District, presented Zeller with the Coast Guard Auxiliary Plaque of Merit ("A" Award) for extraordinary service. The citation ended with: "Your unselfish action, excellent leadership, and complete disregard for personal safety reflect honorably upon yourself and the Coast Guard Auxiliary."

Bolling Douglas

A Navy admiral's daughter, Bolling Douglas joined the Auxiliary in 1960 and founded a flotilla in Augusta, Georgia. Later she moved to a flotilla located on Lake Lanier, about twenty-five miles northeast of Atlanta. Douglas was a familiar figure on the home waters of Lake Lanier, known for her very recognizable boat. She and her husband owned an authentic Chinese junk. A vessel of that type would have stood out on any American waters, but on an inland lake it was especially eye-catching.

For Auxiliary work she owned a more traditional cabin cruiser, the *Finale*. On this boat, generations of Auxiliarists from the area were trained to her high standards in the service's boat crew program. Every mission was multimission as those on board were drilled in marlinspike, communications, and search and rescue techniques.

Within the Auxiliary, Douglas had served in almost every staff office of her flotilla, particularly in the education and operation fields. She had been the commander and vice commander, and later served as division captain. She became Auxiliary operational qualified and attended the national Search and Rescue School, then held at Governor's Island. She also held the navigation advanced rating in the power squadron.

In 1979 while on patrol one day on Lake Lanier, Bolling Douglas and her crew received a call stating that a boat had caught fire at a nearby marina. The Auxiliary facility sped to the scene, where the enflamed boat was at the dock with many others nearby, and a restaurant terrace within yards. Douglas and her crew were able to get a line secured to tow the burning boat farther out into the harbor, away from boats and boaters. Just as they released the line to let it drift out of the marina, it exploded. For their daring action, the members of Douglas' crew were awarded the Plaque of Merit.

Douglas went through the elected ranks and in 1978 was elected vice commodore of the Seventh District. But soon thereafter, the man who had been newly elected as district commodore passed away. The district board, in a special ballot, elected Douglas as the new district commodore. The Coast Guard sent a C-130 to fly her and others to Dobbins Air Force Base, outside

Atlanta, for her official installation in office. Thus Bolling Douglas became the first female Auxiliary district commodore.

This unconventional beginning of her term was followed by the unprecedented mobilization of Coast Guard forces responding to the Mariel boat lift in May 1980, named Operation Key Ring. Taking action almost immediately, the Coast Guard called for Auxiliary assets to augment theirs as Cuban refugees took to the sea. The chief of the Office of Boating Safety contacted Douglas (who at the time was attending her first national conference as commodore), with an initial request for seventy-six Auxiliary facilities and more than 260 members. Commodore Douglas was never slow to take action.

Returning home immediately, she recruited a private pilot to fly her to Miami, then persuaded him to join the Auxiliary. Starting with an initial briefing on 27 May, planning went into the night. The following day Douglas met with senior Coast Guard officers in Miami, flying from there to Key West. As a result of these meetings, the Auxiliary's involvement was scaled back somewhat, to fifty-two vessels and 165 members. To support the mobilization, crew housing, fuel, and docking in the Keys were arranged. By 31 May, an operations center had been set up, and Key Ring Base Radio was on the air on Big Pine Key. The next day two additional radio stations were set up. For the next eighteen days the Auxiliary functioned smoothly, assuming major responsibility for search and rescue in the Keys.

On 17 June with the crisis having subsided, Operation Key Ring ended and Douglas returned to more normal demands as the Auxiliary district commodore. But when her term ended, her service to the Auxiliary was far from over. Requirements for the boat crew program had undergone a complete revision. The need for qualification examiners to test and qualify members as crew, operator, or coxswain resulted in a demand for Auxiliarists experienced in boat handling. Douglas was among the first to step forward and go through the challenging program. So the first female district commodore then became the first female qualification examiner. She traveled all over the Seventh District, where she was known for her attention to detail and the high standards she expected in boat crew candidates.

In addition to the respect she earned from the Coast Guard and the Auxiliary, Douglas is well known in the boating industry. During her long career as a marine surveyor, insurance companies often called her in for challenging claims. The measure of her reputation is evidenced by her service as a member of the National Association of Marine Surveyors. Douglas has worked as a member of the National Boating Safety Advisory Council and served as president of the American Boat and Yacht Council. Currently she is president of the ABYC Foundation.

Betty Wood McNabb

Born in 1909, Betty Wood McNabb was one the first women to join the Coast Guard Auxiliary in June 1941. She and her husband, Lt. Cdr. Harold McNabb, U.S. Coast Guard Reserve, used their houseboat to conduct antisubmarine patrols during World War II. In 1944 she joined the Women's Army Corps, where she was introduced to the medical records field in which she would work for three decades. After the war, McNabb became a nurse and later worked as a medical records consultant for the state of Georgia.

She fell in love with flying in 1951, after stopping by a local airport in Albany, Georgia, to watch a plane take off. A friend asked her if she wanted a ride in his plane. In mid-flight he said, "Now you can take her around." McNabb even landed the plane, remarking how easy it was. She bought a plane that day and her flying career began. McNabb acquired her pilot's license at age forty-three in 1952, and started averaging 400 hours a year of flying time. Since her job required endless hours of travel, she used her first aircraft for that purpose and flew over forty-eight states, five foreign countries, and most of the Caribbean Islands.

In October 1953, the female aviator joined the Civil Air Patrol and rose to the rank of lieutenant colonel. She led both cadets and senior members of Albany's squadron. In September 1955, she became their commander. McNabb was rated to fly single- and multiengine aircraft, single-engine seaplanes, and commercial gliders. She was also rated as an instrument instructor. She ferried commercial aircraft and competed in the women's Powder Puff, Angel, and Petticoat Derbies.

Betty McNabb was the first woman to graduate from the nonresident course at the Air Force War College. She served twice as president of the Ninety-Nines, an international women pilots' organization founded by Amelia Earhart, and as an executive committee member for more than a decade. McNabb was also a member of the Mach Buster's Club, holding the distinction of being one of the first women in the western world to break the sound barrier. This came as a result of the commander of Turner Air Force Base calling her one day and asking if she wanted to fly in an F-100F tactical jet. At 45,000 feet, as they approached the sound barrier, the pilot said she could take the plane through Mach 1, if she wished—which she did.

In 1971 the McNabbs moved from Georgia to her hometown of Panama, Florida. There, in 1973 they joined Coast Guard Auxiliary Flotilla 16 in the Eighth District. Between that time and her last Auxiliary mission in 1991, Betty McNabb logged more than 1,500 flight hours on Auxiliary operations. Virtually every weekend she would climb into her Grumman Tiger and fly along the Florida coast between Pensacola and St. Marks, looking for boats in distress, oil spills, and hazards to navigation. She qualified as a vessel examiner and public education instructor, and served as assistant district staff officer for air operations in the Eighth District. In 1985 she was appointed to the national staff as branch chief for air safety. McNabb also served as the liaison to the Civil Air Patrol in the Eighth District.

In April 1977, she was inducted into the National Aerospace Hall of Honor in Nashville. Her award cited her presentations to school groups; orientation flights for students, teachers, and the handicapped; work in aerospace workshops; counseling in accident preventions for the Federal Aviation Administration; articles on flying; search and rescue work for the Auxiliary and Civil Air Patrol; and a personal twenty-five-year flying safety record.

But McNabb was most proud of three awards: the American Medical Records Association's Distinguished Member Award; the highest Civil Air Patrol award, the Silver Valor Medal; and the Coast Guard Auxiliary's Certificate of Administrative Merit, the Auxiliary's third highest award.

Harold McNabb died in 1982. In a 1987 interview, Betty McNabb said, "flying is so much a part of my life that I'm going to fly as long as I can." She flew her last Auxiliary mission in 1991 at age eighty-two. At the time, she was the oldest female pilot in the Auxiliary. She was still on the roster of Flotilla 16 when she died in 1996.

Nick Kerigan

Auxiliarist Nick Kerigan worked for the investment firm of Morgan Stanley Dean Witter on 11 September 2001. The firm was then located on the fifty-sixth floor of Two World Trade Center. When the attack occurred, Kerigan was on the phone. He heard the crash and through his window saw debris flying. No one knew what had happened. Then the second plane hit Two World Trade, approximately thirty floors above. The building shook, and parts of the ceiling collapsed, blocking the exit corridor.

Kerigan and his coworkers broke open the doors to gain access to the stairway. When they reached the street, policemen told them to go east to Broadway. Approximately a half-hour after they exited their building, they saw it collapse. Kerigan was among more than 4,000 Morgan Stanley employees who successfully evacuated the building.

In the days following this national tragedy, Nick Kerigan, as the First District Southern Region vice commodore, assisted district commodore William Huling in coordinating plans and developing policies. He worked with operations and administrative staff and Cdr. Edward Seebald, the regional director of Auxiliary, to see that the Auxiliary response to the attack went smoothly.

Throughout the New York coastal area, members of the Coast Guard Auxiliary showed up without being called. They came to every single Coast Guard station to do what they could. In many cases, they took over duties of the service members as they responded to the emergency. Auxiliary boats and aircraft conducted both surface and air patrols and assumed search and rescue standby duties at many small boat stations. This gave the active duty force the latitude to redirect Coast Guard small boats toward port security and homeland defense. On the water, Coast Guard Auxiliary boats from Westchester County ran security patrols around the George Washington Bridge, those from Sandy Hook around the Verrazano-Narrows Bridge.

Auxiliary crews backfilled for Coast Guard search and rescue teams at stations New York, Sandy Hook, and New London, taking over as communications watch standers in New London. Another Auxiliarist and licensed psychologist, Dr. Janice Jackson, served as backup to the Critical Incident Stress Management Team throughout the day on 13 September.

Kerigan participated in the operations at Coast Guard Station New York, serving on search and rescue standby. By the middle of October, he had put in "a couple of hundred hours" on Auxiliary duty, as had many other Auxiliarists.

Jeremiah Ray, Thomas Shook, and Terry Minton

About 7:00 PM on Saturday, 15 January 2005, Coast Guard Auxiliarist Jeremiah Ray's telephone rang. It was Coast Guard Group Seattle with an emergency. They had received a cellular phone call from a small boat, aground on the mud flats of a local river some 15 miles north of where Ray's 28-foot Auxiliary boat was moored. Group Seattle told Ray that a family of three in a stranded boat was frightened and cold with no lights, no heat, and a small child on board. Seattle had no assets available and asked Ray if he could respond with his boat and a crew. Ray agreed, even though he and his crew had already completed a seven-hour patrol on Puget Sound earlier that day.

He immediately called his team, Auxiliarists Thomas Shook and Terry Minton, who agreed to meet Ray at his boat. They were under way by 7:30 PM. A winter storm had struck the area, and winds exceeded 20 miles an hour with driving snow, sleet, and hail, and temperatures about 25°. Ray's boat was equipped with a small heater and a good depth sounder, but no global positioning system or radar.

It was pitch black, and visibility in the driving snow was down to about 200 yards as Ray and his crew headed toward the estimated location of the frightened family. Wind-driven waves were up to 4 feet and smashing across Ray's boat, and at one point visibility was almost zero. After traveling in these conditions for two hours, they arrived in the area and, though they could not see the stranded boat, they were able to establish direct cell phone contact.

With depths around 3 feet, Ray's boat risked running aground, but his knowledge and skill enabled them to reach the vessel. Once alongside and with their hands numb from the cold, they had to free their frozen towing gear and the stranded vessel's anchor line. Moving the freezing family onto Ray's boat, they successful pulled the other one off the mud flats and were able to deliver both the family and vessel to safe mooring at midnight. Ray and his crew then struggled back through the night to their home mooring, arriving at 1:45 AM.

For their heroic actions, Jeremiah Ray, Thomas Shook, and Terry Minton were awarded the Auxiliary Plaque of Merit, the second highest award in the Auxiliary, and lived up to the proud tradition of volunteer Auxiliarists.

Buddy Roberts

Hurricane Katrina was still in New Orleans when Coast Guard Auxiliary aircraft commander Buddy Roberts, the liaison at Coast Guard Aviation Training Center Houston, got the call on Sunday, 28 August 2005. There was a need for a video assessment of New Orleans; ABC News had made a request to allow one of their videographers to accompany the mission and film the damage and the Coast Guard in action.

After checking the weather (winds were still 60–70 miles per hour over New Orleans) and his aircraft, Roberts picked up Coast Guard active duty public affairs officer Adam Wine and the ABC photographer and headed for New Orleans. As Roberts piloted his 02A Cessna over the city, he and his passengers could see that more than 50 percent of the city was flooded, and that in several places the storm had breached levees holding back the water. Wine and the photographer documented the damage, rolling their cameras as Coast Guard helicopters extracted victims from the flooded city.

Two days later at midnight, Roberts was called by Coast Guard Aviation Training Center Houston. This time it was to pick up two riverboat pilots from upstream Mississippi River locations and ferry them back to Navy New Orleans, where they would catch helicopter rides to Coast Guard cutters in the Gulf of Mexico for transfer to ships wishing to navigate the Mississippi. First was a stop in Conroe, Texas, to pick up one riverboat pilot, then on to Baton Rouge for another. That was the easy part. Landing at Navy New Orleans had to be done without lights, tower, or electricity at the base. This was no problem for veteran pilot Roberts, the Auxiliary aviation liaison in Houston.

From New Orleans he flew on to Houma, Louisiana, where a Coast Guard rescue swimmer who had been on leave was stranded. With an aids to navigation specialist on board the plane, Roberts made best use of his time by making both a damage assessment of the river and an aerial survey of the aids to navigation from the South Main Pass of the Mississippi all the way to Navy New Orleans. He then transferred personnel to their duty station in Iberia, Louisiana, before returning to Houston. Two more missions followed, moving personnel and equipment from base to base and allowing his aircraft to serve as a photo platform.

From four flotillas in the Houston area alone, eight Auxiliary aircraft participated in the Katrina effort. "To a person I have called out, they have responded," said Roberts. For him, a Hurricane Andrew survivor and veteran pilot, it was but another opportunity to respond when his country called.

The commanding officers of the Aviation Training Center in Mobile, Alabama, and Air Station New Orleans in a joint message applauded the commitment and skills of the Coast Guard Auxiliary Air Wing. These two Coast Guard bases had been at the forefront of providing unparalleled air rescue in the face of probably the nation's worst natural disaster. According to Captains B. C. Jones and D. R. Callahan, "the Aux Air assets, as always, stepped up to the plate and provided outstanding support to the operation." As of 13 September, they said, the Air Auxiliary had seventeen aircraft involved in rescue operations. "The aircrews have flown 56 sorties for a total of 209 hours."

Coast Guard helicopters operating over New Orleans during the first seven days saved an astonishing 6,470 lives (4,731 by hoist) during 723 sorties and 1,507 flight hours. Coast Guard Auxiliary aircraft and their crews enabled their active duty brethren to accomplish these feats. "Their commitment allowed SAR aircraft to stay focused on SAR while still accomplishing necessary logistics missions."

9. COAST GUARD RESERVE

By the 1930s, the Coast Guard was the only armed service that did not have a reserve component. The Army and Navy had sizable organizations of veterans and other personnel who were paid modest salaries to stay in training and make themselves available in a national emergency. With World War II under way in Asia and Europe, Congress passed the Coast Guard Reserve Act of 1939. However, this new Reserve was to be a civilian, volunteer organization focused primarily on assisting the Coast Guard in its boating safety responsibilities. Membership was limited to those who owned boats.

By 1941 the Coast Guard was preparing for war, and Congress restructured the Reserve. Henceforth the service would have two reserve forces. The existing civilian organization was renamed the Coast Guard Auxiliary, and a new military Coast Guard Reserve was created on 19 February 1941. The service Guard expanded to more than 214,000 active duty personnel by the peak of World War II. More than 92 percent were Reservists, serving in all theaters of the war.

As the war progressed, the joint chiefs of staff, following the examples of Great Britain and the Soviet Union, realized that women would have to play a major role in the war effort. Congress created the Women's Reserve of the Coast Guard in November 1942, modeled on the Navy's Women's Reserve that had been formed a few months earlier. Two restrictions placed on Navy women were carried over to the Coast Guard: women were not to serve outside the continental United States; and no woman, officer or enlisted, was empowered to issue orders to any male Coast Guardsman.

Women in the Coast Guard reserve were known by the acronym SPARs, based on the service's motto "Semper Paratus, Always Ready." Most SPAR officers received their training at the academy in New London, and most enlisted SPARs were trained at Palm Beach, Florida.

By 1943, the restriction on giving orders to Coast Guardsmen was abolished, and by September 1944 Congress also abolished overseas-duty restriction. By the end of the war, about 200 SPARs had served in Alaska, and 200 more in Hawaii. Altogether, approximately 11,000 women served in the Coast

Guard Women's Reserve. Shortly after the surrender of Japan in 1945, women's reserve branches of all the services were disbanded. The USCGC *Spar* (WLB-403) was commissioned on 12 June 1944 in honor of women Reservists (and decommissioned in 1997). The last SPAR was discharged in 1947, although the label was still being applied to female Coast Guardsmen in the 1960s. In 2001 the service commissioned another ship by the same name, *Spar* (WLB-206), honoring all those who had served.

Lucas Bobbitt

In spring 1944, Coast Guard Reservist SN1 Lucas Bobbitt was serving in the USS *Leopold* (DE-319), one of thirty Coast Guard–manned destroyer escorts. On 1 March the *Leopold* took up her position, together with other Coast Guard–manned destroyer escorts, guarding a twenty-seven-ship convoy (CU-16) departing New York City for Europe. Commissioned just five months earlier, the 306-foot ship would be making its second convoy across the North Atlantic. Its mission was to protect the convoy from German U-boat attacks.

A little more than a week later, at about 8:00 PM on 9 March, the convoy was about 400 miles south of Iceland when radar detected a U-boat at a distance of 8,000 yards. The *Leopold* broke off from the convoy and headed to intercept the enemy sub. Lt. Cdr. Kenneth C. Phillips, U.S. Coast Guard, the *Leopold*'s commanding officer, ordered his crew to battle stations with orders to "fire on sight." As the *Leopold* got closer, she fired a flare to light the area. As soon as *U-255* was sighted, the *Leopold*'s guns commenced. Only a few rounds had been fired when another submarine, lying in wait, fired a new acoustic torpedo that struck the *Leopold* amidships.

When it hit, Coast Guard Reservist Bobbitt was at his battle station as a part of a gun crew. The explosion knocked him against the breach of the 3-inch gun, and the grating from the deck ripped loose and hit him on the side of his right leg. Bobbitt got up and discovered that the explosion had killed several other gun crew members. He tried to depress the gun to fire at the U-boat, but it was jammed. The explosion had also blown the commanding officer and a number of the crew off the ship and into the water.

Bobbitt soon heard the order to abandon ship, but didn't react right away. He didn't think his ship was sinking, and he was in no hurry to enter the 39° waters of the North Atlantic. But after a few moments, he put on his lifejacket and started to climb down the nettings to a lifeboat. The rush of men to get off the ship was so great that Bobbitt and many others ended up in the ocean. After swimming for about an hour and a half he spotted a life raft, only to discover that it was completely full with no more room. He hung on the side, fighting the cold and trying to stay conscious, until one of the wounded died and was pushed out to make room for Bobbitt.

His ordeal and that of his fellow survivors was not over. They hoped to be picked up by the USS *Joyce* (DE-317), another Coast Guard–manned destroyer escort that had followed them to intercept the U-boat. But the enemy sub was still in the area, and if the *Joyce* stopped to pick up survivors she would be a sitting duck. A British plane flew over and dropped a flare, but was unable to drop depth charges on the U-boat because of fears it would also blow the life rafts out of the water. The winds and waves increased and often washed over Bobbitt's raft, sometimes taking men overboard.

Finally, at about 1:30 in the morning, the U-boat departed and the *Joyce* stopped to pick up survivors. By that time only 5 men were left in the life raft with Bobbitt. The final count revealed that all of the *Leopold's* 13 officers and 158 of her 186 enlisted men had been lost, making Lucas Bobbitt one of only 28 survivors. The sinking of the *Leopold* was the biggest loss the Coast Guard suffered in World War II from enemy action.

SN1 Lucas Bobbitt's ability to hang on for hours in the frigid waters of the North Atlantic personifies the perseverance, commitment, and courage of thousands of Coast Guard Reservists who served during World War II. Many others, like most of those on the *Leopold*, sacrificed their lives for their country.

Vera Hammerschlag

Among the 1,000 commissioned officers of the Coast Guard SPARs was Vera Hammerschlag.

In the summer of 1943, Coast Guard Headquarters decided that long-range navigation (LORAN) monitor stations within the continental United States should be manned by SPARs. In the LORAN system, developed at the beginning of the war, radio signals transmitted from two shore-based stations were picked up by a certain type of receiver-indicator installed in ships and planes. This allowed them to calculate their exact positions. The monitor stations were equipped with the same type of receiver-indicator, but because they were in fixed locations, were able to check the accuracy and general operations of the transmitting stations. SPAR operators would stand watch twenty-four hours a day, taking and recording these measurements every two minutes.

Lt. (jg) Vera Hammerschlag, U.S. Coast Guard Reserve (Women), having worked as an assistant to the naval liaison officer for the LORAN program at the Massachusetts Institute of Technology and therefore familiar with the system, was selected to be in charge of the first SPAR monitor station at Chatham, Massachusetts. She and one enlisted SPAR were assigned to a two-month course at the Massachusetts Institute of Technology. They studied LORAN operation and the maintenance of receiving equipment, the only women in the LORAN section of the Naval Training School at MIT.

Later, ten enlisted SPARs were sent to a one-week course in operations only. The selection of these SPARs was unique. LORAN was so highly classified that not even the training officer had any concept of what the duties of these SPARs would be, or what their qualifications should be. All the SPARs selected were volunteers who had accepted the assignment with a spirit of adventure. It would be the first time SPARs were sent out of the district office.

The LORAN monitor station was located right at the water's edge at the showplace of town, about a mile from Main Street, at the already existing Chatham Lifeboat Station. In front of the station was a vast expanse of white sand, and beyond that the Atlantic. The LORAN station consisted of one small building about 50 feet long and 30 feet wide. This provided sleeping quarters, a recreation room, office space, operations room, repair shop, and storage space. Lieutenant (jg) Hammerschlag arrived in advance purposely, to get the hang of operations and additional technical information. However, she spent the whole week trying to make the small space accommodate twelve SPARs and their gear.

After a week of planning night and day for their arrival, preparing barracks regulations and watch standing schedules, contacting the chaplain and the United Service Organization, arranging for laundry and ordering supplies, Hammerschlag went down in the lighthouse truck to meet the first contingent of SPARs. They arrived from Boston on the morning train.

When Hammerschlag had reported to Chatham, Unit 21 was manned 100 percent by men. The plan was for them to leave for overseas assignments as quickly as the SPARs were capable of taking over. Within one month the station was 100 percent SPARs, with the exception of one male radio technician. He left six months later, when the SPARs felt qualified to accept the responsibility of technical maintenance.

Lieutenant (jg) Hammerschlag was the commanding officer, but she was also the operations and engineering officer, medical officer, barracks officer, personnel officer, training officer—even captain of the head! She had to learn the intricacies of plumbing, a coal furnace, and a Kohler engine that supplied emergency power when the main line went out. Because nor'easters were frequent on Cape Cod, that happened more than once. When Hammerschlag looked at the 125-foot antenna mast, she wondered which SPAR would climb it if something went wrong.

The esprit de corps of Unit 21 was outstanding. The SPARs knew they were participating in a system that was playing a vital part in winning the war. They felt as close to the front lines as it was possible for SPARs to be. The unit became like a family. When one of the members got married, Hammerschlag gave the bride away, the chaplain performed the ceremony in the local church, and all the townspeople turned out for it.

Looking back on her service as the commanding officer, Vera Hammer-schlag said, "Inasmuch as LORAN is considered one of the outstanding scientific developments of this war, it is a satisfaction to know that SPARs were given the opportunity to participate in its operation."

During the war, the monitoring station at Chatham may have been the only all-female-manned one of its kind in the world. A headquarters letter of commendation stated: "The operation of Unit 21 under the SPARs has been carried out in a most efficient manner, and the efforts of the SPAR personnel have contributed greatly to the overall efficiency of the LORAN system during World War II."

Ira A. Bitner

Since 1971 Reservists have been used to augment active duty Coast Guard units as well as retaining their primary mission of mobilization. Since that time, Coast Guard Reservists have performed much of their training on the job at active duty commands, and have become a very visible part of what is today known as Team Coast Guard.

One of these Reservists was SN Ira A. Bitner, who was augmenting at Coast Guard Station Execution Rocks in Long Island Sound, New York, on 27 May 1974. He watched as a small fishing boat with three persons on board capsized on a shoal off the southwest end of Execution Rocks. Seaman Bitner immediately alerted another watch stander of the catastrophe and launched the station small boat.

He skillfully proceeded to the scene through 25-knot winds and heavy 6-foot seas. Arriving on scene, he observed one of the three victims being washed away from the capsized vessel. Quickly throwing life preservers to the two men clinging to the overturned fishing boat, Bitner maneuvered the station boat toward the third distressed man, who disappeared beneath the water before he could reach him. When his search of the immediate area proved futile, Reservist Bitner, aware of the elements' debilitating effects on the other two victims, hastily returned to the capsized boat and single-handedly pulled the semiconscious men from the frigid water. He transported them to shore and returned to the search area to continue his efforts. Shortly thereafter, other Coast Guard and civilian units arrived on scene to join in the search for the missing victim. After an extended search, Seaman Bitner was forced to return to the station due to his dwindling fuel supply, inoperative radio, and a hull cracked by the force of the seas.

Coast Guard Reservist Ira Bitner demonstrated remarkable initiative, exceptional fortitude, and daring in spite of imminent personal danger in this rescue mission. On 9 December 1974 he was awarded the Coast Guard Medal for his heroism.

Sandra Mitten

A forty-nine-year-old grandmother from New Berlin, Wisconsin, PS1 Sandra Mitten was one of only five women in Port Security Unit (PSU) 303, based in Milwaukee. PSUs had been created in 1987 but had never been recalled to active duty until 1990, when Mitten's unit was sent to Camp Perry, Ohio, for last minute staging and additional training. She, like most other members of her unit, thought she would return to her home and be called for duty later. But Mitten was surprised when her unit was immediately activated and given twelve hours to go home before departure for Saudi Arabia. It was the first time in fifty years that Coast Guard Reservists had been activated. Coast Guard units in the Persian Gulf would be responsible for patrolling ports and the waters around naval ships.

Mitten was one of about 300 port securitymen deployed to Saudi Arabia in fall 1990. Her Reserve unit was responsible for waterside security at the port of Dammam, Saudia Arabia, on the Persian Gulf, one of the main ports supplying the multinational forces taking part in Operation Desert Storm and not far from the Saudi airbase at Dhahran. The unit would use a Coast Guard 22-foot patrol boat, powered by two 155-horsepower outboard motors and armed with a .50-caliber machine gun.

Mitten's assignment was as a bow gunner. She had never fired a machine gun until being called up for this mobilization. An employee at a small-engine assembly company back home in Wisconsin, she joked that her job didn't allow her much time to fire the .50-caliber. But not only did she learn quickly, she discovered that shooting was a great stress reliever. Soon Sandra Mitten became one of the best gunners in the unit—so good that she was sometimes referred to as a modern-day Annie Oakley.

Their area in Dammam came under Iraqi Scud missile attacks several times. These could come at any time, and had potential of being chemical or biological weapons. On one occasion, a big piece of a Scud blown up by a Patriot missile fell on the building where PSU 303 ate their meals.

Mitten also resigned herself to the role of grandmother of her unit, with a roommate who was younger than her daughter back home. "When this first started, people started calling me 'grandma,' and I wasn't sure I liked it," she said. "But as time went on, that's all they ever called me. Even the Army guys living at the compound call me that—even people I don't know."

Mitten and the other members of PSU 303 were replaced by another PSU and returned to the United Sates in March 1991. The last of the Coast Guard PSUs would return by summer 1991.

Eric Bowers and Michael Walker

Eric Bowers and Michael Walker had known each other since first grade. They went through Coast Guard boot camp together, and were hired by the District of Columbia's fire department at the same time. Both belonged to the Coast Guard Reserve's Port Security Unit 305, where Eric Bowers was a damage controlman 3rd class and Michael Walker a boatswain's mate 3rd class. Just after the 11 September 2001 attack on the Pentagon, all D.C. fire-fighters were recalled.

Bowers found himself as part of the first D.C. fire company on the roof of the Pentagon, cutting into it to try to vent the fire out of the biggest office building in the world. "It was a tough roof to breach," he said. "Layers of slate, wood, and then concrete. We were up there a long time. I could [see] American Airlines flight magazines fluttering around, from the 757 that hit the building."

Walker was among those who entered the blazing interior of the Pentagon. "A lot more of the building was burned on the inside than appeared from the outside. It looked as if fire blasted down the hallways. Because of the layout of the building, even though I'm on a truck company, for all those hours we were doing engine company work, pulling hoses, dragging hoses." After their taxing day at the Pentagon, during which they never saw each other, early on 12 September they received telephone calls from Coast Guard Reserve PSU 305. They were being mobilized and ordered to New York Harbor.

The Coast Guard Reserve was the first reserve component recalled in response to the events of 9/11. Within twenty-four hours of the attacks, the service, bolstered by Reserve personnel, had greatly enhanced the physical security of the nation's ports and waterways. By week's end, Reservists were well engaged in the service's largest mobilization since World War II, up to that time. The Coast Guard activated over a third of its Reserve force by recalling 2,623 Reservists within one month. At the height of the post-9/11 mobilization, 2,751 Coast Guard Reservists were called to active duty.

Petty Officers Bowers and Walker were part of a unit consisting of 135 Coast Guard Reservists and five active duty personnel based at Fort Eustis, Virginia. After reporting to Fort Eustis, PSU 305's Boston Whalers, fitted with twin 175-horsepower outboards, were loaded on flatbed trucks and sent to New York. At noon Thursday, PSU 305 moved out of Fort Eustis. Once in New York, they operated their boats out of the Military Ocean Terminal in Bayonne, New Jersey. From there the unit's boats escorted the U.S. Navy hospital ship *Comfort* (T-AH-20) into New York Harbor; eventually they stood guard over the ship as it moored along the Hudson River, north of the area of the World Trade Center.

Through mid- to late October, dropping temperatures made life on the open fiberglass gunboats difficult for eight hour patrols. After forty-five days in New York Harbor, Petty Officer Bowers and Walker were released from active duty with the rest of PSU 305, to enjoy two months at home before being recalled again to active duty, this time bound for the Middle East.

But instead, by early January they found themselves at Guantánamo Bay, Cuba. There they were asked to provide waterside security for Camp X-Ray, where al Qaeda and Taliban personnel captured in Afghanistan were being confined. The members of PSU 305 did not return to their Virginia home base until mid-June 2002. Even after that, Petty Officers Bowers and Walker, like all Coast Guard Reservists, knew they had to be Semper Paratus in case they were mobilized again.

Firefighters and Coast Guard Reservists Bowers and Walker served in three of the major sites in the 2000s global war on terrorism. They responded to terrorist attacks in both New York and Washington, then served in Cuba to contain those captured and believed to be terrorists. In the 276 days between 9/11 and 15 June 2002, PSU 305 saw 226 days of active duty.

Scott McKinley

The Coast Guard was already busy responding to the disaster in the wake of Hurricane Katrina when the call came late in the afternoon on 1 September 2005. Coast Guard Reserve Cdr. Scott McKinley took the call. He was commanding officer of Port Security Unit 309, based out of Port Clinton, Ohio. PSU 309's 110 members included 30 police officers and 10 firefighters, plus a variety of other civilian occupations, from cook to lawyer.

They were being assigned to work for Sector Mobile, Alabama, and take up the job of relieving Station Gulfport personnel so they could attend to their families and begin the work of rebuilding their station after Katrina. Gulfport, Mississippi, had been directly in the path of the hurricane. Commander McKinley oversaw the loading of five semitrailers with almost 100 short tons of unit gear, boats and weapons. The unit also brought many cases of bottled water and other supplies.

Three charter buses transported PSU 309 to Mississippi, along with the semitrailers full of supplies. The convoy to Gulfport took almost twenty hours. Upon their arrival they learned that Station Gulfport had been totally destroyed, with only the roof and steel frames remaining. PSU 309 immediately set up a self-contained tent city for berthing at the nearby U.S. Navy Seabees' training base.

Power lines were down everywhere, and there was no electricity. The 95° daytime temperatures made for challenging working conditions. PSU 309 personnel patrolled the storm-damaged Gulfport pier, while rebuilding efforts began on the new station. Other Reserve units, such as PSU 308, home-ported in Gulfport, also assisted.

Commander McKinley's PSU members patrolled the waters of the Pearl River, Bay St. Louis, and the Back Bay of Biloxi looking for those in need of assistance. More than 50,000 pounds of supplies were handed out, including meals, ready to eat (MREs) and water to some 200 stranded Vietnamese fishermen in the Back Bay area. Though PSU 309 logged more than 400 patrols and 1,000 hours of underway time in four weeks in Gulfport, many of the crew felt their most important contributions were assisting those affected by the hurricane. They ripped out water-damaged drywall and insulation and hauled it away. They assisted in locating personal effects strewn by the hurricane. They would not soon forget handing out food to the fishermen or helping to clean out another Coast Guardsman's damaged house.

In later years PSU 309 deployed to the Middle East in support of Operation Iraqi Freedom, to ensure that ports in Kuwait were secure and protect high-value U.S. assets bringing supplies to troops in Iraq.

Jack J. Brown

Coast Guard Reservist CWO4 Jack J. Brown served in the Army Reserve from 1971 to 1977 before joining the Coast Guard Reserve on 5 February 1982. In 2003 the war in Iraq caused the Coast Guard to mobilize its Reserve to a higher level than it had in 2001, and a new highest level since World War II. By April 2003, 4,412 Reservists had been mobilized to active duty. This represented 56 percent of the total Reserve force of 7,836. The Coast Guard had the highest percentage of mobilized Reservists of any of the military services.

Brown deployed to Iraq, where he served as special assistant to the Department of Homeland Security attaché in support of Operation Iraqi Freedom from 27 March to 14 September 2007. During this six-month tour, he faced sixty rocket and mortar attacks involving more than 200 explosive devices. In one rocket attack, Brown selflessly left a protected position to retrieve an exposed coworker. Despite receiving two shrapnel wounds during this courageous action under enemy fire, he quickly returned to duty.

During another rocket attack a month later, Chief Warrant Officer Brown instinctively, and without regard for his personal safety, shielded the Iraqi director of customs police with his body until they could reach a fortified bunker. CWO Brown also led the response to a burning quad-size trailer, heroically entering the structure to evacuate the occupants through a rear exit. After ensuring their safety, he secured the electrical power and aided another colleague in extinguishing the fire.

Brown was the go-to person. He was routinely called at the last minute to jump on board aircraft to attend the Iraqi-Coalition meetings that planned the transfer of missions to the Iraqis in Basrah, Umm Qasr, and the oil platforms. CWO Brown's work helped to improve overall security conditions in Iraq. At the end of his most recent mobilization, since 9/11 he had served more than fifteen months in a combat zone and in excess of forty-three months of active duty time.

CWO Brown was awarded the Bronze Star at a special ceremony at Coast Guard Headquarters on 4 February 2008. Adm. Thad Allen, U.S. Coast Guard commandant, presented Brown with the award before a standing-room-only crowd of family, friends, and shipmates. His Bronze Star marks only the second time the service has issued it since the start of current efforts against terrorism. In September 2007, CWO Brown was presented the 2007 Coast Guard Combat Veteran's Association Person of the Year Award in a ceremony in the commandant's suite at USCG Headquarters.

10. COAST GUARD CIVILIAN EMPLOYEES

Frequently overlooked when talking about Team Coast Guard is the large number of civilian employees who, on a regular basis, make invaluable contributions to meeting the service's missions. There are some 8,000 civilian members of the Coast Guard (2,000 of whom are paid with non-appropriated funds) in 100 locations, representing more than 280 occupations. They are an essential part of the team. Civilians often work behind the scenes, away from the spotlight. But their presence is felt on cutters, small boats, and aircraft. Without them the cutters would not sail, the aircraft would not fly, and the stations would fall into disrepair.

Civilians have also played an extraordinarily important and fascinating part of Coast Guard history. Lifesaving missions, inspection functions, and aids-to-navigation duties all were carried out at one time by civilians. Many of the legendary figures discussed in this book were not military but civilian. Today some civilians serve in a boardroom setting, developing strategic plans or representing the Coast Guard at top-level conferences. Members of the senior executive service not only influence and shape the Coast Guard's future, they also play a leading role in managing current policies and programs. Brad J. Kieserman, chief of the operations law group in the Office of Maritime and International Law at Coast Guard Headquarters, Washington, D.C., serves as a good example of one these.

Others train and educate future service leaders. Dr. Irving King served for many years as a professor at the Coast Guard Academy in New London. Still others, such as Diana Garcia in southern California, accomplish a wide variety of tasks to help Coast Guard personnel and missions. Aside from the stories presented earlier in this book, a few more help to illustrate the numerous ways in which they are valued members of Team Coast Guard.

Brad J. Kieserman

Pennsylvania native Brad Kieserman grew up just outside Philadelphia, in a town called Warminster. In 1986 he enlisted in the Coast Guard and spent seven years as a quartermaster before attending Officer Candidate School.

He became a commissioned officer and eventually a Coast Guard lawyer. Retiring from the service in 2006, Kieserman immediately became a civilian employee at Coast Guard Headquarters. Since that time he has served as the primary national Coast Guard legal adviser for matters of maritime law enforcement, defense operations, search and rescue, and other service missions. Kieserman has also played a key role as negotiator or counsel to U.S. delegations engaged in bilateral or unilateral law enforcement agreement negotiations, including those related to drug interdiction, migrant smuggling, maritime terrorism, coastal security, and fisheries.

For many years the Coast Guard interdicted illegal migrants at sea in the Mona Passage between the Dominican Republic and Puerto Rico, and in the Florida Straits southeast of Miami. With no way to identify anyone who might have been a a re-entering felon or wanted criminal, the Coast Guard had no choice but to simply take undocumented migrants back to the Dominican Republic. The lack of an identification system and consequences also gave potential criminals no reason not to try to cross the Mona Passage again, often multiple times.

Kieserman analyzed this situation, then led and managed the development and execution of an interagency, mobile, biometrics-at-sea program. Fingerprints of possibly illegal migrants are now taken at sea on board Coast Guard cutters. They are sent wirelessly to be checked against the Department of Homeland Security identification database, which also creates permanent records for the next time the same individuals are stopped. This new program has ended years of a catch and release operation.

Under an agreement with the Dominican Republic—the launch point for almost all interdicted vessels—boat captains, crew, and passengers can be returned there regardless of nationality. But with fingerprint identification, those with criminal records, outstanding warrants, or a history of attempted illegal entry may be held for prosecution by the U.S. attorney general's office. The wireless biometrics program has had a significant impact on the number of illegal migrants.

To support the operations of the Fourteenth Coast Guard District in the Western Pacific, Kieserman had secured maritime law enforcement agreements with the Republic of the Marshall Islands, the Cook Islands, Palau, and the Federated States of Micronesia by the end of 2007. These resulted in integrated operations over several million miles of previously unpatrolled fishing grounds. Within the first month of reaching this agreement, Micronesian officers working from the U.S. Coast Guard 255-foot buoy tender *Sequoia* (WLB-215) made seizures of three fishing vessels engaged in large-scale poaching. Other joint patrols and enforcement actions have followed, leading regional leaders and senior U.S. officials to praise the initiative.

In recent years, transnational drug trafficking organizations have dramatically increased their use of stateless self-propelled semisubmersible (SPSS) vessels on international voyages. These hard-to-detect craft now account for the movement of one-third of all cocaine bound for the United States from South America. Previously, when the semi-submersibles were detected the crews quickly abandoned and sank their vessels. They sank so quickly that Coast Guard personnel on scene had no opportunity to recover contraband. They were left with no prosecution options and could only repatriate the "survivors." Kieserman built a compelling case for criminalizing SPSS operation. He drafted a bill and successfully orchestrated an intensive campaign to educate Congress and the public about the threat. SPSS operation is now illegal and crews can be prosecuted, providing an effective legal counter to this change in smuggling tactics.

Irving King

Having grown up in Milo, Maine, Irving H. King entered the University of Maine in 1953. He enlisted in the Army in 1954 and served at Fort Hood, Texas, before returning to the University of Maine in 1956 and earning a bachelor of arts in history in 1959. He went on to earn a master of arts (1962) and Ph.D. (1968), both also from the University of Maine. King began his teaching career in 1962 as a graduate assistant in history. He was appointed assistant professor of history at King's College in Wilkes-Barre, Pennsylvania, in 1963, and taught history there for three years while working on his doctorate from Maine.

In 1966 King accepted a position as assistant professor of history at the Coast Guard Academy. He was promoted to associate professor in 1968 and to full professor in 1976. As a member of the faculty, Irving King served as section head of history and government from 1979 to 1984, and as head of the Department of Humanities from 1985 to 1990. He was also a member of the Williams College–Mystic Seaport Maritime Studies Program in 1991.

As a professional educator, King was the recipient of numerous awards and honors. Among them, in 1975 he was selected for inclusion in *Outstanding Educators of America*; in 1979 he was elected Best History Teacher in Connecticut by the Daughters of Colonial Wars; in 1982 he was included in the ninth edition of *Men of Achievement*, Cambridge, England; in the 1990s he was included in *Who's Who in the East*. In 1991 Irving King was elected to the Connecticut Academy of Arts and Sciences, and in 1993 he was selected for inclusion in *Who's Who in American Education*. During the Coast Guard Academy's 1994 homecoming weekend, King was honored with the Distinguished Faculty Award.

Dr. Irving King

But Professor King's numerous honors over the years cannot begin to describe the scholarship and academic leadership he provided to the academy during his more than thirty years of teaching there. He educated, mentored, and served as an example for thousands of cadets and officers, instilling a desire for lifelong learning and a deep appreciation for both Coast Guard and American heritage. Some of his students became admirals; some continue to publish scholarly articles inspired by his tutelage. At least one, the author of this book, went on to become a maritime historian and history professor.

Professor King's influence shows in a story he told me. "A young officer almost apologetically entered my office one day," he said. "'You probably won't remember me,' the student said, 'I wasn't a very good student. I loved history but was struggling to survive in physics and chemistry. The reason I came to see you is that it's important for you to know that you had a very big impact on my life even though I wasn't necessarily a good student for you.'" Behind his glasses, King's eyes softened. A contented smile brightened his face. "That is when you feel that you're important," he said.

Professor King became a distinguished author and maritime scholar. His painstaking research was groundbreaking in identifying and locating primary historical Coast Guard documents. He authored three books documenting the early service's history: *George Washington's Coast Guard* (1978), *The Coast Guard Under Sail* (1989), and *The Coast Guard Expands, 1965–1915* (1996). His final book received an honorable mention for the John Lyman Book Prize in American History.

Besides educating thousands of officers about the service's history, King has also taught the general public about Coast Guard heritage and preserved it for generations to come. His tenure at the academy was rich, rewarding, and distinguished. He retired in summer 1999 and now resides in Florida.

Professor Irving King serves as an excellent representative for all civilians serving at the academy and at other Coast Guard training centers. They play a key role in developing and inspiring future service leaders.

Diana Garcia

Born in New York City, Diana Garcia grew up in the Bronx. As the wife of career Marine Corps staff NCO GySgt. Sixto Garcia, she traveled far from New York. Before working for the Coast Guard, Garcia worked in Navy housing offices in Roosevelt Roads, Puerto Rico; Dam Neck, Virginia; and Naval Station San Diego, California. She also worked in the private sector as an apartment rental agent and provided legal aid for Section 8 housing.

After her husband retired from the Marine Corps, he accepted a position with Hughes Aircraft, and they moved to the Long Beach, California, area. Diana Garcia began working for the Long Beach Naval Station housing office, soon being promoted to the position of assistant to the director. This was valuable administrative experience, and when she discovered a better-paying position as the housing inspector for the Coast Guard in the Long Beach area, Garcia became a civilian employee of that service in August 1989. In 1997 she became the housing manager and leased housing contract officer for all of southern California and Search Light, Nevada. Finding adequate, affordable housing within a reasonable commute to duty stations today is both her challenge and her joy. Because of Garcia's knowledge and experience in the housing field, she has been of great assistance to countless active duty Coast Guardsmen.

Relocating to the southern California area can be intimidating because of high housing costs. Additionally, the closer lodgings are to the coast—where Coast Guard people work—the higher the price, so often service members live a considerable distance from their duty stations. But before buying or leasing a home or an apartment, Coast Guard members new to the region are required to report to Garcia's office.

In the Los Angeles area, Garcia's office has access to very limited government-owned accommodations. However, she has cultivated a great relationship with the local Air Force and Navy housing complexes, and has been able to get Coast Guard families into these Department of Defense units. Garcia has also put together a strong referral system that maximizes all available rental resources. In her earlier days she had to read the local ads and call on a daily basis to see if rentals were still available. Today, the Internet has made that part of her job much easier. Now she refers personnel to Web sites that advertise rental properties.

Besides the Internet, Garcia has witnessed another major change: in 2000, allowances for housing based on market rental rates for each area were implemented. This has made it much easier for Coast Guard personnel to find appropriate lodgings in expensive areas.

Garcia also handles the leased apartments for Coast Guard personnel on small cutters in the Los Angeles area, and she coordinates assignment to the barracks at Naval Station San Diego for personnel assigned to commands in that area.

Asked what has given her the greatest professional satisfaction, Garcia identifies finding affordable housing for junior personnel. She remembers a young Coast Guardsman who was married with an infant and had just reported to the Los Angeles area with no place to live and no money to rent a motel room. Garcia arranged temporary housing for this young family and expedited their assignment to government-owned housing at nearby Fort MacArthur.

She beams as she tells of helping people to have a place to go to that is not afloat. Garcia also realizes that if service members' families are happy, they can focus more on their assigned duties and be much more productive in their units. Periodically personnel stop by her office to express their gratitude for her efforts. Retired Coast Guard YNMC Wayne Canfield, Pacific area housing program manager, described Garcia as "a cornerstone of support for all our members in southern California."

Civilian members are a vital component of the total force. They are part of a long line of professionals who for more than two hundred years, as naval historian Samuel Eliot Morison puts it, have been called upon "to do a little of everything—the Coast Guard is used to that." The support they provide is essential and is a foundation block under the entire service structure.

These civilians are not just employees; they are members of the Coast Guard. Whether they are shipyard workers, industrial workers, security officers, administrative assistants, accountants, investigators, historians, or any of a host of other positions, all contribute greatly. Without them the Coast Guard could not function. They should not be overlooked, but appreciated and remembered.

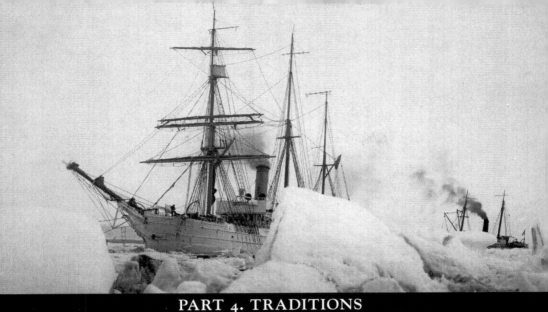

PART 4. TRADITIONS

This nation's oldest continuous seagoing service is rich in traditions. It shares many of these with its sister services, but the Coast Guard has also evolved its own unique customs and practices. The chapters that follow present Coast Stories stories that have made the service stronger and give Coast Guardsmen an extra measure of confidence. This helps them to live up to the traditions of their service for their country and for humanity.

11. SEMPER PARATUS

Semper Paratus, the Latin motto of the U.S. Coast Guard, means "Always Ready." It is part of the everyday vocabulary of service members, whether active, Reserve, Auxiliary, or civilian. The motto serves as a reminder of the Coast Guard's proud tradition of constant preparedness for protecting, defending, and rescuing the public.

Its origin is uncertain, but by the end of the nineteenth century, it appears to have been widely accepted as the motto of the Revenue Cutter Service. The Latin words are found in reverse order in the New Testament. The Apostle Peter, in his first general epistle, writes: "Paratus Semper ad satisfactionem omni poscenti vos rationem" (1 Peter 3:15, "be always ready to give an answer to every man that asks you a reason").

Some believe the Coast Guard use of the term began with an 1836 article in the New Orleans *Bee*, publicly congratulating Capt. Ezekiel Johns on his departure from the revenue cutter *Ingham*. During the previous June, Johns had unofficially involved the *Ingham* in the first overt naval conflict with the Mexican Navy and its warship *Montezuma*. The brief, one-day action made the *Ingham* the only U.S. naval vessel to fire a shot in support of the Anglo-Texans in their rebellion against the Mexican government. Whether the Americans' smuggling of arms and men into Texas was lawful is debatable and complicated, but it gained accolades from the citizens of New Orleans. The *Bee* declared the *Ingham* "a vessel entitled to bear the best motto for a military public servant—*Semper Paratus*." The *Army and Navy Chronicle*, a favored military publication for all officers, reprinted the article. This is where other Revenue Cutter Service officers undoubtedly read and likely agreed that it was the perfect motto and could perhaps be applied to their service as well.

Others believe the saying came out of the Revenue Cutter Service's feats during the Civil War. Indeed, *Army and Navy Journal* (a later publication that began in 1863) editor W. C. Church, writing of the service's value and potential in the 24 November 1864 issue, unknowingly predicted both its name and its motto: "Keeping *always* under steam and *ever ready*, in the event of extraordinary need, to render valuable service, the cutters can be made to

form a *coast guard* whose value it is impossible at the present time to estimate"
(emphasis mine).

"Semper Paratus" appears to have been adopted sometime between
October 1896 and May 1897: a new seal including the phrase appeared on
a general order of the Division of Revenue Cutter Service on 21 May 1897.
By 1900, the motto had become a Revenue Cutter Service watchword. It
was given further official recognition when it appeared in 1910 on the service's ensign. Not just a catchy phrase spoken by Coast Guard members, it is
an integral part of the service's guardian ethos culture. Being always ready to
respond with ability, confidence, and competency requires constant training.
The phrase's precise origin may remain unknown, but there is no doubt as to
who put it to words and music.

Capt. Francis Saltus Van Boskerck received his commission in the
Revenue Cutter Service on 20 May 1891. His long career included twenty-
three years of sea duty. Between 1914 and 1915 he oversaw construction of
the cutters *Tallapoosa* (WPG-52) and *Ossipee* (WPG-50) at Newport News,
Virginia. In 1917 he was captain of the port in Philadelphia and an aide for
the Fourth Naval District at the American routing office there. He was the
first Coast Guard officer to report a German submarine on the Atlantic coast.
After the war, Van Boskerck transferred to the Puget Sound Navy Yard to
supervise repairs on the famous cutter *Bear*. He commanded the *Bear* on the
1920 summer cruise to the Bering Sea and Arctic Ocean.

In 1922, as commander of *Yamacraw*, Van Boskerck was stationed at
Savannah, Georgia, and chased rumrunners off the coast of the Carolinas and
Florida. He wrote the words to the song "Semper Paratus" in Savannah, while
serving as commanding officer. Later he elaborated:

> One day, during the winter of 1922 the inspiration came to me to write
> a song of the Coast Guard. It was one those so-called "flashes" that come
> to people, at times, apparently from nowhere but probably related to
> the subconscious and originate from the great Fund of Mind, whence
> authors, inventors, etc. receive inspiration. And so I went below to my
> cabin on the *Yamacraw* and wrote the words to the song which I named
> "Semper Paratus." I immediately took the text to the ward room where
> I told the officers assembled that, while I had never attempted stray-
> ing into the paths of music I had made a stab at writing the words of a
> song which had as its motive the keeping alive and building of our fine
> traditions, morale of the service and general pride in the Coast Guard.
> I was prepared for criticism and invited it. But I was rather surprised
> at the warmth and enthusiasm with which the words were greeted and
> the advice of the officers to set the words to music.

Capt. Francis Saltus Van Boskerck, author and composer of
"Semper Paratus"

Van Boskerck drew the words from the actual traditions of the Coast Guard.
He wanted his song to be a true anthem of lore and history, to indoctrinate
those who sang it with service comradeship, as emphasized in the last line of
the chorus, "Aye, Coast Guard, we're all for you!" The first and second stanzas
serve as a good summary of the service's heritage.

Stanza 1
    From Aztec Shore to Arctic Zone,
    To Europe and Far East,
    The Flag is carried by our ships
    In times of war and peace;
    And never have we struck it yet,
    In spite of foemen's fight,
    Who cheered our crews and cheered again
    For showing how to fight.

Chorus

> So here's the Coast Guard marching song,
> We sing on land or sea.
> Through surf and storm and howling gale,
> High shall our purpose be,
> *Semper Paratus* is our guide,
> Our fame, our glory, too.
> To fight, to save, or fight and die,
> Aye! Coast Guard, we are for you.

Stanza 2

> *Surveyor* and *Narcissus*,
> The *Eagle* and *Dispatch*,
> The *Hudson* and the *Tampa*
> These names are hard to match;
> From Barrow's shores to Paraguay,
> Great Lakes or ocean's wave,
> The Coast Guard fights through storms and winds
> To punish or to save.

Stanza 3

> Aye! we've been "Always Ready"
> To do, to fight, or die!
> Write glory to the shield we wear
> In letters to the sky.
> To sink the foe or save the maimed
> Our mission and our pride.
> We'll carry on 'til Kingdom Come
> Ideals for which we've died.

Stanza 1: From Aztec Shore to Arctic Zone

In June 1846 nine cutters, constituting the first official squadron of revenue cutters, commenced operations against Mexico in the Gulf of Mexico ("Aztec Shore"). This small squadron performed scouting, convoy, towing, and blockade duties, as well as transporting troops and supplies and carrying mail and dispatches. They sailed mostly between New Orleans and Gen. Zachary Taylor's Army depot at Brazos Santiago, Texas. Just before Taylor's great offensive victory in the battles of Monterey and Buena Vista, the cutters *Legare* and *Ewing* carried a thousand rifles to Taylor at Port Isabel. During the first expedition to Tabasco, the cutter *Forward* provided single-handed artillery support and combined with the cutter *McClane* to blockade the port.

Ever since Alaska became a U.S. territory in 1867, Revenue Cutter Service and later Coast Guard vessels have patrolled the Arctic waters. The service's most famous expedition there was the overland relief provided during the winter of 1897–98 and described earlier in this book. Later, in 1957 the Coast Guard icebreaking cutter *Storis* and buoy tenders *Bramble* and *Spar* became the first American ships to make the passage from the Pacific to the Atlantic Ocean, north of the American continent. And today, Coast Guard polar icebreakers continue to serve in the Arctic Zone.

To Europe and Far East
During World War I, six Coast Guard cutters patrolled European waters between Gibraltar and Great Britain. One, the *Tampa*, presumably struck by a German U-boat's torpedo, was lost with all hands. First Lt. Eng. Charles E. Sugden, U.S. Coast Guard, commanded Naval Air Station Ile Tudy, France. For his distinguished service, the French government awarded Sugden the Legion of Honor (rank of Chevalier). Coast Guardsmen would return to European waters in World War II and the years following.

The newly commissioned *McCulloch*, on a round-the-world shakedown cruise, joined Commo. Thomas E. Dewey's squadron at Hong Kong and participated in the defeat of the Spanish fleet at the battle of Manila Bay on 1 May 1898. In 1922 the *Mojave* (WPG-46) made a cruise to the Far East, hosting the secretary of the treasury. The cutter made port calls in Hakodate and Yokohama, Japan, and in Shanghai, China.

And never have we struck it yet,
In spite of foemen's might,
Who cheered our crews and cheered again
For showing how to fight.

These words, from Van Boskerck's first stanza, refer to an incident involving the captain of the revenue cutter *Surveyor*. Capt. William L. Travis fought valiantly to defend his vessel from attack during the War of 1812, a story to which Van Boskerck alludes in his second stanza.

Stanza 2: *Surveyor* and *Narcissus*

One of the most hotly contested engagements of the War of 1812 was between the cutter *Surveyor* and the British frigate *Narcissus*. The *Surveyor* lay at anchor at the mouth of the York River in June 1813. The cutter took extra precautions by opening her gun ports and running out her six 12-pound carronades. She was prepared for action. But the *Surveyor* would be up against a much bigger ship, the *Narcissus*. The British sent a boarding part of fifty men to capture the *Surveyor*. In the fighting, the Americans killed three British sailors and wounded another seven, while suffering five casualties themselves.

Captain Travis, realizing he was surrounded and outnumbered three to one and further opposition would lead to fruitless bloodshed, surrendered the *Surveyor*. The following day, the British captain returned the Revenue Cutter Service officer's sword with a note stating: "Your gallant and desperate attempt to defend your vessel against more than double your number excited such admiration on the part of your opponents as I have seldom witnessed." The British captain, Lt. John Crerie, later added "the determined manner in which the deck was disputed inch by inch."

The *Eagle* and *Dispatch*

The defense of the cutter *Eagle* against the attack of the British brig *Dispatch* was another dramatic incident in the War of 1812. The *Eagle*, out of New Haven, Connecticut, was sailing in Long Island Sound when the *Dispatch* discovered and chased her. The *Eagle* tried to escape in shallow water. When the *Dispatch* brought her guns to bear, Capt. Frederick Lee beached his vessel off Friar's Head, a 160-foot-high bluff 15 miles northeast of Port Jefferson, New York.

After stripping the *Eagle* of her sails and rigging, the crew carried her two 2-pounders and towed two of her four 4-pounders ashore and up the steep hill. Thus positioned, they prevented the British from landing in boats and taking the *Eagle*. Throughout the day and night and into the next morning, the cutter's crew fought bravely. When they ran out of ammunition, they retrieved spent British rounds and turned them. Finally the *Dispatch* sailed away over the horizon, whereupon the Americans refloated the *Eagle*. But unexpectedly, the *Dispatch* reappeared on the scene and forced Captain Lee to surrender.

The *Hudson* and *Tampa*

The revenue cutter *Hudson*, a harbor tug stationed in New York Harbor when war was declared on Spain in 1898, served with Adm. William T. Sampson's fleet and helped blockade Cuban harbors. On 31 May the *Hudson*, along with the Navy gunboat *Wilmington* (PG-8) and torpedo boat *Winslow* (TB-5), were sent on a reconnaissance mission near Cardenas, Cuba. The *Winslow*, far inshore of the other two vessels, came under heavy enemy fire. The *Wilmington* and *Hudson* arrived shortly thereafter.

Five minutes after firing the first shots, the cutter *Hudson* steamed into action firing on the enemy's battery with its two 6-pounder guns. The *Winslow* began moving erratically and nearly collided with the *Hudson*, which offered assistance to the apparently disabled torpedo boat. But the Navy vessel declined the offer.

Fifteen minutes later the *Winslow's* officers, realizing their ship could not be controlled, requested help from the *Hudson*. The cutter maneuvered through unknown waters while keeping up an intense fire on the shore battery. After thirty minutes the *Hudson* successfully took the *Winslow* under tow. Both vessels were under fire all the while, but the *Winslow* was pulled to safety. For their distinguished service, all of the *Hudson's* officers and crew received medals from Congress. Lt. Frank H. Newcomb, the commanding officer, received a gold medal; each of his officers received silver medals; and a bronze medal was presented to each of the members of his crew.

The *Tampa* was one of six cutters based in Gibraltar during World War I. It was part of a very effective antisubmarine unit that guarded convoys between Great Britain and the Mediterranean. The Navy had praised the *Tampa* for a year's constant convoy-escort duty, in which she steamed an average of nearly 3,600 miles a month. Of the 350 ships escorted, only 2 were lost through enemy action. On 26 September 1918, the *Tampa* left her eighteenth convoy safely in Bristol Channel and turned to follow orders to report to Milford Haven, 60 miles away. But she was attacked by *UB-91*, taking one torpedo. All hands were lost, including 111 Coast Guardsmen (7 officers, 4 warrant officers, and 100 enlisted men), 4 Navy personnel assigned to the *Tampa*, and 16 British passengers. There were no survivors. It was one of worst sea casualties that the United States suffered in this war.

From Barrow's Shore to Paraguay

"Barrow's shore" refers to the 1897–98 Overland Relief Expedition mounted by the Revenue Cutter Service to rescue 275 people on board eight whale ships frozen in the Arctic Ocean near Point Barrow, Alaska that is discussed earlier in this book.

In February 1855 the dictator of Paraguay, Carlos Antonio Lopez, fired at the U.S. Navy survey vessel *Water Witch*. After considerable delay, Congress and President James Buchanan ordered a naval expedition under Capt. William B. Shubrick to blockade Paraguay, destroy the fortifications at Humatia, and seize the capital city, Asuncion. The revenue cutter *Harriet Lane* (later made famous by firing the first naval shot of the Civil War) was transferred to the Navy Department to participate in this expedition and sailed for Paraguay on 7 October 1858. But upon arriving at Corrientes, Paraguay, the ship's officers learned that an agreement had been reached and the conflict was over. The *Harriet Lane* sailed back to New York and was transferred back to the Revenue Cutter Service.

Great Lakes or Ocean's Wave

The chain of freshwater lakes in eastern North America on the Canada-U.S. border—Superior, Michigan, Huron, Erie, and Ontario—forms the largest such group on Earth. The combined surface area of the lakes is approximately 94,250 square miles, and their coastline measures about 10,500 miles. They are sometimes referred to as inland seas or as Canada and the United States' Third Coast—or, the "Eighth Sea."

The Lighthouse Service was the first of the four agencies that would eventually make up the U.S. Coast Guard on the Great Lakes, establishing the Presque Isle Light on Lake Erie in 1819. The need for aids to navigation grew as shipping increased. By 1866 there were seventy-two lights guiding ships to safety. The Lighthouse Service also operated another fleet of ships, known as lighthouse tenders. These provided the means to bring supplies and needed work parties to the scattered and isolated lighthouses. In 1874 the *Dahlia* was the first tender constructed especially for ice on the inland seas.

By the 1820s, Revenue Cutter Service vessels were cruising the Great Lakes enforcing revenue laws and assisting Great Lakes seafarers in distress. And in 1876, eleven Life-Saving Stations were established on Lakes Erie, Ontario, and Huron. The next year additional stations were added, and service was expanded to include Lakes Superior and Michigan. By 1914 there were sixty-two Life-Saving Stations scattered throughout the lakes.

Chorus

The stirring chorus of "Semper Paratus" proclaims, "Through surf and storm and howling gale, / High shall our purpose be," and that "'Semper Paratus' is our guide, / Our fame, our glory, too." The motto guides the service as a whole, as well each of its members. During World War II, a new opening verse and a different chorus were written by Homer Smith, Third Naval District Coast Guard Quartet; Chief Cole; and Lt. Walton Butterfield, U.S. Coast Guard Reserve. They reflect the service's attitude during that war.

> From North and South and East and West,
> The Coast Guard's in the fight.
> Destroying subs and landing troops,
> The Axis feels our might.
> For we're the first invaders,
> On every fighting field.
> Afloat, ashore, on men and SPARs,
> You'll find the Coast Guard shield.

The opening lines of the chorus were also adapted as follows:

> So here's the Coast Guard battle song,
> We fight on land or sea.
> Through howling gale and shot and shell,
> To win our victory.
> "Semper Paratus" is our guide,
> Our pledge, our motto too.
> We're "Always Ready" to do or die!
> Aye! Coast Guard we are for you!

After World War II, the original first stanza replaced the temporary World War II one. The opening two lines of the chorus were once again rewritten and have remained the same since.

> We're always ready for the call,
> We place our trust in thee.
> Through surf and storm . . .

In 1923 Van Boskerck went to the Naval War College at Newport, Rhode Island, and in 1924 became district commander of the Great Lakes District. In 1925 he was selected to be the assistant inspector of the Northwest District.

Soon after his arrival in Seattle, "Captain Van," as he was known to his many friends, became commander of the Bering Sea Patrol during 1925 and 1926. Headquartered at the remote port of Unalaska, he put the words of his song to music with the help of two Public Health Service dentists, doctors Alf E. Nannestad and Joseph O. Fournier. Van Boskerck asked Nannestad to "[pick] out the tune on the piano and [write] the original score." Fournier played violin, nicknamed "The Singing Dentist" because he sang as he worked on teeth.

Mrs. Albert Clara Goss, wife of a local fur trader, let them use her beat-up piano for composing. At that time it was probably the only piano in the whole long chain of Aleutian Islands. Mrs. Goss had a great heart and a fine musical background; she made hers a home away from home for Coast Guard officers. Everyone was welcome, and the regular dinner entrée was baked ham with pineapple. It has been said the song would never have been written without Mrs. Goss' assistance.

Captain Van Boskerck hoped to give "Semper Paratus" as much recognition as the Marines' hymn, "From the Halls of Montezuma," and the Navy's "Anchors Aweigh." He returned to the East Coast in 1927 with his song now composed but still lacking a full score. He was named captain of the Port of

Norfolk. While there, Van Boskerck attended a dance at the Ghent Club given by the Norfolk unit of the League of Coast Guard Women. The nine-piece orchestra played "Semper Paratus." It was wonderfully received with loud ovations and with the audience calling for numerous encores.

In fall 1927, Van Boskerck traveled to Washington, D.C., to confer with Lt. Col. Harvey ("Heinie") Miller, editor and publisher of the magazine *Coast Guard*, about plans for his future after retirement, which was coming in four years. Miller asked if he would like to be the next national commander of the Army and Navy Union and opined that he would make a fine commander, a position never held by a Coast Guard officer. Captain Van thanked him for the honor and promised to consider it seriously.

Then he broached the subject of publishing his song. He carried with him several worn, wrinkled, and smudged sheets of paper upon which were written the words and music of "Semper Paratus." Van Boskerck explained, "In it I have tried to pour forth all the glory, honor, and tradition of the Coast Guard. It is an anthem of Coast Guard lore and history."

Within an hour he had extracted from Miller a promise to do all in his power to "put it over" so that the Coast Guard would have a service song. He was then on his way to attend the Army-Navy football game in New York, but changed his mind and took the night boat back to Norfolk. It was a port he never reached. Capt. Francis Saltus Van Boskerck died suddenly and peacefully shortly before the vessel docked on 26 November 1927.

In light of this unexpected death, Miller found himself in possession of a crudely prepared musical score that lacked completeness and finesse. But he was enthralled by the inspirational quality of the words, which teemed with the essence of Coast Guard valor and accomplishment. Phrases such as "Write glory to the shield we wear / In letters to the sky" and "Through surf and storm and howling gale / High shall our purpose be" seemed to embody the service's ideals.

Miller turned to WO William R. Sima, assistant director of the Naval Academy Band, to prepare a full musical score for orchestral presentation and to arrange the song for publication. Sima, author of the Navy's "Victory March," was to serve in the Navy for thirty-two years. He immediately saw that there was real music in Captain Van Boskerck's efforts, music to match the song's inspiring words, and later claimed to have "polished up the melody and made it into a regular three-minute march." In actuality, Sima changed the rhythm and the melody of the march so much that it is unrecognizable as the "Semper Paratus" known today. Because it was so different from Van Boskerck's original tune, Sima's arrangement never became popular and has fallen into obscurity.

Miller published the words with a piano score in the April 1928 issue of *Coast Guard* magazine, with the lyrics attributed to Van Boskerck. Before doing so, however, he showed a copy of the song to Rear Adm. Frederick C. Billard, commandant of the Coast Guard, for his comments. Billard wrote:

> *The Coast Guard* magazine is doing a commendable bit of work in publishing "Semper Paratus," the Coast Guard march. The words, as written by the late Captain Van Boskerck, are fine and exemplify clearly and with inspiration the record and traditions of our service.
>
> I hope the words and music meet with approval in our service and that the Coast Guard anthem may soon become as popular as the standard marches and anthems of the other branches of our military and naval services.

The Coast Guard Band's first director, Chief Warrant Officer Hayden O. Jenks, arranged Van Boskerck's music for his eighteen musicians in 1930. He was the first person to arrange what would later become the Coast Guard's official march. His arrangement is a very simple setting still used on parade routes.

In 1938 Miller prevailed upon the old Fox Theatre (later Capitol, in Washington, D.C.) to present a gala premiere of "Semper Paratus." Mr. S. J. Stebbens, a great showman and executive, was Fox manager at the time. Well-known orchestrator William C. Schoenfeld arranged the song for the production. It was presented as part of a musical extravaganza featuring an orchestra of 125 musicians and a male chorus, as well as a momentous storm scene with 100 women in nautical costumes, a detachment of armed cuttermen from the CGC *Apache*, and a male quartet in oilskins singing "Semper Paratus."

The show was a great success and, for a while, the song was as popular as it had been in Unalaska. Schoenfeld's arrangement is the one heard today in song medleys and at nearly every concert given by the U.S. Coast Guard Band.

The famous Mathew Lake made a stately arrangement for use during World War II. Also during that war, *Coast Guard* magazine led a campaign to popularize the service song, which was little-acknowledged beyond Washington, D.C. So many people contacted their radio stations that it ranked number sixteen on the popular song charts in fall 1942.

Captain Van Boskerck lies in Arlington National Cemetery on Dewey Knoll, not far from the Coast Guard World War I memorial. His widow, Carlotta Van Boskerck, survived her husband by many years and lived in Greenwich, Connecticut, having seen his wish fulfilled. His words and song are now known by every member of the Coast Guard. From the very beginning of their service, they commit it to memory in boot camp at Cape May, New Jersey, or as cadets at the Academy or Officer Candidate School in New London, Connecticut. Members stand with pride and respect for "Semper Paratus" and what it represents whenever they hear it performed.

12. THE *BEAR*

The heritage of the Coast Guard dates to 1790. Since then, countless ship's crews have added to it. But the service's heritage is perhaps best exemplified by those who served in the first cutter *Bear* during that ship's more than fifty years of service to our country and humanity.

The *Bear*, long the best known ship in the service, is much more than a famous cutter; she is a symbol for all the Coast Guard represents: steadfastness, courage, and constant readiness to help people and ships in distress.

A steam barentine built in Scotland in 1874 and designed for working in heavy ice, the *Bear*'s ribs were exceptionally heavy for a ship of only 198 feet and were closer together than they would have been on a vessel designed for ice-free waters. The *Bear*'s oak planking was six inches thick, steamed and bent to fit the ribs, and fastened tightly with the best Swedish iron. It was in many respects a sailing battering ram. The *Bear*'s early years were spent as a sealer.

The Navy purchased the sealing vessel *Bear* in 1883, with special funds that Congress appropriated to search for the Adolphus W. Greely Arctic Expedition. Under the command of Cdr. Winfield S. Schley, U.S. Navy, the *Bear* rescued Greely and the other survivors and returned them to civilization, gaining worldwide fame for its role. The *Bear* was of no further use to the Navy after Greely's rescue, and she was slated to be sold out of the service.

The Act of 3 March 1885 transferred the *Bear*, lying in the Navy Yard at New York, to the Revenue Cutter Service without cost to the treasury, since special funds had already been laid out for her purchase. The ship went into the Fundy and Murphy shipyard in New York, where she was refitted as a revenue cutter. She then sailed around the Horn to San Francisco, arriving 106 days out of New York. The Treasury Department designated the *Bear* as the Arctic Ocean cruiser and flagship of the Bering Sea Force.

The ship would serve in Arctic waters for forty-one of her eighty-nine years as a cutter. Completing thirty-four cruises to Alaska, her exploits included delivering reindeer to the native Alaskans, protecting seal rookeries, and serving as an ad hoc Alaskan territorial courtroom. Her deck often served as a courtroom, in which justice was dispensed swiftly but fairly.

USRC *Bear* under way

The *Bear* also conducted investigations and undertook crime prevention and law enforcement.

A number of distinguished leaders of the Coast Guard served on board this famous cutter, including the legendary Capt. Michael A. "Hell Roaring" Healy, commanding officer of the *Bear* from 1886 to 1896. Commo. Ellsworth P. Bertholf, the first commandant of the modern U.S. Coast Guard, served on board the *Bear* three times: first during the Overland Relief Expedition, again as the ship's executive officer (1899–1901), and finally as commanding officer (December 1907–December 1910). He is discussed earlier, in the chapter on honor.

Rear Adm. Harry G. Hamlet served in the *Bear* in 1901. He later served as superintendent of the Academy (1928–32) and was responsible for the phrase "Who Lives Here Reveres Honor and Honors Duty" being tiled into the floor of the entrance to Chase Hall. He served as commandant of the Coast Guard from 1932 to 1936.

Capt. Francis S. Van Boskerck commanded the *Bear* on her 1920 summer cruise to the Bering Sea and Arctic Ocean. He would later compose the words and music for the Coast Guard's marching song, "Semper Paratus."

Capt. John D. "Jack" Costello, U.S. Coast Guard (Retired), in researching for a plaque that his academy class (1952) wished to place in Bear Plaza, discovered that no fewer than fifteen future admirals, including four who would be superintendents of the academy and two who would be commandants of the Coast Guard, had served in the *Bear*. The Coast Guard retired the legendary cutter in 1928.

USRC *Bear*

The *Bear* was the ship involved in the Overland Relief Expedition of 1897–98, discussed earlier, and saw service in three wars. She served during the Spanish-American War as a revenue cutter. The *Bear* was a Coast Guard cutter during the World War I, and served in the Navy as USS *Bear* (AG-29) in the Greenland Patrol of the World War II. Before that war she was refitted for Byrd's Antarctic expeditions. Thus she served in both Arctic and Antarctic waters, two of the harshest environments on Earth. Decommissioned by the Navy in 1944, the *Bear* was transferred to the Maritime Commission. She foundered under tow off Chatham, Massachusetts, in March 1963.

In November 1926, after the *Bear* returned from what was then thought to have been the last voyage of this proud ship, the Coast Guard Academy Corps of Cadets unanimously agreed "that a bear was a fitting mascot, representative of the tenacity and timely aggressiveness of the service." The first custodian of this mascot was Cadet Stephen H. Evans, later to become superintendent of the academy. In 1926 Evans returned from leave with a live bear cub.

Bear statue at the Coast Guard Academy

He somehow talked Cdr. Harold D. Sinckley, at the time superintendent, into allowing the bear to remain at the academy.

They named him Objee, short for "objectionable presence." Objee had many homes throughout his tenure at the academy, but the one in which he spent most of his time, and his final home, was the old academy observatory next to Billard Hall. Although he did not sleep in Chase Hall, Objee was often brought into the barracks and turned loose. He bathed in the cadets' showers and was even allowed to eat in the wardroom from time to time. Objee was particularly fond of visiting cadets during study hour. Apparently he lived up to his name, because in 1984, after twenty-seven live Objees, the tradition was ended when the Corps of Cadets was stripped of its right to keep a living bear due to the "objectionable presence" that it imposed on the surrounding community and new animal quarantine laws. The last Objee, a female black bear, was retired from mascot duties and relocated to Widmark Farms, Gardiner, New York. She died there on 21 November 2007.

In October 1997, a life-size bear statue was dedicated in the newly created Academy Plaza behind Chase Hall. A gift of the class of 1952, the statue is alert and vigilant, focused outward from the plaza beyond the academy— to "the challenges graduates will encounter as they strive to perpetuate the standard of service and the traditions established by their predecessors." The area around the statue is now known as Bear Plaza, commemorating not only Objee but also the most famous vessel to serve in the Coast Guard. For morale and spirit, cadets commonly dress up the statue before a big football game or other major athletic event, using jerseys, team hats, war paint, class T-shirts, or various other uniforms and decorations.

On 4 February 1983, a second *Bear* (WMEC-901) was commissioned as a Coast Guard cutter, restoring the proud name to the list of active vessels. It was the first of thirteen 270-foot Famous-class cutters commissioned during the 1980s.

13. CREED OF THE UNITED STATES COAST GUARDSMAN

The January 1946 issue of *Coast Guard* magazine lamented that there was no such thing as "The Creed of a United States Coast Guardsman." It noted that everyone was familiar with "The American's Creed" and that the Marine Corps had its own "Creed of a United States Marine." The article went on to argue that almost every worthy organization had its own personal creed that lent strength and inspiration, yet the Coast Guard did not. As a result, the magazine invited "every writer who sees these words to set himself to the serious and worthy task of creating 'The Creed of a United States Coast Guardsman.'"

A three-man board would study all entries, and the best would be published in the magazine. Readers were reminded that the song "Semper Paratus" was first published in its pages, and a creed to accompany it would be appropriate. Apparently there was little response, because in the following years the magazine published only a very brief creed authored by Edith F. Munro, mother of Coast Guard Medal of Honor winner Douglas Munro.

Vice Adm. Harry G. Hamlet, U.S. Coast Guard (Retired), finally took upon himself to write the creed that is known today. Commissioned in 1896 following his graduation from the U.S. Revenue Cutter School of Instruction, Hamlet served on board the *Bear* during the celebrated 1897–98 relief expedition to the Arctic. He headed the Coast Guard destroyer force in 1925, and later served as superintendent of the academy in New London, Connecticut (1928–32). He wrote "The Mission of the United States Coast Guard Academy" in 1929 and ended his active duty career as commandant of the Coast Guard, from 1932 to 1936.

Hamlet later wrote that the idea for a creed had come to him many years earlier, while serving on board the revenue cutter *Tahoma* in the Bering Sea. The *Tahoma* had been the first Bering Sea Patrol vessel to return to Unalaska and was en route home after a bleak cruise, when new orders turned her about for additional duty. At that point Hamlet decided a creed was needed as a morale builder. However, it was not until he retired that he found the opportunity to put his idea into writing. "The Creed of a Coast Guardsman," which

Capt. (later Vice Adm.) Harry G. Hamlet, author of the
"Creed of a Coastguardsman."

he wrote in 1938, was first published in the *Coast Guard Bulletin* in its April
1950 edition.

> I am proud to be a United States Coast Guardsman.
> I revere that long line of expert seamen who by their devotion to duty
> and sacrifice of self have made it possible for me to be a member of a ser-
> vice honored and respected, in peace and in war, throughout the world.
> I never, by work or deed, will bring reproach upon the fair name of my
> service, nor permit others to do so unchallenged.
> I will cheerfully and willingly obey all lawful orders.
> I will always be on time to relieve, and shall endeavor to do more, rather
> than less, than my share.

I will always be at my station, alert and attending to my duties.
I shall, so far as I am able, bring to my seniors solutions, not problems.
I shall live joyously, but always with due regard for the rights and privileges of others.
I shall endeavor to be a model citizen in the community in which I live.
I shall sell life dearly to an enemy of my country, but give it freely to rescue those in peril.
With God's help, I shall endeavor to be one of His noblest Works . . .
A United States Coastguardsman.

Since its publication, this creed has waxed and waned in popularity. During certain periods recruits were required to commit it to memory while in boot camp; at other times they were not. Some heard it only at award ceremonies and retirements. But for others it became the foundation that guided them, both enlisted and officers, throughout their careers. Regardless of its popularity or familiarity, however, its inspiring words are still valid today.

Harry G. Hamlet retired on 1 September 1938 after reaching the mandatory age of sixty-four and was promoted from rear admiral to vice admiral because of his more than forty years of service. He died on 24 January 1954 and is buried in Arlington National Cemetery.

14. GUARDIAN ETHOS

The term "guardian" is relatively new in referring to the Coast Guard or those who serve in it. It first appeared in Robert Ervin Johnson's magisterial history of the service, *Guardians of the Sea*, published in 1987. Johnson used it to describe the service as a whole.

In January 2002, *Coast Guard Publication 1: America's Maritime Guardian* was promulgated to align with *Joint Publication 1*, the capstone doctrine for U.S. armed forces unified action; and with *Naval Publication 1*, which describes how naval services operate as an integrated force across a range of operations. The Coast Guard publication is designed to tell men and women of the active duty, Reserve, and Auxiliary service what their organization is all about—its history, ethos, values, and reason for existence. It is the service's first publication to synthesize who members are, what they do, and how they do things. Throughout its pages, the Coast Guard is described as "America's Maritime Guardian."

At the direction of the commandant of the Coast Guard, and in partnership with the Master Chief Petty Officer of the Coast Guard, in 2007 Training Center Cape May was charged with refining the curriculum for enlisted recruits to better internalize the service's culture, character, and core values. That May, following visits to Navy, Army, and Marine Corps training locations, Capt. Sandra Stosz (commanding officer, Coast Guard Training Center Cape May) and Cdr. Thomas McCormick (training officer) discussed how each of the other armed services had a warrior ethos. The Air Force was at that time teaching its newly developed "Airman's Creed" that expressed its version of this warrior ethos. Commander McCormick suggested that the Coast Guard needed a "Guardian Ethos" to provide the foundation for a service identity—something that would commit recruits to the Coast Guard and internalize the service's characteristics as depicted in *Coast Guard Publication No. 1*.

With roots in many different predecessor agencies, the Coast Guard has indeed historically lacked a singularly defined identity. This lack of consistent identity has caused confusion with the public because of the wide spectrum of both authorities and competencies resident in the service's mission requirements. The guardian-ethos idea was not intended to replace "The Creed of a Coast Guardsman," which is a contract an individual makes with the service. The ethos defines the essence of the Coast Guard and is the contract that the service and its members make with the nation and its citizens.

That August 2007, the Training Center's CMC Bruce Bradley, was directed to establish a local grassroots working group to develop the "Guardian Ethos." A key member of his group was ET1 Sean Edward Ross. In September the draft was distributed for comment throughout the Gold Badge network. MCPO-CG Skip Bowen distributed it at that October's Senior Executive Leadership Conference.

During this process the "Guardian Ethos" was created. At its heart is the belief that every man and woman in the Coast Guard is a guardian. It is now learned, and since April 2008, every recruit shouts it out upon graduation. Academy cadets, officer candidates, and enlisted personnel all recite the "Guardian Ethos."

In an op-ed piece in May 2008, Adm. Thad Allen, commandant of the Coast Guard, said: "This is really the essence of the Coast Guard today, though it dates back to the days when the Coast Guard was the Steamboat Inspection Service, the Revenue Cutter Service, the Life-Saving Service and Lighthouse Services. We have a proud history of serving the nation and our communities in the maritime domain both in wartime and peace. And our core values remain focused on saving lives and protecting both people and the environment. We will always be America's maritime guardian."

"The Guardian Ethos"
I am America's maritime guardian.
I serve the citizens of the United States.
I will protect them.
I will defend them.
I will save them.
I am their shield.
For them I am Semper Paratus.
I live the Coast Guard core values.
I am a guardian.
We are the United States Coast Guard.

In July 2008, Admiral Allen formally introduced the ethos to the entire Coast Guard. He believed it would assist the service in tying its military, maritime, multi-mission character into a more tangible service identity—one that would resonate with those in the Coast Guard, their external partners, and their customers as well. He firmly proclaimed that the men and women of the Coast

Guard are guardians. According to Allen, the guardian ethos is the essence of our service; it is who we are.

Like guardian angels, the Coast Guard is often unnoticed. Each and every member of the service's family—the storekeeper providing logistical support, an Auxiliarist on a routine patrol, a Reservist deployed to Bahrain, a civilian employee repairing a buoy, or a retiree recruiting young people to the academy—they are all guardians.

Members of the Coast Guard are not only guardians of the maritime public and the environment, they are also guardians of each other. They protect, defend, and save each other as well as serving the maritime public. They have a proud tradition of being each others' guardians by looking after their own.

PART 5. SEA CHEST

A type of wooden trunk in which sailors historically stored their personal possessions, sea chests were often extremely well built. Their design varied, depending on the era in which they were produced and the nation from which they originated. Some were quite ornate, with elegant carving and beautiful construction, while others were plain and relatively simple. Many had a distinctive profile, with a large bottom and slides slanting up to a smaller top. Some sea chests had curved tops; others were left flat for ease of storage, and many included drawers or shelves for storing small and especially important items. Typically, the chests were equipped with sturdy locks and heavy handles so they could be moved easily. Some families saved sea chests that had belonged to their ancestors.

Storage in a ship is often limited, so sailors were expected to fit all their possessions into these chests. They were typically kept in bunkrooms, butted against the wall or in another location as out of the way as possible. Usually they contained a varied assortment of unrelated items that might tell something about the owner.

Any number of things could be held in a sea chest, including eating utensils, extra clothes, souvenirs from various journeys, and mariner's papers detailing a sailor's skills and official position on board ship. Sailors also kept in their chests references from former employers and mementos of home. Rummaging through their sea chests, sailors could trace their careers, where they had been, ships in which they had sailed, actions in which they had taken part, and shipmates they would always remember.

In that sense, the miscellany that follows belongs in the sea chest of this book. Together they tell some important and interesting things about our Coast Guard.

15. COAST GUARD FIRSTS

Members of the Coast Guard can be proud of being part of an organization that claims so many firsts. This book covered Hopley Yeaton in the earlier chapter "Revenue Cutter Service." He was the first seagoing officer to receive a commission from the federal government. What follows are but three of many more examples, all worthy of being remembered.

In the field of technology the Coast Guard (through its predecessor the Revenue Cutter Service) holds the distinction of making the first wireless radio transmission from a service ship, and of being the first to employ wireless telegraphy for tactical purposes. A Coast Guard pilot, Elmer Stone, flew the first aircraft across the Atlantic in 1919, eight years before Charles Lindbergh's more well-known transatlantic solo flight. And three Coast Guard vessels—the *Storis* (WAG-38), *Spar* (WAGL-403), and *Bramble* (WAGL-402)—were the first American vessels to transit the Northwest Passage and circumnavigate North America.

Maritime Radio

The period between the end of the American Civil War and World War I saw dramatic, world-changing technological developments. The first incandescent electric light banished darkness forever at Thomas Edison's Menlo Park laboratory in 1879. Motorboats and motorcars by 1895 had traveled a few epoch-making miles. But many believe that the crowning miracle of the century was Guglielmo Marconi's establishment of wireless communication by electromagnetic waves in 1898. By 1915, wireless telegraphy had revolutionized communication at sea. The Coast Guard played a pioneering role in the use of this new technology.

In 1899, the San Francisco newspaper *Call* was eager to be the first to report the return of the U.S. Army troop transport *Sherman* from the Philippines. The paper had lookouts at the beach who would telegraph updates overland to the news office. There was a great desire to get the news even earlier—from the San Francisco lightship, some nine miles off the entrance to the Golden Gate. Reporters had tried visual signals, but the frequent fog made those unreliable most of the time. One week of failed signaling between Claus Spreckel's Building and Telegraph Hill, followed by five weeks of experimentation at the beach, culminated in successful over-water transmissions between the yacht *Lurline* and a shore station.

Through the courtesy of the federal government, a wireless transmitting apparatus was placed on board San Francisco's lightship number 70. This new lightship, under the command of Master Aber Lowell, had been placed in service a year earlier. She was 122 feet overall in length, with a composite hull made of steel frames and topsides with a wooden hull. Her two masts were topped by lantern galleries. The receiving instruments were placed in the basement of the Cliff House restaurant. On 22 August, a tugboat came alongside the lightship and offloaded the wireless apparatus and antennas, including a dynamo to provide electricity for the equipment. A telegrapher also came on board the lightship to operate the apparatus. The equipment was tested on 23 August during daylight hours.

At noon the following day, another tugboat brought a technician on board to make slight adjustments to the transmitter, enabling it to perform satisfactorily. A breathless crowd awaited the signal at the Cliff House. There Lewis McKisick and H. J. Wolters manned the shore station, as everyone waited for the return of California's war veterans.

Shortly after five o'clock on 24 August 1899, the telegrapher on the lightship sent the words, "Sherman in sight." This was the first use in the United States of wireless on board a service ship—Lightship 70. It followed Marconi's first ship-to-shore transmission by a year. Lightship 70 stayed in service off San Francisco Bay until 1930.

The smuggling situation was always a challenge to Coast Guard units on the Pacific. There was a heavy demand for Chinese laborers and for opium. This was especially acute in the Pacific Northwest, where smuggling vessels only had to pick up their cargo in Victoria, British Columbia, and sail the short distances through numerous channels to a variety of landing sites.

Capt. Dorr F. Tozier, commanding officer of the U.S. revenue cutter *U.S. Grant*, faced an uphill fight. Early in 1903, the Pacific Wireless Telegraph Company extended service to the Puget Sound area. Captain Tozier recognized the advantages of using wireless telegraphy to keep constantly in touch with his sources of information in Victoria, British Columbia, and Port Townsend, Washington; and to direct the movement of his two 65-foot launches, the *Guard* at San Juan Island and *Scout* at Port Townsend. Captain Tozier convinced the local collector of customs of the value of placing the technology on board his revenue cutter.

In July 1904 the *Grant*, a 163-foot, three-masted, iron-hulled vessel commissioned in 1871, was laid up for repairs at Quartermaster Harbor, Washington.

San Francisco Lightship No. 70

During that time, a dynamo was mounted in the upper engine room to generate electricity to power the wireless apparatus. A radio shack was constructed on deck, abaft the foremast. On 18 August, Chief Engineer H. C. Wentworth came on board to attend the trial use of the wireless.

At 11:00 AM they got under way in Puget Sound with an operator from the local telegraph office, who knew nothing about the apparatus itself. Nevertheless, during the cruise he successfully used the wireless to contact the launches and Port Townsend. By 1 April 1904, regular scheduled radio communication was in effect—but before that date, the wireless had been used on numerous occasions to handle confidential, tactical messages in an improvised code. Thus the revenue cutter U.S. Grant, while cruising in the Straits of Juan de Fuca and Puget Sound, became the first U.S. ship to employ wireless telegraphy for tactical purposes.

It soon became clear that radio would play a major role in the history of the service. Within the next few years, cutters, together with the world's naval and merchant fleets, made radio their own. The first reference to radio in service law appeared in the Revenue Cutter Service Regulations issued by the commandant, Capt. Worth G. Ross, in 1907. The "Wireless Act of June 24, 1910" required any steamer carrying fifty or more persons to be equipped with an apparatus capable of sending and receiving radio messages.

U.S. revenue cutter *Grant*

The first use of wireless in a dramatic rescue occurred on 23 January 1908, when the radio operator of the White Star liner *Republic* sent the message that they had been rammed and were in danger of sinking twenty-six miles southeast of Nantucket Island. Immediately four revenue cutters started from distant parts of the coast for the distressed steamship. The cutter *Gresham* (WPG-85), learning of the collision, steamed to the *Republic* at full speed from Provincetown, Massachusetts. Finding the ship the next morning, the *Gresham* began towing the *Republic* and beached her in the nearest shoal water to the south of Nantucket Island.

The weather worsened, however, and the captain of the *Republic* ordered all hands to abandon ship and head to the *Gresham* in their lifeboats. Meanwhile a sister cutter, the *Seneca*, alerted by the wireless, arrived on scene to assist the *Gresham*. When the two cutters had picked up the last of the *Republic*'s crew, the *Gresham*'s wireless sent out its happy message: "All hands saved." Radio operators became the new heroes.

By 1910, seventeen cutters boasted wireless capabilities, and acting Secretary of the Treasury Charles P. Hilles took pains to inform Congress that these installations had "proved a most important and potent factor" in relief and rescue work. By 1915 the entire cruising fleet of the Revenue Cutter Service was "on the air," standing continuous guard on the radio distress frequency and thus bringing to the voyaging public a new measure of comfort and security.

Elmer Stone, pioneer aviator

Transatlantic Flight

Elmer "Archie" Stone was a Coast Guard officer and one of the founders of the Coast Guard aviation service. Born in 1887 in Livonia, New York, Stone was appointed a cadet in the Revenue Cutter Service and graduated from the Revenue Cutter Service Academy with the Class of 1913. Commissioned just ten years after the Wright Brothers' famous flight, Stone convinced the Coast Guard in 1916 that it would greatly benefit from having an aviator. He was sent to Pensacola, Florida, where on 10 April 1917 he won his wings to become Naval Aviator No. 38.

During World War I the Coast Guard was temporarily integrated with the Navy, and Stone was assigned to the Navy Bureau of Construction and Repair's aircraft section as an engineer and test pilot. Then and later, he was one of the best. That would lead to his key role in one of aviation history's most forgotten milestones, which took place in 1919.

On 1 April 1913 the London *Daily Mail* announced that it was offering a prize of about $50,000 to the first person to fly across the Atlantic. Only one aircraft could be used, and all intermediate landings had to be made at sea.

The starting and finishing points could be anywhere in Newfoundland or the British Isles, and the total elapsed time could not exceed seventy-two consecutive hours.

Several years passed with no one being able to meet the challenge. On 31 October 1918, Cdr. John Towers, U.S. Navy, formally proposed to Adm. William S. Benson, chief of naval operations, that the Navy attempt the first transatlantic flight the following spring.

The U.S. Navy was determined to be the first to make that flight, although as a government agency it refused to consider itself or any of its personnel eligible for the *Daily Mail* competition. The prize the Navy wanted was the immortal honor. The service's tests convinced the Navy that the new NC-1 aircraft, designed for transatlantic operations from the start, could be successful. These "flying boats" were built during World War I as a joint venture between the Navy and Curtiss Aeroplane and Motor Company (Glenn Curtiss), hence the NC designation. The flying boats came to be unofficially called Nancies and were at the time the largest biplanes in the world.

Although the aircraft was not ready until after the Armistice was signed, it turned out to be the best long-range plane built until that time. The Curtiss-designed hull would become the prototype for the great Catalina PBY hulls of World War II. The Nancies had 126 feet of wingspread, only 4 feet shorter than a modern Boeing 707. They were originally powered by three engines, but a fourth was added as a pusher on the centerline for the planes the Navy would use.

Secretary of the Navy Josephus Daniels approved the request on 4 February 1919 and put Towers in command. Towers formed NC Seaplane Division One, which consisted of NC-1, NC-2, NC-3, and NC-4. The Navy's Seaplane Division One was in direct competition with three teams of British pilots who would be flying from a base in St. Johns, Newfoundland. Among the pilots that Towers chose was Coast Guard 1st Lt. Elmer Stone. He would be the only non-Navy man on this mission.

Before the attempted flight, the NC-2 was badly damaged and deleted. In the early morning hours of 5 May, a gasoline fire destroyed the NC-1's starboard wings, so the NC-2's wings were used as replacements. On 7 May, chief machinist's mate Edward Howard, engineer on NC-4, lost his hand in a spinning propeller and was removed from the flight. He was replaced by chief machinist Eugene S. Rhoads as the engineer on the NC-4.

The NC-1 and NC-3 flew from Rockaway Beach, Long Island, to Halifax, Nova Scotia, and then on to Trepassey, Newfoundland. The NC-4 had to turn back with engine problems, and after being repaired barely made it to Trespassey in time for the leg across the Atlantic to the Azores. The three seaplanes took off from Newfoundland on 16 May 1919. Each carried a wireless radio with a range of 350 miles that would also allow them to talk among themselves. The pilot of the NC-4 was Coast Guard Lt. Elmer Stone. The aircraft commander and navigator was Lt. Cdr. Albert C. Read, U.S. Navy. The copilot and the other members of the crew were all Navy personnel.

The 1,110 miles from Trepassey, Newfoundland, to Ponta Delgada, on the island of Sao Miguel in the Azores was the most challenging of the flight, which was made under adverse conditions. In open cockpits, at altitudes from 100 to 3,000 feet, the pilots fought fog and icing conditions both day and night, with none of the all-weather instruments now considered necessary for safe flight.

All three aircraft counted on twenty-two Navy destroyers placed 50 miles apart along the path as both aids to navigation and possible rescue ships in case they had to land in the open ocean. After flying for more than fifteen hours at 80–90 miles per hour, the NC-1 and NC-3 were forced to land at sea on 17 May—before reaching the Azores. The NC-1 touched down at 1:00 PM in twelve-foot seas and nearly broached on several occasions, before being rescued by the Greek freighter *Ionia* that night at 11:00. Taken under tow, the NC-1 sank. The NC-3, also damaged from its sea landing, sailed into Ponta Delgada after water-taxiing 205 miles in fifty-three hours.

The NC-4, piloted by Coast Guardsman Stone, was the only aircraft that made it all the way and landed at Horta, on the Azores island of Fayal, on 17 May. During this longest leg of the flight, Stone and his Navy copilot had flown for fifteen hours in an open cockpit at seventy miles an hour. With all the crews once again assembled and watching, the NC-4 lifted off ten days later from Horta and flew to Lisbon, Portugal, with Stone at the controls. The Portuguese government knighted Stone and the Navy personnel that same day, with the Order of the Tower and Sword.

The final leg of the journey was from Ferrol, Spain, to Plymouth, England. Stone flew the NC-4 toward the tip of Brittany. Passing over Brest, France, he piloted the NC-4 almost due north to Plymouth. Crossing the English Channel the visibility fell to almost zero, and Stone and his Navy co-pilot had to take the NC-4 down to within fifty feet of the water's surface to remain below the cloud layer. The rest of the flight to Plymouth was made barely above the water.

As they reached the coast of Britain the fog suddenly thinned, and sun appeared overhead. Twenty-five minutes later the NC-4 was circling Plymouth, overflying Drake's Island and the citadel; as she passed over, various colored Very flares shot up to mark the plane's passage. From the harbor came the now-familiar chorus of whistles and sirens and bells. At 1:27 PM on 30 May 1919, Stone wheeled the NC-4 around in a wide circle to eastward, then brought

The NC-4, the first plane to fly across the Atlantic Ocean

her around with her nose into the west wind for her touchdown in the waters off the Corinthian Yacht Club.

The NC-4 landed at Plymouth, being the first aircraft to successfully fly across the Atlantic Ocean. Stone and the other crews were feted by the great and wealthy, the titled of Great Britain and the Lord Mayor of London. The British government awarded Stone the British Air Force Cross on 9 June 1919. He received a written commendation from then–Assistant Secretary of the Navy Franklin D. Roosevelt, dated 23 August 1919, that stated: "I wish to heartily commend you for your work as pilot of the Seaplane NC-4 during the recent trans-Atlantic flight expedition. The energy, efficiency, and courage shown by you contributed to the accomplishment of the first trans-Atlantic flight, which feat has brought honor to the American Navy and the entire American nation." The NC-4 is displayed today at the National Museum of Naval Aviation at Pensacola.

Stone received a promotion to the temporary rank of captain on 25 September 1919. On 30 March 1920, he was appointed as Coast Guard Aviator No. 1. He was awarded a Navy Cross for "distinguished service in making the first successful trans-Atlantic flight" on 11 November 1920. On 2 September 1921, he reverted to his permanent rank of first lieutenant. On 1 October 1921, Stone was awarded the Victory Medal with Aviation Clasp, and on 23 May 1930 the president awarded him a congressional medal especially designed for the occasion, for "extraordinary achievement in making the first successful trans-Atlantic flight."

Even though this flight took place eight years before Lindbergh's, virtually no one knows about it. The American who is asked today about the first transatlantic flight will very likely insist that it was Charles Lindbergh in 1927. The NC-4's flight, its timeless lessons and legacy remain largely forgotten or ignored. But every Coast Guardsman can be proud that the pilot of the NC-4, the first plane to fly across that Atlantic, was a fellow service member, Elmer "Archie" Stone.

After his daring feat, Stone worked with the Navy's Bureau of Aeronautics for the next six years as a test pilot. Here he assisted in the development and installation of the catapults and arresting gear of the new aircraft carriers USS *Lexington* (CV-2) and *Saratoga* (CV-3), equipment that is to this day used on aircraft carriers. On 27 February 1926, he piloted a powder-catapulted amphibious plane from a barge anchored in the Potomac River. The powder catapult, which Stone helped develop, received its power from the discharge of a 3-inch blank shell. His flight marked the first time a plane was catapulted using powder rather than air pressure. The Navy Department later commended Stone for his valuable services as both test pilot and developer of the catapult and deck arresting gear.

Detached from the Navy Department on 21 September 1926, Stone was immediately sent to sea as the executive officer of the CGC *Ossipee* (WPR-50). Following that tour of duty, he assumed command of the Coast Guard destroyer *Monaghan* (CG-15) at New London, Connecticut. Unlike many other Coast Guard officers, Elmer "Archie" Stone never lost his interest in aviation. In May 1932 he became the commanding officer of the Coast Guard aviation unit at Cape May, New Jersey. He continued to develop his skill at making open-ocean landings until he was arguably the best seaplane pilot in any of the world's naval services.

In 1933, when the Navy dirigible *Akron* (ZRS-4) went down off the Atlantic coast in a storm with only three survivors of the seventy-six on board, Stone was the only available pilot willing to attempt a landing in the heavy seas. He accomplished this successfully, but was too late to save any more lives. In December 1934 he set a new world speed for amphibian aircraft: 191.734 miles per hour in a new Grumman JF-2 "Duck" Seaplane (CG 167). Elmer Stone arrived in San Diego in 1935 and relieved Lt. Luke Christopher as the commanding officer of the air-patrol detachment in San Diego. But this tour of duty would be a short one, because of Stone's untimely death a year after his arrival. On 20 May 1936, at the Naval Air Station in San Diego, Cdr. Stone served as an observer at the Navy trials of a new type of flying boat. He walked over to a concrete hangar abutment and sat down on. At age forty-nine, Elmer Stone fell over with a heart attack and died almost instantly. He is buried in Arlington National Cemetery.

Stone was a pivotal figure in the establishment and development of aviation for the Coast Guard and Navy. He was a favorite of many famous aviation figures of the day, including Eddie Rickenbacker; aircraft designers Anthony Fokker, Igor Sikorsky, and Alexander P. de Seversky; and the Prince of Wales. On 26 January 1983, the new multipurpose building that housed Facilities Engineering and the Coast Guard Reserve at the Coast Guard Air Station, San Diego, was dedicated to the memory of Cdr. Elmer F. Stone. The station also pays tribute to the service's first aviator with a statue in front of the building bearing his name.

On 12 May 1983, Commander Stone became the first Coast Guard aviator to be enshrined in the Naval Aviation Hall of Honor at the National Museum of Naval Aviation in Pensacola. The NC-4 is also on display.

Northwest Passage

Beginning with Norse explorers in the tenth century, mariners from Europe searched for a Northwest Passage across the top of North America that would give them quicker access to Asia and its markets. None was successful. The Northwest Passage is actually several passageways through the complex archipelago of the Canadian Arctic.

As Cold War tensions between the Soviet Union and Western democracies intensified in the early 1950s, the possibility of a Soviet air attack over the North Pole led to another attempt to determine the feasibility of a Northwest Passage. Such a transit would make possible an increase in the number of early warning radar stations across the Canadian Arctic. The U.S. Coast Guard was given the assignment to find a usable passage through which deep-draft vessels trapped in the Arctic by ice or war could escape. The Coast Guard was also tasked with conducting a detailed hydrographic survey of this passage.

On 1 July 1957, the Coast Guard 230-foot icebreaking cutter *Storis* (WAG-38) , and the 180-foot buoy tenders *Bramble* (WAGL/WLB-392) and *Spar* (WAGL/WLB-403), both of which had hulls strengthened for ice operations, rendezvoused in Seattle and then departed. They traveled through the Unimak Pass on their way to Point Barrow, Alaska, where they began their attempt to break through the historic Northwest Passage. The goal of this adventurous mission was to sail through the Bellot Strait, a frozen passageway thought to be wide enough for merchant ships, and to locate escape routes for vessels trapped in the Arctic. They would be aided by charts created during an unsuccessful 1956 Coast Guard attempt to find a passage through these tricky northern waterways.

The leader of this Coast Guard expedition was Cdr. Harold L. Wood, commanding officer of the *Storis*. The three cutters crossed the Arctic Circle on 10 July and arrived at Point Barrow on 12 July. Their progress along the northern coast of Canada's Northwest Territories was slow and at times extremely dangerous. Sometimes the cutters struggled to maintain headway through

The U.S. Coast Guard cutter *Storis* (WAG-38), flagship of the Northwest Passage

heavy ice. The situation came to a near-crisis on 29 July, when the *Storis* met hard, fast ice that could not be moved. Even explosives failed to free the ship. She was finally able to free herself the following day, when a small crack was revealed in the floe. After making a 200-yard trip to open water and turning the *Storis* around, Captain Wood freed the other two cutters.

They passed through a series of straits and gulfs named for Norwegian and British explorers and royalty, reaching the west edge of Bellot Strait on 4 September. There they were joined by the Royal Canadian Navy's modi-fied *Wind*-class icebreaker, HMCS *Labrador*. On the morning of 6 September 1957, the four vessels transited the seventeen-mile strait. The passage was clear of ice and took only two hours. Once through it and into the ice-free waters of Prince Regent Inlet, the vessels steamed north of Baffin Island and into Lancaster Sound, crossing the Arctic Circle on 12 September.

From there they steamed south into Baffin Bay and through the Davis Strait to the Labrador Sea. After replenishing fuel and provisions at Argentia, Newfoundland, the three Coast Guard cutters proceeded to their home ports, having completed a 4,500-mile journey. The *Spar*, first to leave its home port, was the first to return, arriving in Bristol, Rhode Island, on 24 September. The *Bramble* arrived back in Miami on 1 October, and the *Storis* steamed to Seattle by way of the Panama Canal later that same month. When the cutters reached

The four commanding officers of the vessels that constituted the convoy through Bellot Strait, 6 September 1957, meet on the deck of the Canadian icebreaker HMCS *Labrador* before their historic transit. From left: Cdr. Harold L. Wood, Capt. Thomas C. Pullen, Lt. Charles V. Cowing, and Lt. Cdr. Harry H. Carter.

their home ports at the end of their Arctic voyage, they also became the first vessels to circumnavigate the North American continent.

In addition, these three Coast Guard vessels became the first American ships to make the transit of the Northwest Passage and the first to successfully make a convoy through the passage. The *Bramble* and *Spar* became the first (and only American) buoy tenders to make the Arctic voyage. The *Spar* was decommissioned in 1997 and the *Bramble* in 2003. The *Storis*, later reclassified as a medium-endurance cutter and used for search and rescue missions and fisheries law enforcement patrols, became the oldest commissioned Coast Guard cutter still in active service. She was not decommissioned until early 2007.

16. COAST GUARD IDENTITY

Ensign

Nine years after Congress established the Revenue Cutter Service, it provided that cutters and boats engaged in revenue collection should display a distinguishing and unique ensign. Approved 2 March 1799, an act of Congress created the Coast Guard ensign as the revenue flag of the United States. The adoption of the distinctive flag had been inspired by ship owners' concerns that a vessel claiming to be a revenue cutter and ordering a merchant vessel to heave to might actually be a pirate. Congress therefore directed President John Adams to prescribe the special ensign, provided a $100 fine for its unauthorized use, and authorized the commanding officer of any cutter flying the ensign to use deadly force against vessels that failed to heed his instructions.

Secretary of the Treasury Oliver Wolcott's order was for an ensign and pennant of "sixteen perpendicular stripes—the number of states in the Union when this ensign was officially adopted—alternate red and white; the union of the ensign to be the arms of the United States in a dark blue on a white field." It soon became familiar in American waters and served as a sign of authority for the Revenue Cutter Service.

Outside American waters, the cutters displayed the national ensign. However, this revenue flag was later adopted to fly over U.S. custom houses. President William Howard Taft issued an executive order in 1910, changing the revenue cutter ensign by adding an emblem such that a "distinguishing flag now used by vessels of the Revenue Cutter Service be marked by the distinctive emblem of that service, in blue and white . . . over the center of the seventh vertical red stripe." The emblem referred to was the seal of the Revenue Cutter Service. It included the motto Semper Paratus, giving that motto further official recognition.

Cutters then began flying the U.S. flag as their naval ensign, and the revenue cutter ensign, now shifted to the flag-signal yard, became the service's distinctive flag. Five years later, when the service merged with the Life-Saving

Service and became the United States Coast Guard, the Revenue Cutter Service's ensign became the distinguishing flag on all Coast Guard cutters, continuing to this day the legacy of that predecessor service. The emblem used was changed on the order of Secretary of the Treasury Andrew Mellon in 1927, from that of the old Revenue Cutter Service to that of the Coast Guard, which since 1915 had become an independent bureau of the Treasury Department.

When President Harry S. Truman prescribed a new presidential seal in 1945, the ensign was changed to conform to this. The thirteen stars previously arranged around the eagle by a semicircular arc were placed in their present position above the eagle's head. This emblem has been redesigned several times since, most recently by the deletion of the motto above and below the shield in 1966.

Even when they are not conducting law enforcement missions, Coast Guard vessels nevertheless fly the distinctive ensign from the head of the forward-most mast. On board cutters in commission with a single mast, it flies immediately below the commission pennant. At shore installations it is displayed from the starboard yardarm of the flag mast.

The colors used in the Coast Guard ensign today, as in the Revenue Cutter Service, are all symbolic. Red stands for youth and the sacrifice of blood for liberty's sake. Blue represents justice and a covenant against oppression. White symbolizes a desire for light and purity. Intended in 1799 to identify the federal authority of the cutters for vessel boarding, examination, and seizure, and to enforce the laws of the United States, the Coast Guard ensign is never carried as a parade or ceremony standard.

Racing Stripe

The Coast Guard has long struggled with recognition by the American public. The now-well-known diagonal "racing stripe" was one way of making the service's cutters and aircraft more recognizable. Retired Vice Adm. Thomas Sargent recalls in his memoirs that "in 1962, Admiral Edwin Roland was appointed Commandant and brought to the office a breath of fresh air and much innovation." He further notes, "James Read was the Assistant Secretary of the Treasury and had charge of the Coast Guard. He and Eddie [Roland] became good friends, and Jim Read had great regard for the Coast Guard. Between them, they considered that the [Coast Guard] had remained in the background far too long."

Since image building had played an important role in the recent election of President John F. Kennedy in 1960, the industrial design firm of Raymond Loewy and William Snaith was hired to redesign the exterior and interior of the presidential plane. Kennedy was so pleased with the new look that he approved their proposal for improving the worldwide visual identification of the U.S. government.

Capt. Benjamin F. Engel was appointed to head a board in late 1962 to find and develop a new Coast Guard recognition image. Loewy and Snaith submitted several proposals. Besides Captain Engel, Rear Adm. Paul Trimble, headquarters chief of staff, and Capt. Thomas Sargent, chief of civil engineering, were also involved in evaluating proposals. The design firm suggested the current stripe of a wide Coast Guard orange color bar forward of a narrow blue bar, with the service's emblem superimposed. The slash or racing-stripe design canted at 64 degrees from a horizontal line. The color blue represented the seagoing heritage; orange was internationally identified with search and rescue.

The commandant approved this design in 1964. It was adopted service-wide on 6 April 1967, to be followed by the words "Coast Guard" painted in block letters. This new identification was placed on all service boats, cutters, and aircraft, with the exception of the *Eagle*. Many believed that placing the racing stripe on this tall ship would detract from its beauty and historic appearance. However, when the *Eagle* was scheduled to lead the 1976 maritime parade into New York Harbor as a part of Operation Sail, Coast Guard officials decided to add the stripe to her otherwise unadorned white hull. This would distinguish her from foreign sailing ships visiting for the nation's bicentennial celebration. The decision generated a major controversy, with many in the sailing community decrying the new paint job. The *Eagle* thus became the last Coast Guard unit to receive the racing stripe.

Today, the identifying stripe remains on all service craft. Many foreign services have also adopted the symbol, in its original colors or modified, including the Canadian Coast Guard, the Italian Guardia Costiera, the French Maritime Gendarmerie, the Indian Coast Guard, the German Federal Coast Guard, and the Australian Customs Service. Auxiliary vessels maintained by the U.S. Coast Guard also carry the stripe in inverted colors.

Uniform

For generations, Coast Guard personnel wore uniforms that were often confused with those of the much larger U.S. Navy. The early history of Revenue Service uniforms is vague to nonexistent. In any event, the early outfit must have been similar to that of the Continental Navy. As the years passed, the Revenue Cutter Service attire continued to be similar to and patterned on U.S. Navy uniforms.

New regulations issued in 1864 provided that a small embroidered national shield was placed above the stripes on the sleeve. This shield would become the distinguishing mark for Revenue Cutter Service uniforms, to distinguish them for those of the Navy. When the Revenue Service and the Life-

Saving Service combined to form the U.S. Coast Guard in 1915, the new service had two uniforms. To keep up the esprit de corps of former Life-Saving Service personnel, the Coast Guard authorized a special "surfman's" outfit for these men. This apparel consisted of a single-breasted blue coat with four buttons, four pockets, and peaked lapels along with special collar devices. The cap was the same as that authorized for chief petty officers except for the cap device, which was the emblem of crossed oars superimposed on a circular life buoy. The Coast Guard decided to keep this unique surfman's uniform on the books at least until 1943. By 1941, the only major difference between Navy and Coast Guard uniforms concerned this surfman attire.

By the 1920s, two major changes were seen in regular (non-surfmen) Coast Guard attire. First was the adoption of the double-breasted service coat similar to that still worn by U.S. Navy officers and chief petty officers, with the familiar shield device above the rank stripes. Enlisted men below the rating of chief petty officer adopted the Navy-style crackerjack uniform with white duck hat, though the traditional Donald Duck flat cap remained standard.

Since the service's uniform was identical except for the small Coast Guard shield on the right sleeve, headquarters developed a distinctive hat for enlisted personnel to wear instead of the Navy "Dixie-cups." Unfortunately the flat hat (nicknamed the Donald Duck) did not have a brim and wasn't too popular. The Navy discontinued it in 1963.

As for Navy flat hats, the vessel name was printed on the hat's ribbon but always included the letters "CG" after the ship's name, for example, USS Manning, CG.

In 1941, for the first time, Coast Guard uniforms became officially a modification of the Navy's. The garments themselves were the same as those of the Navy; only the distinguishing corps devices, buttons, shoulder marks, and the familiar shield identified them as Coast Guard. The officer's cap device for the Coast Guard was the most obvious difference, consisting of a large spread eagle with shield, holding in its talons a single horizontal anchor. The Navy's device had, and still has, a smaller eagle over crossed anchors. Also, the naval eagle was silver, whereas the Coast Guard's was gold.

In the Coast Guard, the national shield continued in its placement above the sleeve rank stripes of the officer's uniform coat. During the 1960s the vessel's name was replaced by the words "U.S. Coast Guard" on the hat ribbon of every Coast Guard flat hat. The only distinguishing device on enlisted uniforms, if the flat hat was not being worn, was the Coast Guard shield at the bottom of the right sleeve of a chief petty officer's coat, and of the crackerjack jumper. If the cuffs were rolled up on the jumper, there was no visible way to distinguish a Coast Guardsman from a Navy sailor.

SA Carl "Sandy" Schwab in 1966, wearing the Coast Guard uniform of the time.

On 1 April 1967, the Coast Guard was transferred from the Treasury Department to the newly created Department of Transportation. Shortly after taking over as commandant in June 1970, Adm. Chester R. Bender formed a board of officers to design a new universal formal uniform that would be different enough from the Navy to clearly distinguish the Coast Guard as a completely separate armed service. His goal was to raise the visibility of the Coast Guard as a service that could and did stand on its own. It would be a dramatic change from a long-standing tradition of wearing uniforms of the Navy, with only small identifying marks such as the Coast Guard shield and the anchor and shields on the officers' and chief petty officers' uniforms. Admiral Bender also stated that one of his purposes was to update the apparel to be consistent with contemporary society.

Senior officers were generally unenthusiastic; nonetheless, the board's deliberations resulted in a single-breasted, royal blue officer uniform. Admiral

Bender, aware of the long-standing dissatisfaction of most enlisted Coast Guard personnel with their old uniforms, also wanted the board to replace it with one similar to that worn by officers and chief petty officers. He believed the traditional jumper was demeaning for old enlisted men, and detracted from the authority of petty officers engaged in maritime law enforcement. The uniform that the board recommended—similar to officers'—included appropriate insignia for all enlisted personnel.

The only difference now between the uniforms of officers, chief petty officers, and enlisted personnel would be in the rank insignia and cap devices. Everyone would now wear a combination cap, with varying devices. Many believed this better reflected the service's valuing of its enlisted members, even though it occasionally caused saluting confusion among members of other armed services. The new single-breasted uniform was somewhat similar to that of the former Life-Saving Service.

The new royal blue coat had four pockets, and trousers matched. The shirt was light blue, the tie royal blue, and the dress shoes black. The warm-weather shirt was short-sleeved and light blue, with shoulder bars for officers and pin-on metal collar devices for chief petty officers and petty officers. Non-rated personnel wore no collar devices. In a departure from the U.S. Navy convention, and Coast Guard tradition that followed that convention, all petty officers E-6 and below now wore red chevrons, and all chief petty officers wore gold. Also unlike the Navy, officers and CPOs did not wear khaki; all Coast Guard personnel wore the same color uniform.

The reaction to the new "Bender Blues," as they came to be known, was not entirely favorable. Some noted that it was quite similar in cut to the Air Force's class A uniform, only of a deeper blue color with Coast Guard insignia. With a light blue shirt the same as that worn by Air Force personnel, they noted, now Coast Guard personnel would be confused with that service instead of the Navy, especially in the summer. Others lamented the lack of the traditional seagoing officer's double-breasted coat. The uniform also did away with the tradition of distinguishing between first class petty officers and chief petty officers. Previously, when a first class petty officer advanced to chief, he shifted from the enlisted uniform to the khakis that were the trademark of that rate. Now, only the cap device marked this significant transition. But enlisted personnel widely supported the new coat and tie uniform.

In 1972, the current Coast Guard dress blue uniform was introduced for wear by both officers and enlisted personnel; the transition was completed during 1974. Since that time, service members have never been confused with those of the Navy. Today the only uniforms that remain identical to the Navy's are the officer's summer white service and full dress uniforms. Coast Guard personnel are, however, still occasionally confused with those of the Air Force.

Coast Guard Auxiliary uniforms evolved until by 1967 they were like the service's officer uniforms, except that stripes on sleeves and shoulder boards were silver rather than gold, buttons were silver rather than gold, and they had a cap device to distinguish them from officers. The Auxiliary shield is silver with the letter A in its center; commodores wear shoulder boards identical to those of Coast Guard flag officers except for their silver, rather than gold, color. Today, Auxiliarists are often mistakenly saluted by personnel who are unfamiliar with the Coast Guard Auxiliary.

The transition to Bender Blues necessitated a change to the Auxiliary's cap device, because it was very similar to what all enlisted Coast Guard personnel (E-6 and below) wore. The new emblem needed to eliminate the possibility of confusing these two devices and identifying both Auxiliarists and Coast Guard petty officers as law enforcement officers. In reality, only petty officers have that authority. After much discussion, the new Auxiliary cap device was selected to represent the close relationship of the Coast Guard and its Auxiliary. The traditional Auxiliary seal was incorporated with the spread wings of the Coast Guard commissioned officer's eagle, surrounded by the wreath of excellence taken from the Auxiliary AUXOP device—but all in silver. There is no horizontal anchor at its base, as there is on the commissioned officer's cap device.

17. BATTLE STREAMERS

There is no doubt the Coast Guard cherishes its many peacetime activities, but it is also justly proud of its service in the wars of the United States. The "system of cutters" was only seven years old when several of its fleet fought in the Quasi-War with France. In this and the War of 1812, these small, lightly armed cutters proved their worth against experienced European warships.

Battle streamers are 2¾-inch-wide-by-4-foot-long cloth ribbons that have been attached to the ceremonial version of the Coast Guard colors since 1968. Each is unique in its combination of colors and represents an individual war, campaign, or theater of operations. They commemorate Coast Guard heroic actions in naval engagements throughout the history of the service, serving as reminders of sacrifice, service, and a proud heritage. Battle streamers symbolize Coast Guard personnel's dedication for more than two hundred years.

Viewed together, they provide a summary of the operational battle history of the Coast Guard and Revenue Cutter Service. The first six stand for the honors that accrued to the Revenue Cutter Service before 1915, when the service was merged with the Life-Saving Service to become the Coast Guard. On the 178th anniversary of the service—4 August 1968—the commandant, Adm. Willard J. Smith, affixed the first set of battle streamers ever to adorn the Coast Guard colors.

The ceremonies were held, appropriately, at Portsmouth, New Hampshire, the community to which President George Washington turned when he appointed Hopley Yeaton master of one of the first revenue cutters and tendered him the first commission as a seagoing officer in the service of the federal government. On that occasion, his words best summarize the streamers' purpose: "From this date on, these streamers, together with others which may be bestowed on the Coast Guard at some future date, will adorn the Coast Guard Ceremonial Color whenever and wherever it may be unfurled. Let these Battle Streamers forever stand as a living memorial and a lasting tribute to our gallant personnel, who, by their deeds and heroic action, served the Coast Guard and their nation with glory and distinction in its hour of need."

Each battle streamer is listed below, followed by a brief description of the war, campaign, or theater of operations it represents and representative examples of Coast Guard involvement.

Maritime Protection of the New Republic
Streamer: eight red (scarlet) and eight white alternating stripes

For the heroic actions of the U.S. Revenue Cutter Service, forerunner of the Coast Guard, which served as the only maritime defense force protecting our young nation from 1790 to 1797. Most notably the Revenue Cutter Service fought against French privateers who were seizing British and Spanish ships in American waters. The service undertook actions of great value to the United States, including efforts to prevent maritime smuggling. This secured a reputation for excellence that the U.S. Coast Guard today continues to embody. This is the only battle streamer unique to the Coast Guard.

French Naval Battle (Quasi-War with France)
Streamer: light blue with two groupings of red, white, and blue stripes

During the period 1790–97, the Revenue Cutter Service assumed the task of protecting American trade in the absence of a regular Navy (the U.S. Navy was not founded until 1798). The first international challenge to the young United States was this undeclared naval war with France. Congress authorized President John Adams to employ revenue cutters to operate with the newly created Navy Department to protect American mercantile interests. The ten-vessel Revenue Cutter fleet engaged French privateers who preyed on American merchant vessels.

The first action between rival ships of the two nations occurred in November 1798. Although outgunned and outnumbered, the cutters distinguished themselves. The *Eagle* captured five French vessels and recaptured seven American vessels. The *Pickering* captured *L'Egypte Conquise*, a vessel with twice the armament and three times the complement of the cutter. Revenue cutters actually captured more enemy ships than did the Navy, accounting for eighteen of the total twenty-two taken.

War of 1812

Streamer: scarlet with two white stripes

Twelve revenue cutters were called upon to participate in "the second battle of independence" from Great Britain. When war was declared, the United States could only muster sixteen naval vessels and about a dozen cutters for coastal defense, against Britain's powerful navy of six hundred warships. All the revenue cutters were small and lightly armed and could not risk engagement with the larger British warships. They did, however, seize a number of the enemy's small ships, protect American merchant ships from British privateers, and capture British merchantmen. The war was barely a week old when the cutter *Jefferson* captured the first prize to fall to the American fleet, the merchantman *Patriot*. Later the cutter *Vigilant* captured the British privateer *Dart* off the east end of Block Island, New York. In all, the cutters captured fourteen enemy merchant ships.

Operations against West Indian Pirates

Streamer: cobalt blue center with stripes of black, white, black, and old gold

Piracy in the Caribbean was at its worst between 1818 and 1825. Privateers raided Spanish shipping during many Latin American fights of independence from Spain. As the number of Spanish merchantmen decreased, privateers attacked ships of other nations, becoming no better than pirates. Soon they posed a serious threat to U.S. shipping. To protect American seamen, the Navy Department established the West Indies Squadron, to be augmented by revenue cutters. The *Louisiana* and *Alabama* were among those that played a significant role in the effort, serving off the southern coast and the Chesapeake. On 31 August 1819 these two cutters were boldly attacked off the southern coast of Florida by the pirate ship *Bravo*, commanded by Jean LaFarge, a lieutenant of the notorious Jean Lafitte. The short battle was terminated by the cutters' boats boarding the *Bravo* and carrying her decks in a hand-to-hand struggle.

African Slave Trade Patrol, 1820–61

Streamer: cobalt blue center with strips of white, cobalt blue, white, apple red, white, and cobalt blue edge.

In the middle years of the nineteenth century, many Americans spoke out against the slave traffic flowing from Africa to the Western Hemisphere. The U.S. Navy joined Great Britain's Royal Navy to establish the African Slave Trade Patrol, which for more than forty years hunted and ran down slavers who plied the Atlantic with their cargoes of human misery. At the same time, paradoxically, even though the United States had abolished the trade in January 1808, slaves already in the country were still bought and sold openly, and slavery was still legal in southern states.

Revenue cutters were also engaged in fighting the slave trade, patrolling off the U.S. coast while Navy vessels patrolled off the west coast of Africa. The *Harriet Lane* cruised between New York and Cape Florida on this patrol, while other cutters patrolled the southern coast of the United States.

Indian Wars, 1835–42

Streamer: scarlet with two black stripes

The 1835 massacre of a U.S. Army detachment by the Seminole Nation resulted in the deployment of American forces to the Everglades of Florida. The maneuverability and shallow draft of the revenue cutters proved beneficial in the performance of myriad duties, including transporting troops, armament, and supplies; and landing cuttermen to fortify settlements and pursue Seminole raiding parties into the treacherous Everglades. In addition to trying to intercept supplies intended for Indians, cutters also guarded the coast of Florida to prevent the exportation of slaves to Cuba. As a result of this blockade, the Seminoles had only five kegs of powder left by April 1842. The following month, Secretary of War John Spencer declared an end to hostilities. Nine cutters participated in these conflicts: the *Dallas, Dexter, Jackson, Campbell, Washington, Jefferson, Madison, Van Buren,* and a second *Jefferson.*

Mexican War, 1846–48

Streamer: green with one stripe

In June 1846 nine cutters, constituting the first official squadron of revenue cutters, commenced operations against Mexico in the Gulf of Mexico. This small squadron performed scouting, convoy, towing, and blockade duties, as well as transporting troops and supplies and carrying mail and dispatches. During the first expedition to Tabasco, the cutter *Forward* provided single-handed artillery support, and combined with the cutter *McClane* to blockade the port.

Civil War, 1861–65

Streamer: blue and gray, equally divided

During the American Civil War, fifty-seven revenue cutters not only carried out their many peacetime duties, they also worked with the Army, Navy, and Marines to bring the tragic war to its conclusion. Revenue cutters were called upon to assist in the crucial blockading of more than three thousand miles of Confederate coastline, cutting vital southern supply lines. They guarded harbors on both the East and West coasts of the United States and fought off Confederate privateers.

The first maritime shot of the Civil War, fired by the revenue cutter *Harriet Lane* across the bow of the Confederate vessel *Nashville* during the bombardment of Fort Sumter, marked the beginning of the Revenue Cutter Service participation in the war. The *Harriet Lane* would later participate in the attack on Hatteras Inlet, the Union's first victory, and serve as Commo. David Dixon Porter's flagship during the seizure of New Orleans. The cutter *Miami* participated in the capture of Norfolk, Virginia.

Spanish-American War, 1898

Streamer: yellow with two blue stripes

The sinking of the U.S. battleship *Maine* in Havana Harbor in 1898 crystallized American sympathy for those seeking Cuban independence from Spanish rule. The Revenue Cutter Service was called upon, and eight cutters took part in the blockade of Havana. The *McCullogh*, under the command of Capt. Daniel B. Hodgson, was a part of Commodore Dewey's fleet at the Battle of Manila Bay. The only death among the United States forces at the battle was Chief Engineer Francis B. Randall, who died of heat stroke in the engine room of the *McCullogh*.

Four cutters patrolled the U.S. West Coast against raiders, and seven others worked with the Army guarding principal ports from Boston to the Mississippi passes. Eight revenue cutters served in Adm. William T. Sampson's fleet, blockading Cuban harbors. During the battle of Cardenas, Cuba, the cutter *Hudson* performed heroically, as discussed in the earlier chapter about the Revenue Cutter Service.

World War I Victory, 1917–18

Streamer: double rainbow

Protection of the Allies' supply convoys was vital to victory in World War I. In mid-1917, six cutters formed Squadron 2 of Division 6 of the Atlantic Fleet Patrol Forces. These vessels escorted many convoys between Gibraltar and Great Britain, and engaged German submarines in the Mediterranean. Other large cutters performed similar duties in home waters, off Bermuda, in the Azores, in the Caribbean, and off the coast of Nova Scotia.

The CGC *Seneca* and the CGC *Tampa*, both of which have been discussed earlier in this book, were among Coast Guard vessels and personnel who distinguished themselves in this war. A total of 192 officers and men of the Coast Guard lost their lives in the performance of their duties during the war.

It has long been believed that the Coast Guard suffered the highest percentage of deaths of any of the U.S. armed forces in World War I. It was recently discovered that the claim was based on statistics that included the

Marines as part of the Navy. When the Marines are considered separately they had the highest percentage of deaths. Next came the Coast Guard, with a higher percentage than either the Army or Navy.

Yangtze Service, 1926–27, 1930–32

Streamer: dark blue with two groupings of yellow and red stripes

The Navy protected U.S. citizens against bandit and warlord forces in turbulent China during the first part of the twentieth century. Severe floods along the Yangtze River valley brought the U.S. Asiatic Fleet into action to also aid millions of Chinese left homeless and hungry. I have been unable to determine why the Coast Guard has this battle streamer. Possibly a lone Coast Guardsman served in this area during the period.

American Defense Service, 1939–41

Streamer: yellow with two groupings of red, white, and blue stripes

With the beginning of World War II in Europe, President Franklin Roosevelt required patrols off the entrances of U.S. ports as part of his neutrality proclamation. Coast Guard small craft patrolled every U.S. port, guarding against sabotage and other covert activities by the Axis powers. Shortly after the fall of Denmark to the Nazis, the United States signed an agreement with the Danish government in exile, pledging to defend Denmark's colony of Greenland from invasion by the Germans. In May 1941 the cutter *Comanche* (WATA-202) disembarked an armed Coast Guard detachment to guard Greenland's cryolite mine, on the southwest coast near Cape Farewell. A short while later the cutter *Northland* (WPG-49) made the first naval capture of WWII: the German-controlled sealer *Buskoe*, and later captured a Nazi radio station set up on Greenland soil.

World War II: American Campaign, 1941–46

Streamer: blue with two groupings of white, black, red, and white stripes; with red, white, and blue stripes in the center

Throughout World War II, Coast Guardsmen guarded the ports and harbors and patrolled the beaches of the United States. During the early months of U.S. participation in the war, most German U-boat victims were in the western Atlantic. Coast Guard cutters participated in both transatlantic and coastal convoys, protecting merchant ships and attacking U-boats. Temporary Reservists and Coast Guard Auxiliarists manned small boats, including offshore sailing yachts, in coastal antisubmarine warfare patrols. On 9 May 1942, the 165-foot cutter *Icarus* (WPC-110), patrolling off of Cape Lookout, North Carolina, sank U-352 with depth charges, accomplishing the second naval submarine kill of World War II. Another 165-foot cutter, the *Escanaba*, performed heroically, as discussed earlier in this book.

World War II: Asiatic-Pacific Campaign, 1941–46

Streamer: gold with two white, red, and white stripe groupings; with blue, white, and red stripes in the center

The war in the Pacific began with Japan's attack on Pearl Harbor, Hawaii, 7 December 1941. The cutter *Taney* (WPG-37) was present that day and manned her guns within minutes of the attack. Although the *Taney* was unscathed, she did ward off five planes headed for the cutter. Coast Guardsmen fought alongside the Navy throughout the war in the Pacific, in the thick of it, at all the places with bloodstained names such as Guadalcanal, Kwajalein, Eniwetok, Saipan, Guam, Peleliu, Leyte, Iwo Jima, and Okinawa. Coast Guard coxswains played an integral part in American amphibious operations in the Pacific. Coast Guardsmen manned troop transports and escorted convoys as well. Signalman 1st Class Douglas Munro was the only Coastguardsman to ever have been awarded the Medal of Honor and he is discussed in the earlier chapter "Honor."

Philippine Defense, 1941–42

Streamer: red with two white stripes

Awarded for Coast Guard participation in the defense of the Philippines between 7 December 1941 and 5 May 1942. Coast Guard Lt. T. James Crotty, U.S. Coast Guard, was among defenders of the Philippines during this period. He carried out special demolition work during the retreat of American and Filipino forces from Bataan to Corregidor. He then served as the executive officer of the USS *Quail* (AM-15), which swept clear channels to the island and also bombarded Japanese forces on Bataan. Crotty was captured by the Imperial Japanese Army after the surrender of Corregidor in May 1942. He died later that fall while a prisoner of war, of diphtheria. Crotty was the only documented Coast Guard prisoner of war during the 20th century.

Philippine Liberation, 1944–45

Streamer: red with one blue and one white stripe

Coast Guard personnel manned cargo ships, landing ships, and patrol frigates throughout the campaign to liberate the Philippines from Japanese occupation. They participated in the Leyte, Lingayen, and Luzon operations, helping to land troops on the beaches and fighting off kamikaze pilots. Of the 738 vessels participating in the Leyte campaign, 35 were Coast Guard–manned and 7 others carried Coast Guardsmen in their Navy crews. Of the 685 vessels participating in the Luzon operation, 16 Coast Guard–manned vessels took part, as well as Coast Guardsmen serving in 7 other vessels with Navy crews.

Philippine Independence, 1941–45

Streamer: blue with yellow border stripes and red, white, red center grouping

The Philippine Independence ribbon was awarded to all Coast Guard personnel who qualified for both the Philippine Defense and Philippine Liberation ribbons.

Philippine Presidential Unit Citation, 1941–42, 1944–45

Streamer: red, white, and blue

Awarded by the president of the Philippine Republic to Coast Guard service members serving in units engaged in either the defense or the liberation of the Philippines. Cdr. Chester R. Bender, U.S. Coast Guard, became the air-sea rescue adviser and liaison officer with the Far East Air Force Headquarters in the Philippines shortly after its liberation from the Japanese. He remained there for the rest of the war, and in the 1970s became commandant of the Coast Guard.

World War II: European-African–Middle Eastern Campaign, 1942–45

Steamer: green and brown with three stripe groupings: green, white, and red; white, black, and white; and a center grouping of red, white, and blue

A major task of the Coast Guard in World War II was antisubmarine warfare. Coast Guard cutters and Coast Guard–manned naval vessels destroyed German U-boats and rescued more than four thousand survivors of torpedoings. The cutter *Alexander Hamilton* (WPG-34) was torpedoed and sunk off Iceland in January 1942, the first major Coast Guard loss in the war. Another major task of the service was operating the landing craft that hit the beaches at North Africa, Salerno, Anzio, Normandy, and southern France.

French Croix de Guerre, World War II, 1944

Streamer: red with four green stripes

Twelve individual awards of the Croix de Guerre were made to Coast Guard service members for their involvement in the liberation of France. Among the recipients was Capt. Alfred Richmond, senior Coast Guard officer on the staff of the commander, Naval Forces Europe. Richmond helped plan the invasion of Normandy. He was presented the Croix de Guerre with Palm "for exceptional service" rendered.

World War II Victory, 1941–46

Streamer: red with rainbow border groupings and two stripes

Victory in World War II hinged on preventing enemy submarines from cutting sea lanes, the amphibious capability to land soldiers and Marines onto enemy-held territory, and the ability to sustain them by sea once ashore. The Coast Guard played a vital role in all these, contributing greatly to the Allied victory.

Navy Occupation Service

Streamer: white borders with a black and red stripe

Awarded to several Coast Guard vessels, including the *Buttonwood* (WAGL-306), *Bibb* (WPG-31), and *Chincoteague* (WAVP-375), for occupation of the territories of U.S. enemies during and subsequent to World War II.

Korean Service, 1950–54

Streamer: light blue bordered on each side with white; white center stripes

In June 1950, Communist North Korean forces invaded South Korea. The United States, within the framework of a UN resolution, responded. Although the Coast Guard did not operate under the Department of the Navy in the Korean conflict, the service instituted a port security program in response to an executive order, manning a total of five Pacific weather stations in support of Korean operations. Coast Guard cutters served as open-ocean weather stations, providing ground troops with information on weather patterns and serving as communication platforms. Another vital role of the Coast Guard was to provide search and rescue for downed pilots. Twenty-two cutters served in the Far East Theater of Operations. A number of LORAN stations were constructed to improve navigation in Korean waters, including one at Pusan, Korea. A negotiated truce was signed in 1953. Communist aggression had been stopped, and the Republic of South Korea remained free to pursue a democratic form of government.

China Service, 1937–39, 1945–57

Streamer: yellow with two red stripes

On 12 December 1937, Japanese aircraft attacked and sank the USS *Panay* (PR-5). After World War II, the United States returned to provide transport for Chinese Nationalist troops and carry food and supplies from Shanghai up the Yangtze to fight near-famine conditions in the interior.

On 18 January 1953, a Coast Guard Martin PBM-5 *Mariner* aircraft was dispatched from Sangley Point Coast Guard Detachment in the Philippines to assist survivors of a Navy plane crash in Chinese waters. After making an open sea landing and recovering all survivors, the aircraft was able to take off. But an engine failed and crashed, with the loss of the five crew members as well as the four Navy aviators they had rescued.

Navy Unit Commendation

Streamer: green with two groupings of blue, yellow, and red stripes

Awarded to Coast Guard units during World War II, and to seventy-four Coast Guard units constituting Squadrons 1 and 3 and Divisions 11, 12, and 13 for actions in Vietnam.

National Defense Service

Streamer: red with yellow center and two groupings of white, blue, and white stripes

Since the National Defense Service Medal was created in 1950, it has been presented to any member of the armed forces who served during a time when a national emergency has been declared. This includes American engagements in Korea (1950–54), Vietnam (1961–74), the Persian Gulf (1990–95), and the efforts against terrorism beginning in 2001.

Armed Forces Expeditionary

Streamer: light blue with border groupings of green, yellow, brown, and black; red, white, and blue center grouping

Awarded for post–Korean War services in which foreign opposition was encountered or hostile action imminent. Three Coast Guard vessels and one shore unit conducted operations in support of the crisis in the Dominican Republic; and fifteen Coast Guard vessels, five shore units, and one special flight participated in the Cuban Missile Crisis of October 1962. In addition, Coast Guard service members manned seventeen 82-foot craft engaged in Operation Market Time in Vietnam as early as 1965.

Vietnam Service

Streamer: yellow with green borders, three red stripes

Coast Guard duties in Vietnam, beginning in April 1965, were numerous. In successful but dangerous efforts to limit supplies to the Viet Cong, Coast Guardsmen of Squadron 1 boarded all suspicious craft and searched for munitions and other contraband. Twenty-six 82-foot Coast Guard patrol boats deployed to Vietnam and cruised more than four million miles on patrol between May 1965 and August 1970. Large cutters also deployed to Vietnam as Squadron 3. These high-endurance cutters cruised off the shore and took part in more than 1,300 naval gunfire support missions.

Other Coast Guardsmen conducted extensive aids-to-navigation operations, port security and explosive loading operations, and merchant marine safety operations. Coast Guardsmen also installed and operated five LORAN-C stations in southeast Asia during the war in Vietnam. Coast Guard aviators voluntarily served with high honor and distinction with the U.S. Air Force Aerospace Rescue and Recovery forces in Southeast Asia, in the dual role of aircraft commanders and instructor pilots out of Tuy Hoa and Da Nang, Vietnam, as well as from Thailand and the Philippines. They regularly risked their lives flying into harm's way to save airmen in peril of death or capture. Eight thousand Coast Guardsmen served in Vietnam. Seven were killed, including one of the eleven aviators, and sixty-three were wounded.

Coast Guard Unit Commendation

Streamer: nine stripes of blue, yellow, red, green, white, green, red, yellow, and blue

Established in 1963 the Coast Guard Unit Commendation is the highest peacetime unit award presented by the commandant to any unit that has distinguished itself by valorous or extremely meritorious service not involving combat but in support of Coast Guard operations, that renders the unit outstanding compared with other units performing similar service.

Coast Guard Meritorious Unit Commendation

Streamer: nine stripes of blue, white, green, white, light blue, white, green, white, and blue

Awarded by the commandant to any unit that has distinguished itself by valorous or meritorious achievement or service not involving combat but in support of Coast Guard operations, that renders the unit outstanding compared to other units performing similar service, but at a level below that of the Coast Guard Unit Commendation. First awarded in 1973.

Army Meritorious Unit Commendation

Streamer: scarlet

Awarded by the secretary of the Army to the Coast Guard Port Security and Waterways Detail Vietnam for its operations in securing port areas and supervising the handling of ammunition and explosives in Vietnam between 15 October 1966 and 15 April 1967. Explosive loading detachments near Saigon and at Cam Ranh Bay worked around the clock.

Navy Meritorious Unit Commendation

Streamer: green with two groupings of yellow, blue, and yellow; red center

Awarded by the secretary of the Navy to any unit distinguishing itself under combat and non-combat conditions. The Navy Meritorious Unit Commendation has been awarded to fifty-nine Coast Guard afloat units for services in Vietnam, Iraq, and elsewhere.

Republic of Vietnam Armed Forces Meritorious Unit Citation, Gallantry Cross with Palm

Streamer: red with gold center and eight double red stripes with palm

Awarded to various Coast Guard afloat and shore units in recognition of meritorious service in Vietnam. Lt. Eugene Hickey received this award for gallantry in action in command of the CGC *Point White* (WPB-82308) during the Soi Rap encounter.

Republic of Vietnam Meritorious Unit Citation, Civil Actions Medal 1st Class Color, with Palm

Streamer: dark green with two broad red stripes; two narrow red stripes in center, and palm

Awarded to various Coast Guard afloat and shore units in recognition of meritorious civil action service in Vietnam. The most recurring service came in the form of medical care rendered by an effort called Medical Civil Action Program. The Squadron 3 cutters, with the doctors and hospital corpsmen, were best equipped to treat a range of ailments. Village house calls soon became a normal part of a patrol. Coast Guardsmen also helped at orphanages, built homemade playground sets, and carried out countless other helpful acts.

Southwest Asia Campaign

Streamer: black center with stripes of myrtle green, chamois, old glory red, white, old glory red, blue, chamois, and black

Awarded to various Coast Guard units for service in support of Operations Desert Shield or Desert Storm between the dates of 2 August 1990 and 30 November 1995. A total of ten four-person Coast Guard law enforcement detachments served in theater to support the enforcement of UN sanctions by the Maritime Interdiction Forces. The first boarding of an Iraqi vessel conducted by a Coast Guard law enforcement detachment occurred on 30 August 1990. Approximately 60 percent of the six hundred boardings carried out by U.S. forces were either led by or supported with these Coast Guard detachments and a seven-man liaison staff headed by a captain. The commandant designated Vice Adm. Howard B. Thorsen as operational commander for the Coast Guard forces deployed in theater.

Also, in August 1990 President George Bush authorized the call-up of members of the selected Reserve to active duty in support of Operation Desert Shield. Three Coast Guard port security units consisting of 550 Reservists were ordered to the Persian Gulf, in the first involuntary overseas mobilization of these units in the Reserve's fifty-year history. A total of 950 Coast Guard Reservists were called to active duty. Among their other duties, Reservists supervised Ready Reserve Force vessel inspection and supervised the loading of hazardous military cargoes. In response to the Iraqi action of setting ablaze oil wells and pumping stations in Kuwait, some offshore, two HU-25A Falcon jets from Air Station Cape Cod departed for Saudi Arabia. Part of the interagency oil spill assessment team, they were equipped with Aireye technology, which precisely locates and records oil as it floats on water. Two HC-130 aircraft from Air Station Clearwater accompanied them, transporting spare parts and deployment packages. The Falcons mapped more than 40,000 square miles in theater and located "every drop of oil on the water."

Kosovo Campaign
Streamer: five stripes of blue, red, white, blue, and red

In the summer of 1999, the CGC *Bear* (WMEC-901) deployed to the Adriatic Sea in support of Operation Allied Force and Operation Noble Anvil, NATO's military campaign against the forces of the former Republic of Yugoslavia. The *Bear* served in the USS *Theodore Roosevelt* (CVN-71) battle group, providing surface surveillance and search and rescue response for the sea combat commander, and force protection for the amphibious ready group operating near Albania. The cutter provided combat escort for U.S. Army vessels transporting military cargo between Italy and Albania. This escort operation took the *Bear* up to the Albanian coastline, well within enemy surface-to-surface missile range.

Department of Transportation, Secretary's Outstanding Unit Award

Streamer: thirteen stripes of orange, blue, white, blue, orange, white, blue, white, orange, blue, white, blue, and orange

On 3 November 1994, the secretary of transportation bestowed his highest award, the Secretary's Award for Outstanding Achievement, on the Coast Guard for a period of high-tempo operations from 1 October 1993 to 30 September 1994. As the secretary intended this recognition for the service as a unit, the commandant authorized the ribbon bar only, with gold frame, to be known as the Secretary's Outstanding Unit Award. It was again presented to specific units for their outstanding performance of duty in New York Harbor following the terrorist attacks on the World Trade Center from 11 September through 22 October 2001.

Global War on Terrorism Expeditionary

Streamer: fifteen stripes of bluebird, old glory blue, white, old glory blue, bluebird, golden yellow, bluebird, scarlet, bluebird, golden yellow, bluebird, old glory blue, white, old glory blue, and bluebird

Awarded to numerous ashore and afloat units deployed overseas in direct service to the efforts against terrorism that began 11 September 2001. Before June 2005, the medal was awarded for service in Iraq and Afghanistan. Petty Officer Nathan Bruckenthal, a damage controlman, was on a security mission in the Persian Gulf on 24 April 2004 when suicide bombers initiated a waterborne assault on the Khawr al Amaya oil terminal. Bruckenthal was severely wounded while defending the Iraqi terminal and later died from his injuries. He was serving on board the USS *Firebolt* (PC-10) on his second tour of duty in support of Operation Iraqi Freedom. Bruckenthal was the first Coast Guardsman killed in combat since the Vietnam War. For his actions, he was posthumously awarded the Bronze Star Medal, the Purple Heart, and the Global War on Terrorism Expeditionary Medal in April 2004.

Global War on Terrorism Service

Streamer: blue with yellow, red, and white stripes

Awarded to numerous ashore and afloat units in action and support of efforts against terrorism in home-based operations such as Noble Eagle. Since 2005, this blanket term has effectively awarded the Global War on Terrorism Service Medal to most personnel of the U.S. armed forces who performed service in direct support of efforts after September 2001.

Coast Guard Presidential Unit Citation

Streamer: nine stripes of white, orange, white, corsair blue, white, corsair blue, white, orange, and white

The citation was awarded for meritorious achievement and outstanding performance in response to Hurricane Katrina from 29 August to 13 September 2005. Coast Guard personnel were responsible for rescuing more than 33,000 people, beginning cleanup operations of 9.4 million gallons of oil, repair and replacement of more than 1,800 aids to navigation, and providing assistance and hope to hundreds of thousands of displaced citizens. For this specific award, members authorized for the award wear the ribbon with hurricane device.

Afghanistan Campaign

Streamer: thirteen stripes of emerald, scarlet, black, white, scarlet, white, old glory blue, white, scarlet, white, black, scarlet, and emerald

The war in Afghanistan that began 7 October 2001 as Operation Enduring Freedom was launched by the United States with the United Kingdom in response to the 9/11 attacks. A Coast Guard Redeployment Assistance Inspection Detachment was attached to the Army's 1179th Deployment Support Brigade based out of Camp Arifjan, where the bulk of the redeployment operation is located. They ensure that containers packed and loaded in

Iraq and Kuwait are safe to be shipped to the United States, assisting the Army in identifying hazardous materials. In 2006, Lt. Cdr. Vasilios Tasikas deployed to Kabul in support of Operation Enduring Freedom. There he was assigned to the International Law Branch at Combined Forces Command Afghanistan, providing advice on international maritime law.

Iraq Campaign

Streamer: eleven stripes of scarlet, white, green, white, black, chamois, black, white, green, white, and scarlet

The Iraq War, also known as the Second Gulf War, and Operation Iraqi Freedom began 20 March 2003, with the U.S.-led invasion of Iraq. The multinational force was composed almost entirely of troops from the United States and United Kingdom, though several other nations participated. At the height of combat operations, 1,250 U.S. Coast Guard personnel served in Operation Iraqi Freedom; 500 of them were activated Reservists. Coast Guard port security units, law enforcement detachments, national strike force, cutters, and a variety of other units and personnel deployed to support Iraqi Freedom. Cutters were assigned to provide escort and force protection to battle groups and Military Sealift Command convoys passing from the Strait of Gibraltar to the eastern Mediterranean.

INDEX